# The
# Cult of Ra

Stephen Quirke

# The Cult of Ra

*Sun-Worship in Ancient Egypt*

With 97 illustrations

Thames & Hudson

*Frontispiece: Stela showing a lady named Taperet worshipping the falcon-headed sun god Ra. Her offerings are piled high on the altar, and in return she receives sun rays shown as flowers of many colors. Thebes. 22nd Dynasty.*

© 2001 Stephen Quirke

First published in hardcover in the United States of America in 2001 by Thames & Hudson Inc., 500 Fifth Avenue, New York, New York 10110 thamesandhudsonusa.com

Library of Congress Catalog Card Number 2001087367
ISBN 0-500-05107-0

Designed by Liz Rudderham

Printed and bound in Slovenia by Mladinska Knjiga

# Contents

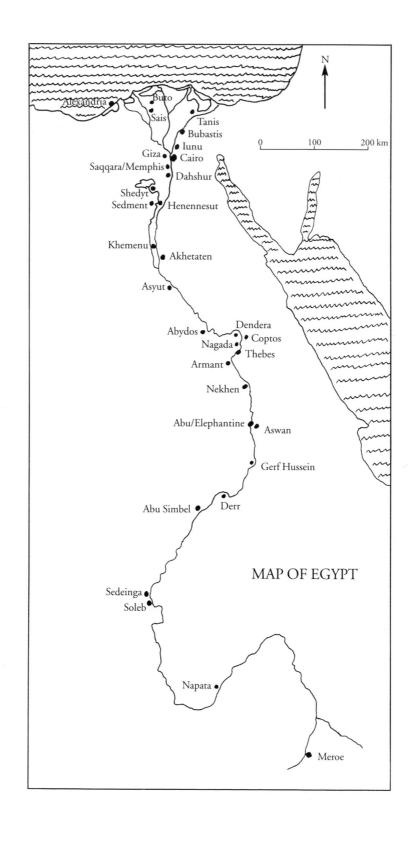

N

Buto
Alexandria
Sais
Tanis
Bubastis
Iunu
Giza
Cairo
Saqqara/Memphis
Dahshur
Shedyt
Sedment
Henennesut

0    100    200 km

Khemenu
Akhetaten

Asyut

Dendera
Abydos
Coptos
Nagada
Thebes
Armant

Nekhen

Abu/Elephantine
Aswan

Gerf Hussein

Abu Simbel
Derr

MAP OF EGYPT

Sedeinga
Soleb

Napata

Meroe

# Preface

## The importance of the mythology, cult and city of Ra

Ancient Egypt exerts an extraordinary fascination for the modern age, combining the familiar and the mysterious. At the kernel of the civilization stands a special relation between the divine father figure of the sun god, ruler of creation, and his solitary offspring on earth, the reigning king of Egypt. Without an understanding of this focal point, we risk losing the significance of every trace of the Egyptian past. For example, the hieroglyphic monuments often immortalize a wife, mother or daughter of the king, and such images and inscriptions draw the modern historian irresistibly to reconstructing royal genealogies, family power struggles and political usurpation. Yet, the Egyptians produced the monuments not as historical documents, but for the religious purpose of perpetuating kingship. In this mythical aura the king plays the part of gods, above all Ra the solar creator and Horus the god of kingship, and therefore a woman styled 'king's wife' becomes his Hathor, goddess of sensuality, while the 'king's mother' must be Nut, goddess of the sky. As the king dies, he repeats the fate of Osiris, ruler of the underworld, and so his former consort must be Isis, the sister-wife of Osiris in myth. These equations emerge in the costume and headgear of the king and his kinswomen. The ritualized meaning of 'king's wife', 'king's mother' can also be seen in the rarity of 'king's sisters' and the virtual absence of 'king's brothers': such omissions only make sense if we accept that the hieroglyphic record presents us with myth, constructed on the model of the sun in creation. As a direct consequence, we need to understand the place of the sun in Egyptian civilization before we can begin to know anything about ancient Egypt.

On this premise, this book follows a path through the principal dimensions of the Egyptian sun. After a brief description of kingship from the Egyptian point of view, Chapter One addresses the evidence for the beliefs concerning the sun god, in Greek parlance the 'mythology' of the sun. Chapter Two then explores the ways in which this solar creator received worship, uncovering both the more widely used sun hymns and, astonishingly, the innermost mysteries of the cult. Here, thanks to research over recent decades by Jan Assmann, we encounter the precise words pronounced by the Egyptians in a kingly project to keep the sun moving through the sky, and thereby the universe in existence (*ill. 1*). The fruits of these investigations amount to an extraordinary act of revelation. Rarely does human society yield its secret core with the depth of detail now accessible to us from the hieroglyphic inscriptions and sacred manuscripts, preserved by chance. Chapter Three moves to the geographical heart of the cult, the city named Iunu by the Egyptians, and known to the Greeks as Heliopolis 'city of the sun'. Now a barren terrain engulfed by the urban explosion of contemporary Cairo, the site once functioned as the first home of the sun god on earth, with a vast precinct for Ra on a scale surpassing even ancient Thebes. The chapter gathers together the remains that have been scattered over the world since the Hellenistic and Roman rulers of Egypt began to dismantle the solar temples 2,000 years ago. If the architecture on the site of Iunu has long since vanished, it stands reflected in Egypt's most famous monuments, as explored in Chapter Four. The pyramids and obelisks are today symbols of Egypt, but they once reflected the power of the sun god and sun king. Against this background, Chapter Five then investigates the extraordinary story of Akhenaten, most single-minded of the sun kings. By excluding all other cult from kingly monuments, Akhenaten has gained modern titles such as the first believer in one god, and the first individual. His reign reveals much of the essence of Egyptian kingship and religion, and inevitably raises a host of new questions for future excavation to answer. Above all, the reign confirms the central importance of the sun cult for our appreciation of ancient Egypt. This book aims at highlighting that message, and providing a general readership with the insights from recent excavation and research.

## A note on names

The form of Egyptian names used in this book requires some explanation. The many variants for the same toponym reflect the rich diversity of Egyptian history. A single place can have had a series of names in its long history, moving from ancient Egyptian to ancient Greek to modern Arabic: Waset became Thebes, then Luxor, and Mennefer became Memphis, then Mit Rahina. Iunu itself was Heliopolis in Greek, and is now in the Cairo districts of Matariya and Ain Shams. However, not even personal names used in one period are exempt from these confusions. This variety also echoes the long history of the country, though in a slightly different way, as follows.

In ancient Egypt the bulk of the population seems to have spoken the Egyptian language, now extinct outside its use in the Coptic Church, the Christian Church in Egypt. Before Christian times, the language was

1 *Temple relief showing, on the left, Ramesses II offering to Ra. On the right the throne-name of the king, Usermaatra, takes the form of an image of the goddess Maat holding the hieroglyph 'user' (meaning 'mighty') and wearing the sun disk. Abu Simbel. 19th Dynasty.*

written in the hieroglyphic script and its cursive versions, hieratic and demotic. These provide the consonantal skeleton, but not the vowels, because a native speaker of the language would not need them. This is difficult for Europeans to grasp, but the same is true of other languages: still today, Hebrew and Arabic newspapers can omit vowels, without losing the power of communication. Unfortunately, the lack of vowels does complicate the ability of non-native-speakers such as ourselves to reconstruct the precise original sound of ancient Egyptian words. For example, the Egyptian word for pyramid is spelled mr: an ancient Egyptian is not available to tell us which vowels belong before, after or between the two consonants. We might read meru, mar, mur… Much research remains before we can be confident that we are anywhere near the original pronunciation, let alone begin to perceive differences over time or between regions. Already in the 5th century BC the Greek historian Herodotus was providing Hellenized versions of Egyptian names, and later classical writers added an array of Greek forms. These were known in Europe before Jean-François Champollion deciphered the hieroglyphic script in 1822, and they are often preferred to the Egyptian hieroglyphic skeleton, not least because the Greek script does provide vowels. Some Egyptian names, usually in a Latinized form of the Greek version, entered European literature so long ago that it would be difficult to reintroduce the Egyptian original, even if we knew how to pronounce it. The deities Osiris, Horus, Isis and Anubis all figure in the Western reception of Egypt, first in Roman times, then during and ever since the Italian Renaissance.

I prefer to use wherever possible a form reflecting as closely as possible the consonants written down by the Egyptians in the hieroglyphic script. This can serve as an anchor for reference, even if we must use classical Greek or Latin forms in instances such as Osiris. Where a weak consonant can reasonably be written in English as a vowel, I use a vowel; where consonants cluster in a manner difficult to pronounce, I insert 'e' as a neutral glide vowel. Thus I write Amenhotep in preference to the Hellenized Amenophis, and Iunu rather than Heliopolis. The example of Amenhotep indicates the limits to my aim for transparency: the 'o' is derived from later indications that the word included such a vowel, and helps simply to break the monotony of the repeated glide 'e'. It might be better to write Amenhetep, but too many 'e' insertions would probably leave a trite impression of this beautiful language. Consistency must continue to be an aim beyond achievement. If the names in the book sometimes seem alien to the reader, the following account of consonants may help to explain the reasons for my choice, and perhaps to bring the reader closer to the Egyptian hieroglyphic forms. Modern English and ancient Egyptian share 17 consonants: 14 written with a single letter – b, p, f, m, n, r, h, w, y, s (originally separate z and s), k, g, t and d – and three often written in English with two letters – sh as in 'sheep', tj as in 'ch' in chin, and j as in the 'j' and 'dg' of 'judge'. More difficult are the seven Egyptian consonants for which modern English has no written equivalent: these have become the source for many different variants in modern alphabetic writings of ancient names.

1. The glottal stop (3 in transliteration, conventionally 'a' in Anglicized versions of names) – if you pronounce a word like 'bottle' without the double t, the 'stop' in place of the double t comes close to the ancient sound

2. a sound between the glottal stop and 'y' (conventionally 'i' in Anglicized versions of names, but often 'a' at the beginning of words – this is the sound at the beginning of the names of the gods Amun and Aten)

3. the sound of the modern Arabic 'ayin', a deep guttural effect – it is the first sound in the Arabic word 'Arab' or Arabic names such as Omar and Iraq

4. a second, stronger 'h', found in modern Arabic, but not in European languages (usually written in Anglicized names as 'h')

5. a sound found in modern Arabic, but also as the 'ch' of Scottish 'loch' (usually written 'kh' in Anglicized versions of Egyptian names)

6. a softer version of the preceding, like the soft 'ch' of German 'ich' (usually written 'kh' in Anglicized versions of names)

7. a form of 'k' pronounced deep in the throat, found in modern Arabic but not in English (usually written 'q' by convention in Anglicized versions of names)

These consonants form the surviving skeleton of Egyptian as recorded in hieroglyphic inscription and cursive manuscript, and are followed as closely as possible throughout this book. Note, however, the few cases where a form preferred in Thames & Hudson publications contradicts these rules: Ramesses rather than Ramessu or the short version Ramses (the additional s in Ramesses comes from Greek versions), Piramesse rather than Per-Ramessu or Per-Ramses (Pi is the Coptic form of ancient Egyptian Per- 'house of'), and Ahmose and Thutmose rather than Ahmes or Djehutymes/Thutmes (the o before se at the end is suggested by Coptic).

## A note on Egyptian chronology

Ancient Egyptian history ranges over 3,000 years, from the first recorded nation-state around 3000 BC to the arrival of Alexander the Great in 332 BC, or the death of Cleopatra in 30 BC. Within this immense time span, periods of national unity alternated with periods of political disunity and civil war. Four main periods of unity stand out in the record, labelled by Egyptologists as the Old, Middle and New Kingdoms and the Late Period, separated by centuries during which no one king ruled the whole land, labelled the First, Second and Third Intermediate Periods. In the 1st millennium BC foreign powers made Egypt a province of larger empires, in periods of Assyrian, Sudanese (Kushite), Persian, Macedonian and finally Roman occupation. These periods rarely have precise boundaries, particularly in earlier ages. The country tended to slip rather gradually into a condition of disunity at the end of a period of national unity, and there are also no exact dates fixing key moments in the processes behind the repeated unifications of the country. Historians can therefore only give approximate dates for the broader periods and corresponding phases in the development of the material culture and technologies of Egypt. For the individual reigns and the groupings of kings into 30 'dynasties' there are more gaps than secure points in the surviving record. Nevertheless, references to positions of stars and the moon have allowed Egyptologists to build up an impression of accuracy for the 12th Dynasty (the core of the Middle Kingdom) and the 18th Dynasty (for the New Kingdom). For periods after the 18th Dynasty the increasing contacts with Western Asia and the Mediterranean world provide a more solid base for estimating the exact or absolute dates of reigns. It would be wrong to imagine that chronology no longer poses any problems, and it seems fundamentally erroneous to cast history, our knowledge of the past, as such an exact science. Our knowledge of the past, whether of this morning or of 4,000 years ago, must remain philosophically a combination of probabilities. Where our poets chart the possible and impossible, and scientists chase the dream of the exact, of certainties, the historian faces the task of assessing the most probable. At present our most probable dates for ancient Egypt rest on the evidence accumulated over two centuries of Egyptological research since the French Revolutionary Expedition to Egypt in 1798–1801. The kinglists from which chronologists began must now make room for less regal bedfellows, often requiring more labour-intensive specialization. Our datings for the late Middle Kingdom depend not on grouping names of kings alone, but more solidly on vast banks of data, such as typologies of coffins, analyses of alloys in metals, studies of handwriting, and study of archaeological finds in stratigraphic sections on excavation. Taken together, these widely varying source materials provide support for a 'most probable' time-line. The reader needs only to remember that a single discovery tomorrow could drastically change the entire carefully elaborated construction we have made of ancient time.

## Short chronological outline

| | |
|---|---|
| Predynastic Periods | |
| Badarian | about 4000 BC |
| Naqada I | 4000–3500 BC |
| Naqada II | 3500–3100 BC |
| Early Dynastic Period | 3100–2686 BC |
| Old Kingdom | 2686–2181 BC |
| First Intermediate Period | 2181–2025 BC |
| Middle Kingdom | 2025–1700 BC |
| Second Intermediate Period | 1700–1550 BC |
| New Kingdom | 1550–1070 BC |
| Third Intermediate Period | 1070–664 BC |
| Late Period | 664–525 BC |
| Persian Period | 525–404 BC |
| Late Dynastic Period | 404–343 BC |
| Second Persian Period | 343–332 BC |
| Macedonian Period | 332–305 BC |
| Ptolemaic Period | 305–30 BC |
| Roman Period | 30 BC – AD 395 |
| Byzantine Period | AD 395–641 |
| Islamic Periods | AD 641– present |

# COSMIC KINGSHIP – THE BRONZE AGE AS THE AGE OF RA

## Decoding ancient Egypt

Since at least the 5th century BC, when the Greek commentator Herodotus wrote his narratives, ancient Egypt has operated in European consciousness as a projected alter ego. This can be ascribed in large part to the external appearance, the self-expression of human beings in their art. For us, ancient Egyptian art carries a strange familiarity, in the succinct rendering of human and animal figures, yet the underlying conventions of this art differ markedly from European tradition. The immortalizing purpose of Egyptian art stands at odds with the bodily perspective developed by the ancient Greeks, and the spatial perspective refined in the Western European Renaissance. For centuries after the introduction of Greek art into Egypt, the Egyptians retained the two systems of depiction side by side, Greek art for civic or Greek religious contexts, but ancient Egyptian art for the eternal, in temples and, above all, in the land of the tomb. Use of the ancient art evaporated along with the hieroglyphic script and the institution of ancient Egyptian kingship only when the country moved into the Christian world, by the 4th century AD. From the modern standpoint, the ancient Egyptian rules for depiction become a curio; its forms are recognizable, yet alien to the rules of spatial perspective endorsed by the optical illusion of 20th-century photography. Our age is of course conscious of the limitations of

**2** *Stela showing King Amenhotep II offering to the falcon-headed Ra-Horakhty, beneath the winged sun disk with two protective serpents wearing the White Crown. Found at Iunu in 1946. Cairo JE 88214. 18th Dynasty.*

perspective, its inability to deliver any promise to capture 'reality'. We are aware of its partiality: each photographic depiction represents, physically, only one point of view. In a world of diversities joined, other systems of depiction can become more attractive than perspective, by indicating dimensions not visible from one point, or only apparent after thought or dream. This attraction applies as much to ancient Egyptian as to abstract art: the icons of the century include the gold mummy-mask of Tutankhamun as well as the black squares of Malevich. Ancient Egypt has become another reminder that life and sight imply the hidden as well as the seen, and that the hidden is often the more important.

Egypt has been adopted then as alien kin, mirroring the interplay of opposites at the heart of European civilization. Already in the Bible, before that Near Eastern text became one of the conflicting foundations of Europe, Egypt plays a double role. For Joseph and Jacob, it is the land of plenty, where famine victims find food; for Moses it is the land of idolatry from which the enslaved must flee, in the original homeward trek of Judaism. Such oppositions assume different guises in the reception of Egypt. The classical authors of Greece and Rome sought in the age-old civilization on the Nile a source of arcane or primeval knowledge. This was, after all, the land from which Greece received its stimulus, in the 6th century BC, to develop the sculptural depiction of the human body, leading eventually to the rules of bodily perspective. However, other writers from the northern shores of the Mediterranean saw Egypt as the contemptible other, most violently in the attack on Egyptian religion by the Roman satirist Juvenal. These two threads of Europe's past, Judaeo-Christian and Graeco-Roman, underwrite modern perceptions. Both had been active within Egypt itself as part of the multi-ethnic society there across the thousand years from the arrival of Alexander the Great in 332 BC to the Islamic conquest in AD 640–1. In AD 1099 the First Crusade re-established for a century Christian states on the eastern shore of the Mediterranean, only intensifying the divide between the European West and a hostile East. During the European Renaissance and Reformation, the rise of Ottoman Turkey finalized this cold war-style partition. After the conquest of Egypt by the Ottoman ruler Selim I in AD 1517 it lay within their empire, still on the land and sea routes of Europeans to more exotic others, India and China.

Throughout the medieval and early modern periods, Egypt was both present in Europe and absent: present in the biblical and classical texts, but absent in image and in its own words. There were few Egyptian monuments outside the country, other than some sculpture and the mighty obelisks brought to Italy by the Roman emperors. It was dangerous to travel even within Europe, on roads infested by brigands, still more so to take to the high seas, where pirates threatened slavery or death. The hardy voyager who reached the shores of Egypt safely, for pilgrimage or trade, would rarely receive official permits for travel south of Cairo. Until Napoleon landed an entire army near Alexandria in 1798, Europeans in Upper Egypt remained rather a rare sight. With the dawn of modern Egypt under the industrial and agricultural revolutions of its forceful Albanian governor Mohamed Ali, Egypt became safer to visit, in terms of both personal security and medical control, at the same time that the Napoleonic wars made land and sea routes safe from bandits. After the introduction of steamboat timetables from European ports to Alexandria, in the mid-19th century, it became relatively easy for more affluent Westerners to visit the monuments of Egypt. The forgotten majority in the Western world who could never afford to travel were exposed to ancient Egypt first through the antiquities brought out of Egypt during industrialization, then through the reporting of scientific discoveries, above all the tomb of the boy-king Tutankhamun in 1922. The architecture and art of the ancient Nile entered every Western city, in the design of cinemas, factories and cemeteries, in the films that built on 19th-century perceptions of Egypt, and then through mass tourism and the blockbuster exhibitions, again pre-eminently of the Tutankhamun treasure. These have sealed the contemporary reception of ancient Egypt in the Western world as one of the most familiar faces of the other. It seems accessible in its artistic self-expression, a source of wonder and inspiration for everyone from the amateur photographer to Henry Moore in the 20th century, as it was in the preceding for everyone from the amateur painter to the Arts and Crafts movements.

And yet, this familiarity is, as everything must be in a human society, a construct of our times for the purpose of our times. We wish to piece together and revive the king of ancient Egypt, and his court and times, like the body of Osiris. Before we can do this, we have first to remove, or at least to be conscious of, our existing prejudices and preconceptions. Some might call this an act of deconstruction, but it cannot be an illusory mission to obtain a blank, free field of perception. We should aim at knowing where we stand, in order to assess how far we may be able to see. With this mental preparation, we can move towards a different Egypt. This land will be recognizable because it was inhabited by human beings with, relative to other animal species, the same physical capacities, needs and limitations as the rest of the species, including ourselves. It will also tend to be 'foreign', but on its own terms. Behind the familiar face of Tutankhamun, there moves a structure of power so different from our own that only by radically adapting our ways of thinking can we begin to recognize it. The king is a sun, and the women in his circuit receive and stimulate him as the maternal sky swallows the sun disk, to give birth to it the next morning. The court is not that of an oriental empire, whether Persian, Turkish or Chinese, but of a kingdom on the Nile, Africa's greatest river, cutting through the Sahara, the planet's most arid desert. The land kept alive by this king is a river bank regulated by the rhythms of an annual miracle, the Nile flood. Its people farm, trade and craft their lives in a solar system different from our own and yet the same. My aim in this book is to narrate that system, as it appears to me from the sources in 2000.

## Human life in the Bronze Age – a different world

When the modern world considers the past, there are two general models at hand to explain any feature of human society, be it political, religious or economic. Neither seems to provide the definitive answers often claimed by historians. The first is the mirage crudely labelled 'primitive man', a suspect category forged by the modern mind out of the historical circumstance that some human societies employ less complicated technologies than others. The second is our perception of our own society, with its long and continuing story of technological developments. It should not be necessary to say, but it is often forgotten, that ancient Egypt belongs to neither of these. It was not engaged in its environment with the immediacy of the hunter-gatherer, nor had it left that environment as far from sight as the post-industrial city-dweller. When we consider beliefs or kingship in ancient Egypt, we move into the world of the Bronze Age and the early Iron Age, along a thousand kilometres of river valley and delta. Here urban life had flourished for centuries already, and farming had arrived 2,000 years before the formation of the first nation-state, about 3000 BC. In this river kingdom, the annual flood of the Nile guaranteed the food supply, and the resulting population was immense; the wheel was useless, as boats provided transport and the most rapid form of communication. The immediate neighbour was the alien desert, where settled life was impossible other than in the few oases, and there only on a small scale; ordered life ended at the precise edge of the fields watered by the river and its flood. Yet the desert offered its own bounty to the inhabitants of the valley. Its rare flora and fauna supplemented the richer fare of the Nile with an exotic range of goods, its mountains and plateaux held semi-precious stones and gold, and its dead roads led out to fabled lands and seas, the 'land of the god' of ancient Egyptian texts. The urbanized kingdom of Egypt dominated its environment perhaps to an unprecedented degree, but did not control life there to the extent possible in our web of nation-states in the 21st century AD. The world retained its mystique. Disease could rarely be defeated and its causes were only understood in the more obvious instances: scorpion and snake bite, for example, or where direct injuries could be observed. Plague, on the other hand, remained the work of the raging goddess Sekhmet, rather than of rats and their guests. We have to strip ourselves of so much intellectual baggage before we can approach this ancient kingship on its own terms: we have to leave behind our photographic eyes, our printed books and papers, our maps and our watches that tell us so firmly where we are in space and time.

A key difference between this vanished Bronze Age world and our own lies in the mechanism by which the rulers deliver promises. Following the world wars of the 20th century, the European-style welfare state is expected to deliver prosperity, security and wellbeing through an annual budget, in which the resources of the nation are calculated to meet the competing demands of different sectors. These calculations rest on two to three centuries spent forging specific institutions with their own local 'cultures', the sum of their attitudes and practices. The names of these institutions fill our lives and our street maps, sometimes foregrounded, sometimes invisible as background noise: hospital, post office, prison, bank, police station and army barracks, printing press, school and museum, sports stadium and theatre, each in its own compartment but serving the same people. When a new technique appears, or a new technology, its own institutional space arrives too, and affects the rest. All are subject to standardized cycles of local, national and international budgets. Bronze Age hierarchical societies had none of this web of expenditure. There were no institutional spaces for hordes of prisoners detained for crimes, large numbers of patients awaiting treatments, or great crowds of spectators. The activities were there, but their institutional form or expression was different. Pre-eminent among these institutions was the mechanism of rule.

## Ancient Egyptian kingship

In ancient Egypt the early state revolved around a personalized individual centre, for which we use the term kingship. As in other Bronze Age worlds, ancient Egyptian kingship delivered those familiar paternal promises of the state, for abundance, security and wellbeing. Yet it did not attempt this in an annual budget for funding buildings or personnel. Instead, it stood one step closer to the earth, fusing what we would separate as religion and politics, in a formula by which the king offered the fruits of the earth to the gods, in return for their blessings for humankind. According to this formula, all kingly action was cult, whether cutting a canal, endowing a temple or fighting at the borders. The principal beneficiary of this cult was the creator, in ancient Egyptian terms the sun god, named Ra (*ill. 2*). From about 2600 BC, the king bore the title 'son of Ra', and this is interpreted literally in a literary tale of about 1600 BC and in the famous cycle of narrative art first found in the temple of the queen who made herself king, Hatshepsut (about 1450 BC). The sun god chooses the woman to bear his next manifestation, takes the form of her husband, impregnates her, and supervises the birth of the child and its ka or sustaining energy. Taken literally, this implies that the king is not a human being, but a manifestation of the sun god with the outward form and mortal lifespan of a man. Automatically all our preconceptions about rulers fail. The European concept of dynasty, as a family tree, has no meaning if each king is a direct issue of the sun god. Instead there is a single line of individual manifestations of Ra. There is no royal blood, only the divine solar king and the human women with whom the sun god has contact. This is why Egyptian texts mention only the formal positions 'wife of the king', 'mother of the king', 'daughter of the king', 'son of the king', and very rarely 'sister of the king'. There can be no 'father of the king', and certainly no 'brother of the king'. This is not a human family, but the fallout from a cosmic intervention of the sun god into the lives of those on earth. In the few surviving kinglists from ancient Egypt, the hieroglyphic versions present an unbroken line, and the one manuscript version interrupts the sequence only where the unity of the country failed. In one or two instances the ancient texts refer to a group of kings as a House, like a European dynasty, but only where the country was divided. Thus, around 2100 BC the rulers in the north could take the name 'House of Khety', that being the most common birth name of the kings in that group. We know nothing about the royal succession in practice, and in that instance do not know whether the various kings called Khety were biologically related at all, let alone a line from father to son. Our view of this kingship can suffer from the coincidence between the European concept of dynasty as family line and the Egyptian social custom favouring succession of father to eldest son in profession. Fathers aimed to hand down their position to their children, and eldest sons were expected to support their aged fathers and to maintain their offerings in the ancestor cult after the father's death. This must have played a powerful part in the political succession from one king to another: if every father wanted to see his biological son reach the father's position, a strong king would be in the best place to see this happen. There are instances throughout Egyptian history where the older king places his successor on the throne beside him as co-regent, to ensure a smooth succession. Yet the sporadic practice of co-regency, never discussed in Egyptian texts, reminds us that there was no mechanism for succession in theory, and that each new king appeared like the sun at dawn, revealing himself in the rising but already a kingly being before that revelation to humankind. The politics are as hidden as in any religious theory of succession. Even the Hellenistic history of Egypt by the priest Manetho groups the kings of Egypt into 'dynasties' first by their place of rule and burial (and therefore by the god or goddess protecting that place), and only occasionally and secondarily by family. For example, the 18th Dynasty appears to comprise kings from four unrelated 'families': the first from the family line of the late-17th Dynasty king Taa; the second from that of Thutmose I, a family of unknown relation to the first, while the two kings at the end of the 18th Dynasty, Ay and Horemheb, were from possibly two more separate families. Modern historians spend much time speculating on kinship ties between these strands of the 18th Dynasty, but the Egyptian sources remain silent. The king in Egypt is the sun, and this eclipses all politics.

Oleg Berlev has noted the nuance in two innocent-seeming phrases often used in the ancient texts to describe the ruler and his heavenly counterpart. The king is often the 'good god', while the creator is the 'great god', but the words 'good' and 'great' imply, when paired, 'younger' and 'older'. This establishes the key relationship in creation, between the sun god as the elder partner in the sky and his issue on earth, the junior partner. Exactly such a pairing may have facilitated the practice of appointing a co-regent, where the senior and junior kings would have echoed the relation of celestial to earthly sovereign. This solar paternity or, better, substitution casts each king as a male, and indeed only rarely in 3,000 years did a woman assume the mantle of kingship. In each case the woman may have ruled alongside a man throughout her reign. This is documented for Hatshepsut, ruling alongside her nephew Thutmose III. It may also be true of the only other two women known to use kingly titles between 3000 and 300 BC – Sebeknefru (about 1800 BC), who may have reigned with Amenemhat III and/or IV, and Tausret (about 1200 BC), who may have reigned with Sety II and Siptah. Whether or not they ruled alone, their ascension to kingship is exceptional. An intriguing aspect of their rule is the special status of Hatshepsut's daughter, Neferura, whose name signified 'perfection of Ra'. Berlev has seen this as a possible new beginning in the theory and practice of kingship, moving from the exclusively male tenure of the office to a mysterious alternative, perhaps complementary, line of 'daughters of Ra'. If this was Hatshepsut's intention, the plan foundered with her death. We rely principally on hieroglyphic inscriptions for our knowledge of individuals at the royal court, but these aim to secure eternal life, not to provide news bulletins of events in political life. We cannot tell from the absence of hieroglyphic references to Neferura whether she was removed, or died young of natural causes. She could simply have receded into invisibility for want of a mythic role at court, deprived of space in the eternal, hieroglyphic record. Similarly, personal politics cannot be read automatically in the decision, at some point late in the reign of Thutmose III, to remove the images and names identifying his aunt as a male ruler. The images offended a cardinal principle of the regular system, that the ruler is son of Ra. In modern parlance, they were religious figures, and would have been removed for religious rather than political reasons.

Here the inadequacies of our language become apparent: our questions are misplaced, so the answers are inappropriate to the setting of Bronze Age Egypt. This is nowhere clearer than in one remarkably direct description of kingship by the Egyptians themselves, attested on a dozen hieroglyphic monuments, the earliest in the same temple to the cult of Hatshepsut as eternal ruler. Jan Assmann brought this text to the attention of Egyptologists, under the new name of 'the King as Priest of the Sun'. Its succinct statements provide a profile of rule, far from our own image of either our own times or the distant past. This climactic passage explains why the creator installed a ruler for men.

> Ra has placed the king on the earth of the living for ever and eternity,
> in order to judge humankind, to satisfy the gods,
> to make Right happen and to annihilate Wrong,
> such that he gives divine offerings to the gods, funerary offerings to the
>    blessed dead.
> The name of the king is in the sky like that of Ra, he lives in joy like Ra-
>    Horakhty.
> Nobles rejoice when they see him; the populace gives him praise
>    in his role of 'the Child'.

The most important task here lies in securing justice on earth, not so removed from modern-day concerns. However, the strategy given particular emphasis is the making of offerings. One of the most widely used titles before the name of the king is Lord of Making Offerings. This no longer plays a major role in contemporary Western consciousness, yet it occupies the fulcral position in this Egyptian account of the relation between heavenly and earthly power. The preceding lines take us still further from late-21st-century attitudes, into as extreme a theory as the divine birth of the king. The king, and he alone, holds special knowledge of the created world. This is the key to his difference when set against human men and women. Knowledge is power. He knows the created forms and their different manifestations. He knows the cosmic circuits of sun, moon and stars. He is the sole initiate of the creator, and on this rests his pivotal role between gods and humankind. Before proceeding any farther in the study of Egyptian belief, the reader needs to reread and contemplate the words of this composition from the 2nd millennium BC, to understand how far we are travelling before we reach this particular human society. Together the divine birth cycle and this exposition of kingship present a remarkable symphony. The king acts for the sun on earth. He is a part of the very stuff of the sun. As his mortal human vessel gives way, he 'flies to the sky and unites with the sun disk', as the literary masterpiece the Life of Sanehat expresses it.

As in ancient Egyptian myth, this special position does not protect him from jealousy or attack. There is every chance that at any moment another issue from the sun god might seek to claim the throne before the present king has returned to the sun disk at the end of the lifespan of his human mortal body. In one episode told of the gods, Geb rebels against his father Shu. Both are legitimate rulers, each the offspring of the sun god, but the timing of their rule is in dispute. Similar legalistic claims pervade the tales of battles between the gods Horus and Seth, in their bid for kingship. These tales, investigated more fully below, bring a religious background to that most political of manoeuvres, the murder of a ruler. It could happen at any time: order could descend into chaos, the flood might fail, and there might be plague. Divine kingship did not remove these dangers from the world: it had to live with them. A large part of its resources went into strategies for achieving permanence for what is good, echoing the persistent obsession with survival that animates creation. According to this world of sun kings, the trained hands of sculptors and painters (women were not trained for these tasks in Egypt) could physically create that divine harmony, just as the trained chanter could effect and realize harmony by pronouncing the correct rituals. Training is the prerequisite: ancient Egyptian art employs a complex series of proportions and interrelations to arrive at its unmistakable final images, and only years of training combined with artistic talent could bring life to the image. The ritually fashioned and dedicated object itself became, in the Egyptian language, a 'permanence', *mnw* from the word *mn* 'to remain, to endure'. From a small vase to a temple or even, as we see with Akhenaten at Amarna, an entire city, the works of kingship took physical form in these 'monuments', the weak translation Egyptologists convention-ally use for *mnw*. Often an inscription in hieroglyphs emphasizes the need for such tangible permanence, with the formula 'the king has made this as his *mnw* for the god (or goddess), that he may achieve life eternally' (*ill. 3*). This is what must be done to inherit eternal life. In perfect union with the system of art, the hieroglyphic script itself expressed and served this perma-nence. Every time hieroglyphs were used, the material entered a transcendental plane, a world of eternity. The outlines and proportions of the figures are those found in formal art, and the very language is pared down to its immutable essentials, the consonants – vowels are not rendered, and image- or meaning-signs remove any ambiguity from the strings of consonants. For example, there is possible ambiguity in writing the sound of the three consonants m+n+w. They could, without the vowels, be understood as the physical sign of permanence established by the king, the 'monument', but might also signify hard stone, the material most likely to achieve that permanence. In order to separate the two meanings of the same sound, the Egyptians could add a sign determining the general meaning in each case. They could specify the general idea of 'monument' with a book-roll for abstract ideas, and the specific idea of a type of stone with a rectangle indicating a quarried block.

**3** *Stela showing King Sety II offering to Amun-Ra. The inscription below records the full five names of the royal titulary, ending with 'son of Ra' Sety (II) and the phrase 'given life, stability and power like Ra eternally'. There follows the classic formula 'he has made a monument (mnw) for his father Amun-Ra'. Temple of Amun, Karnak (Thebes). 19th Dynasty.*

This system of writing is one of the most elegant solutions for capturing a language in two dimensions, as great an aesthetic achievement as the system of formal art used to capture images. A religious aim, to secure harmony for ever, underlies the success of this unitary system of art and writing. It is not easy for modern readers to absorb the implications of hieroglyphic writing. First, this is inscription, not the printed book, and it remains tied to its place like a ritual: each hieroglyph forms part of a religious act perpetuated for eternity but inscribed into a particular place. Secondly, it is not secular, and cannot be historical in intention: there is no wish to provide objective eye-witness accounts of events, in the style of European positivism; instead the inscription drives out evil from the world and establishes for eternity what is good. This does not imply that the modern historian cannot use hiero-glyphic inscriptions to reconstruct a passage of events. It does mean that (s)he must first consider their context and original religious purpose within a Bronze Age world where the sun king ensures divine harmony. Hiero-glyphic inscriptions and formal ancient Egyptian art deliver a vast treasury of information on the past, but not on our terms or directly in response to our questions. The decoding of this civilization requires of us some of that intimate knowledge claimed for the king, of how the world and in particular the heavens move, of a very different solar system.

# CHAPTER ONE

# THE MYTHOLOGY OF RA

## The evidence for Egyptian myths

At first glance the modern investigator may feel overwhelmed by the torrent of visual imagery and host of inscriptions and manuscripts, scattered throughout the Nile Valley and along a time-line of over 3,000 years. Nevertheless, all these disparate sources provide substantially consistent evidence for a single, coherent picture of creation as an act of the sun. This allows us to draw a character sketch of the sun and accompanying gods that can act as a guide to the literary and artistic output of those three millennia, from the Step Pyramid in the 27th century BC to the latest temple reliefs in the 3rd century AD. For a 21st-century world, the poetic vision of the ancient Egyptians may perhaps best be translated into the language of the natural sciences, as James Allen rationalizes the texts in his *Genesis in Egypt*, summarized below. Without such translation into a contemporary idiom, we may find it difficult to take the ancient expressions of belief seriously. If we lose anything in the process, at least the channel of communication opens up between the ancient words and images on the one side and our contemporary configurations of belief and knowledge on the other. It can also be claimed that the creation beliefs express a philosophy of nature in that they answer the same questions as modern physics and biology – where do we come from? How (as well as the ethical why) does the world exist?

Perhaps the greatest danger in translation, or the greatest loss, lies not in the language but in the medium of communicating the ideas, the script. Since the end of the 18th century, we have generally circulated and received ideas by the medium of the printed text, copyrighted and authored. This communications technology has already yielded in part to the computer in the delivery of a vast new scale of generating, retrieving and manipulating words and numbers. Nevertheless, still at the start of a new millennium, our subconscious habits remain those of the printed text, finished and assigned an authority, an author. The advantages of this medium are likely to ensure its survival alongside online and offline computerized communication – Internet and CD-ROM. Therefore we need to continue to wrestle with the hidden assumptions and prejudices sown by our familiarity with the world

4 *Painting in outline, depicting Ra falcon-headed in the company of Sety I. The hieroglyphs above the god name him as Ra-Horakhty. Tomb of Sety I, Thebes West. 19th Dynasty.*

of the printed book. This struggle with ourselves applies especially to our investigation of peoples without the printing press, such as the ancient Egyptians. When examining ancient Egyptian inscriptions and manuscripts for evidence of beliefs, we need to remain aware of the context in which they survive. Often the particular localized use of a motif may dictate the precise manner in which it is formulated. In order to take account of these influences, we need to see clearly the type of source material to which each inscription or manuscript belongs. Here we may briefly summarize the sources for creation beliefs. There are repeated references to solar creation in funerary compositions from the late Old Kingdom to the Roman Period, where the birth of the world serves as a model for the eternal regeneration of the mummified body. Sun hymns of the New Kingdom comprise an additional, more lyrical body of inscription devoted to the sun god as supreme instance of life. On the walls and ceilings of temples, hieroglyphic inscriptions and scenes include the earliest surviving version of perhaps the most famous depiction of creation from Egypt, the vast arched body of the sky goddess Nut on the ceiling of the main chamber in the Cenotaph of Sety I at Abydos. Such images become more frequent later, on the funerary papyri and painted coffins produced in spectacular abundance at Thebes during the 11th and 10th centuries BC. Surviving rituals in the cursive hieratic script include an intricate description of the creator, preserved in one late dynastic papyrus known (after its first modern owner and his lawyer) as Papyrus Bremner Rhind. Such is the range in date and type of the source material for seeing the sun through ancient Egyptian eyes.

## The names of Ra

The various compositions reveal a vision of the unfurling of the world, redolent in poetic phrasing where none of the mystery of existence is lost. As the sum of all matter this first appearance of the sun god could be named Atum, meaning 'the All', but as the sun, source of life and energy, he could be named more specifically as Ra, the main word in the Egyptian language for 'sun' (*ill. 4*). Both terms are used in Coffin Text 335 (the same composition as the later Book of the Dead 'chapter' 17), one of the most frequently attested incantations from the period 2000 BC to the Roman Period (cited here from the coffin of Sebekaa):

FORMULA FOR GOING FORTH BY DAY IN THE UNDERWORLD BY THE
HONOURED [NAME OF THE DECEASED], HE SAYS:

The spoken came to be: Mine is All [Atum] in my existence, alone
I am Ra in his first risings. I am the great god who came into being of himself,
He who created his names, lord of the Nine Gods [i.e. of all gods],
He who has no opponent among the gods,
Mine is yesterday, and I know tomorrow – *it means Osiris.*

These different terms are sometimes combined, for example in the divine name Ra-Atum, where two aspects of divine creation are to be invoked at the same time. Far the most common of such compound names is Ra-Horakhty, using the concept of Horus, god of kingship, as embodiment of divine kingly power: we might loosely paraphrase this favourite Egyptian name for the sun god as 'the sun as the sovereign power in the horizon' (*akhty* = 'he of the horizon'). The horizon as home of the creator becomes the focus for one late Middle Kingdom prayer, labelled in Egyptology as Coffin Text 788, and found inscribed on the east face of the pyramidion, the capstone for the king's pyramid:

Open the face [i.e. the sight] for [the name of the deceased],
That he may see the lord of the horizon,
That he may cross the sky,
And may he [the lord of the horizon] cause that he rise as the great god, lord
    of Time,
An indestructible star,
May he be stellar among the stars.

## The scarab as solar symbol

At the beginning of creation, the Egyptians imagined that the sun must have arisen out of nothingness. This mystery could be expressed as an act of spontaneous self-creation, for which the Egyptians used the word *kheper* 'to come into being', 'to take new form'. Accordingly, one of the names of the sun god was Khepri 'the one who comes into being', and a frequent epithet for a creator god is *kheper-djesef* 'he who comes into being of himself', the self-created. To express this aspect of the sun god, the Egyptians used a humble analogy from their observation of nature, the beetle pushing a ball of dung along the ground (*ill. 5*). The sight of the sphere rolling as if self-propelled seems to have provided a parallel in the Egyptian mind for the great solar sphere moving through the heavens, and the link with the creator was confirmed by the notion that the eggs of the beetle would hatch from the dung-ball, as if the beetle were spontaneously regenerating itself. From the late New Kingdom, the sun god could be depicted as a being with a male human body and a dung beetle for a head. The analogy may strike a modern audience as rather crude or undignified, but today we have moved too far from contact with the earthiness of nature. Instead the motif should remind us how the Egyptian world interlocked the minute and the mighty, the one a possible microcosm embodying the other. Similarly, in the 5th century AD, one of the great fathers of Egyptian Christianity, the abbot Shenute, did not hesitate to find analogies in the behaviour of flies and ants to remind his congregation of the workings of the divine in human life. In ancient Egyptian iconography, the scarab became one of the most popular motifs in art on the smaller scale, thanks to a development in writing and administrative practice at the end of the Old Kingdom. From the beginnings of the Egyptian state, around 3100 BC, for a thousand years the Egyptians used the cylinder seal, a device imported from Mesopotamia for impressing the mud sealings securing documents or commodity containers. At the time that the Egyptian kingdom began to lose its political unity, around the 22nd century BC, the cylinder seal began to be replaced by stamp seals of various forms. By the beginning of the Middle Kingdom, when unity was restored shortly before 2000 BC, the scarab had been widely adopted as the most appropriate symbol and most practical form. The religious significance of the beetle made it a perfect guarantor for the act of sealing, of great importance in the ages before technology provided better security in the form of locks and keys. In form, the features of a scarab can be relatively easily cut from a small oval piece of steatite, leaving the underside flat for the design to be impressed on the sealing. After about 1700 BC the signet ring replaced the scarab as the means of sealing documents with a motif or inscription. Yet the scarab continued to be used in Egypt as a solar amulet in life and in burial, sometimes in the larger form placed on the chest as a 'heart scarab', down to Ptolemaic times. Outside the Nile Valley the form was already being imitated in Minoan Crete and then in Western Asia before 1700 BC, and during the 1st millennium BC it became one of the most popular items of amuletic jewelry, surviving its usage in ancient Egyptian art.

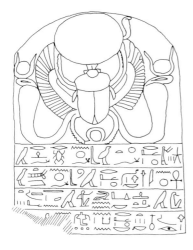

5 *Stela of a goldsmith of Amun, inscribed with a 'hymn to Ra when he rises till the moment he sets in life', beneath an image of a winged scarab raising the sun disk between protective cobras. Both name and title of the goldsmith referred to the god Amun, and were therefore mutilated under Akhenaten (see Chapter Five). Brussels E 6252. 18th Dynasty.*

## *Benu* bird of Ra, the 'phoenix' of Egypt

In addition to the scarab, the Egyptians drew a variety of other motifs from the landscape of the Nile – a bird alighting on dry ground, for example, or a lotus flower opening as the flood water recedes. Both images would fill the landscape in the annual experience of the Egyptians, when the late-summer Nile flood subsided during the autumn. The flood left behind it a valley covered in fertile mud, the silt brought downstream by the torrent. This created a new beginning physically every year. The primeval mound, first dry land of creation, seems to receive focus in cult, and in religious literature, in the form of a mysterious sloped stone called the *benben*. Repeating the consonants b+n, this word derives from the root weben 'to shine', as does the name for the bird of solar creation, the *benu*, forerunner of the phoenix of classical Greek myth. The sources for the *benu* deserve some extended comment, as this is one of the recurrent motifs in sun worship, and beautifully illustrates the way in which the Egyptians used the natural environment for imagery to speak of the divine.

The Greek account of the phoenix requires some untangling, to extract elements attested in ancient Egyptian sources. These do not provide antecedents for its most dramatic theme, of a bird that burns itself and rises from the ashes. However, there are strands linking the Greek phoenix with the Egyptian *benu*. Both are birds of the sun, both take form of themselves, rather than being born from other creatures, both undergo death, and both become symbols of regeneration. Another feature shared by the Egyptian and the later solar bird is the theme of periods of time. According to the Greek writer Herodotus, the phoenix went through its fiery cycle every 500 years. Intriguingly, the Roman author Tacitus refers to a cycle of 1,461 years, which is four times 365 and a quarter. This number carries hidden significance for Egypt, where the ancient calendar rounded off the actual solar year to 365. The earth in fact takes 365 and a quarter days to go around the sun, but the round number has advantages for accountancy, and the Egyptians did not feel the need to add a day in the manner of our leap year. Every 1,461 years the New Year of the Egyptian calendar would coincide again with the 'real' New Year of the solar, and so of the agricultural calendar. This suggests a Nilotic origin for the phoenix at least in the version recorded by Tacitus. Yet it may not be wise at this stage to insist upon too close an identification of the classical phoenix with the ancient *benu* bird of the sun. By the time Tacitus or even, six centuries earlier, Herodotus wrote their accounts, the Greek world had met, absorbed and influenced an extraordinary array of oriental traditions, including those of Syria and Persia, Mesopotamia and Anatolia, as much as those of Egypt.

From Egyptian sources we may draw the character of the *benu* separately from the fabulous phoenix with its own distinctive, if related resonance. The depictions (*ill. 6*) show the *benu* as a bird in the heron family, possibly a specific type, but often indistinguishable from the ordinary heron (Egyptian *shenty*). In the funerary papyri of the New Kingdom and later, two formulae seek to provide the deceased with the ability to take the form, in one case of a heron (Book of the Dead 'chapter' 84), in the other of the *benu* bird ('chapter' 83). The two scenes, side by side, may introduce details to separate the birds, such as a pair of tufts at the crest and/or the breast of the *benu*. However, these may be symbols of distinction, rather than accurate representations of two separate bird species in nature. In these illustrations the *benu* generally has light blue feathers. The bird produced a sound evoked in Egyptian literature: a harpist's song from the late New Kingdom compares the voice of the deceased to that of the 'divine *benu*'. Any physical presence of the bird in Egyptian temples cannot be demonstrated, but there were several places named 'Domain of the *Benu*'. The most important of these stood at the central city of the sun, Iunu (see Chapter Three), but there were others in the 7th and 18th provinces of Upper Egypt, that in the 18th giving its name to the local city. There were also shrines for this sacred bird at Edfu, Ihnasya and Sais, at least by the Late Period. This indicates that the *benu* shared the destiny of the sun cult itself, radiating out from its centre at Iunu to reach, by the end of ancient Egyptian history, every corner of the land. The religious literature names the benu *ba* (or 'soul'), 'form' or 'image' of Ra. From at least the reign of Tutankhamun, the heron appears on heart scarabs, the amulets protecting the heart as source of life in Egyptian elite burials. The bird embodies the radiance emanating from the sun, and one rare New Kingdom funerary composition (Book of the Dead 'chapter' 29B, known from only three manuscripts) places the hopes of survival beyond death on this single solar force:

**6** *Painting on a tomb-wall showing the deceased in the presence of the benu bird, on the boat of the sun disk. Tomb of Irinefer, Deir el-Medina, Thebes West. 19th Dynasty.*

FORMULA FOR [RECITING OVER] A HEART OF CORNELIAN
RECITED BY [NAME OF DECEASED] –

I am the benu, *ba*-soul of Ra,
He who leads the blessed to the Underworld,
He who has Osiris return to earth,
To do what his *ka*-spirit desires,
Who has [name of deceased] return to earth,
To do what his *ka*-spirit desires.

Whether image, soul or offspring, the motifs refer to the effect, the consequence of the existence of the sun. This makes them appropriate to the birth of time, where the first rising of the sun brings not only light but the possibility of existence, the bubble of space and movement within the inert masses of the uncreated void outside. The hieroglyphic script uses the image of a heron perched on a stick to write the word 'flood', presumably from the common sight of the birds clinging to wood above water during the season of the high Nile, every summer. Perhaps in a sense the *benu* means the shining of the sun at the water, on the first moment of creation: the heron is the tangible incarnation, for Egyptian art, but the word itself may in origin be the 'shining' *webenu*. Certainly, in the Egyptian sources, the *benu* presides over the flood, and this provides much of the power of the symbol, in its combination of the solar and the fertile. These motifs mean so much more in the valley of the Nile, with the periodic flood, precisely under the heat of the midsummer sun. This may account for the surprising control ascribed to the *benu* in a line from the same widely attested Middle Kingdom composition on creation cited above, Coffin Text 335:

> I am that great *benu* bird which is in Iunu, the keeper of the inventory of what exists –
> *it means Osiris – what exists means the Time-cycle and the Time-line.*

The gloss does not provide any explanation for the preceding phrase in the way we expect from an encyclopaedia entry. Instead, as throughout this remarkable composition, it expands the base of reference, as if feeling its way around an invisible divine form. Each divine feature corresponds to another, and the combination becomes the source of any enlightenment or 'clarification'. The glosses work more like examples given to illustrate different uses of one word in a modern dictionary, as opposed to the definitions given there for the word. Here we learn that the *benu* in Iunu presides over the inventory of existence, echoing the role of Osiris (in terms of fertility?) and the expanse of time in both its aspects, circular and linear.

## The sun in all creation: the Litany of Ra

Among the finest of Egyptian religious compositions, the Litany of Ra provides perhaps the most explicit demonstration of the unity of creation in its creator. According to this belief, creation unfurled out of the sun god, Atum or 'All', fissioning over time into a world of different features within which Ra or 'the sun' remained the principal figure. The Litany of Ra gives voice and image to this belief, in a series of 75 acclamations of Ra 'in' each of 74 forms in his creation. The composition is best known from Thebes, where it appears first in the tomb of the king during the New Kingdom, before variations occur on Third Intermediate Period papyri. The images illustrating the words of acclamation achieve a unity out of the multitude by giving most of the 74 manifestations of the sun god a mummiform figure (*ill. 7*). The differences between each form appear either in the head of the figure, or simply in its name. Several names refer directly to other gods and goddesses.

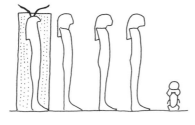

7 *Five of the forms of the sun god figured in the Litany of Ra: from right to left Khepri as a scarab lifting the sun disk, the goddesses Nut, Tefnet, and Nephthys, and the primeval waters Nun depicted as a ram-headed figure in darkness. Tomb of Thutmose III, Valley of the Kings, Thebes. 18th Dynasty.*

For example, one form of Ra is the god Horus, another is the goddess Isis. Clearly, then, all creation derives from the one creator, and, in a certain sense, remains a part of that divine being, even if the individual elements take on lives of their own. Curiously, at the heart of the sequence stands 'the pig', deliberately selected for this position, it appears, despite the generally observed but unwritten rule banning the animal from religious writing and illustration. The pig is as omnivorous as man, and thereby violates the usual demarcation in nature between carnivores and herbivores. This reminder of the human condition perhaps demanded that the pig never be mentioned – quite apart from the fact that it would have been dangerous to eat the meat of a scavenging animal in such a hot climate. After all, scavenging dogs, cats and rats were never demonized in ancient Egyptian art in quite the same way as the pig. The appearance of the pig at the centre of the acclamations to forms of the sun god must have seemed all the more striking, a disturbing reminder that creation includes at its heart the capacity to devour and destroy.

## The feminine aspect of creation, and the family of Ra

Although the sun god consistently appears as the creator who created himself, numerous sources indicate that the stimulus to this creation takes the form of a divine female complement. In general terms the feminine complement to the solar creator is the goddess Hathor, but for the aspect of aide to creation the Egyptians used a more specific name, Iusaas 'She who grows as she comes'. As we see later, in the account of Iunu, city of the sun, the sacred precinct of Ra included prominent architectural space for the cult of the feminine in creation, in its different guises as Hathor, Iusaas and a sometimes separated epithet Nebethetepet 'Lady of the Field of Offerings'. Originally the two names denote a single entity, but after the Middle Kingdom Nebethetepet and Iusaas can appear as separate goddesses, as if to emphasize two separate aspects of the feminine complement to creation, abundance (Nebethetepet) and growth (Iusaas). For example, in a painting illustrating the good deeds of Ramesses III on Papyrus Harris, the two goddesses appear side by side, following the two aspects of the solar creator also separated into the divine sovereign Atum and the falcon-headed Ra-Horakhty. The role of Hathor, or more generally of the feminine principle in creation, underwrites much of kingly court ritual. In their titles and iconography the women around the king relate to him as Hathor relates to Ra. Later we see another key female character added to the solar drama, the figure of Nut, goddess of the sky. Still later in the unfurling of creation comes the great healer, Isis. Hathor, Isis and Nut provide the substance behind the ritual titles 'king's wife/mother/daughter', often read too literally as kinship terms in Egyptology. This mythical ambience provides the basis

**8** *Stela showing a woman and her daughter offering to a lion-headed goddess named in the hieroglyphic inscription as Mestjet, 'eye of Ra'. This is the only evidence for the name, but the depiction of the 'eye of Ra' as lion-headed goddess is widely attested. From Abydos. 21st Dynasty.*

for understanding how Egyptian kingship operated, particularly in such radically innovative times as the reign of Akhenaten (see Chapter Five).

The first division in creation was the opposition of dry and moist, expressed as the issue of a male and a female child from the sun god. The Egyptian words for 'dry', Shu, and 'moisture', Tefnet, appear in the accounts of creation as god and goddess, the first generation after the sun god. This second act of self-generated creation could, like the first, be envisaged in various ways, this time linked to the physicality of the integral male human body. Thus it came about through his mouth, as spit, or his hand, as mastur-bated semen. These physical motifs derive in part from associations between words. The word-links (inaptly named 'wordplay' in Egyptology) violate our dearly held philological faith in etymology. In our sciences of language, we construct family trees for words, and derive meanings from their history. Against this, the ancient Egyptians linked words not because they shared origins, but because they shared consonants, or structure. The interest is not in the past behind each word, but in a present perceived as immutable and god-given. Words correspond to the created matter of creation. In this view, we receive a mystery, hidden information, from the fact that Shu 'dry (air)' echoes in sound *ishesh* 'to sneeze out' (transitive), and that Tefnet 'moisture' shares two consonants with *tef* 'to spit'. These words and relations between words correspond somehow to created features and the relations between them. All creation belongs to the divine, including language and script. The creation is a mystery, but these words are a part of the mystery, and can help to convey it. The word-links work as curiously in our eyes as the mystic cal-culations of more recent radical thinkers on creation, such as Khlebnikov in the early 20th century. Out of these reflections on existence emerge extraor-dinary poetry and art, and these may guide us to our own reflections more sensitively than laws of philology.

Among the most eloquent writings on the origins of the world may be found in the Coffin Texts, columns of cursive hieroglyphs covering the inner sides of the finest coffins from elite provincial cemeteries of the early Middle Kingdom, from about 2000 to 1850 BC. The most perfect of these masterpieces of craft and art survive from the cemetery of the nobles of Khemenu (modern Ashmunein), the cult centre of Thoth, god of knowledge. The city lies in Middle Egypt, midway between Memphis in the north and Thebes to the south, across the Nile from the site later chosen by Akhenaten for the city to his refined version of the sun god. We know little of Middle Kingdom Khemenu beyond the evidence from the tombs, but the quality of the work suffices to demonstrate its importance. Other coffins of the same period from other cemeteries vary in quality from the finest to more clearly provincial work, developing the same and similar traditions. The images and words probably drew from the output of the king's court, but the cemeteries for the Middle Kingdom royal residence did not survive the turmoil of the Second Intermediate Period. Thus we rely on these second and third rungs of the hierarchy for the preservation of what we might call Middle Kingdom philosophy, the intellectual speculation on the origins and meaning of life. The Coffin Texts include a particular group of compositions to which we might loosely apply the label 'Liturgy of Shu' (CT 75 to 80). As god of the air, Shu represents the essential difference between the animate and the inanimate body. Air, or more specifically breathing, is the quality of being alive, and the 'Shu Liturgy' aims to secure for the dead body the possibility of continuing to live. The original manuscripts are lost, and there survive instead the coffin sides, to which the artists of the word adapted the liturgies recited at the funeral. Out of an undifferentiated matter the sun god emerged with the twin principles of Ankh 'Life' and Maat 'What is Right'. Here Shu can be aligned with the grammatically masculine Egyptian word Ankh 'Life', and Tefnet with the feminine word Maat 'What is Right'. This account of creation gives a succinct poetic view of the world. In effect, life and justice existed embedded within the creator before this unfurling, and they take shape as the two complementary physical forces in life, the enduring dry and the corroding moist. The following excerpts from two compositions within the Liturgy illustrate the way in which the Egyptians applied their creation beliefs to the trauma, and the practicalities, of embalming and the funeral procession.

For the first, we may take the version on the coffin of Mesehty, a governor of the strategic city Asyut in Middle Egypt during the early Middle Kingdom (Cairo CG 28118).

FORMULA OF THE BA OF SHU, FOR TAKING THE FORM OF SHU
[TITLE OF THE COMPOSITION NOW NUMBERED CT 75]

I am the *ba* of Shu, the god who took form of himself,
I am the *ba* of Shu, invisible of form.

I took form as the limbs of the god who took form of himself.
I am the one in the flank of the god – I took form in him.
…
I am the one amid the gods of Unending,
One who hears the words of the gods of Unending.

Here the governor Mesehty obtains life for his body after death by a bold strategy typical of Egyptian funerary literature. The verses identify him directly with Shu, the air, not in general terms but precisely at the moment of creation. The rebirth of Mesehty receives the same assurance as existence itself: in the midst of lifelessness, the inert body belies appearance, and stirs with new and divine life.

The second excerpt can be cited from a more southerly source of the period, the coffin for a man named Iqer, excavated by Ernesto Schiaparelli at Gebelein and now preserved in the Egyptian Museum, Turin. The phrasing fuses in the clearest manner the two worlds of creation theology and funeral directives.

FOR EMERGING TO THE SKY, FOR BOARDING THE BOAT OF RA,
FOR TAKING THE FORM OF A LIVING GOD
[TITLE OF THE COMPOSITION NOW NUMBERED CT 76]

O eight gods of Unending, keepers of the regions of the sky,
You whom Shu fashioned from the fluids of his flesh,
You who tie together the ladder for Ra-Atum,
Come towards your father in me, tie the ladder for me,
For I am the one who created you and fashioned you,
Just as I was created by your father Atum.
…
It is I, Shu, created by Atum who took form of himself.
I was not made in the womb, I was not assembled in the egg,
I was not born in birth.
My father Atum spat me out as spittle [*ishesh*] of his mouth,
Together with my sister Tefnet.
She emerged after me, and I was clothed in the breath of life of the throat.

For Iqer, and for any other Egyptian man or woman receiving this funeral liturgy, solar creation provides the means for infusing the inanimate body with breath. The phrasing recasts death as the origin of life, just as in myth the sun regains at midnight the energy for dawn birth. When the bearers of the coffin raise it aloft, they become the deities surrounding the germ of life at the beginning of creation. The breath for the corpse is the very god Shu, and by this means the Egyptians transformed the moment of loss of life into the very source of existence. This remarkable strategy reveals the depth of belief in the creative roles of Ra-Atum, Shu and the other deities in this cycle.

In the next step discernible across the various sources, abstract principle becomes tangible. Shu and Tefnet couple to produce the earth god Geb and the sky goddess Nut. Unlike their parents, or indeed Ra, Geb and Nut have names of their own which are not identical with the features of the environment that they represent (the Egyptian for the earth is *ta* and for the sky *pet*). Geb is a divine presence in the earth on which humans walk, and Nut is the divine, maternal aspect of the sky above them. In the Egyptian view of the world, these gods are not in the world, rather they constitute the framework of that world. Geb and Nut suffered the fate of separation from each other by Shu, the dry air between heaven and earth. Yet with the help of the moon god Thoth they won five days outside the regular year, and on these Nut gave birth to their children: their eldest, the perfect Osiris, the two sister-goddesses Isis and Nephthys, and, violently torn from his mother, the anarchic Seth. Ever since, in the ancient Egyptian view, the year contained besides its 12 months of 30 days each a liminal period of five extra days. This gave the total of 365 days by which the Egyptians reckoned the years of their kings, and from that all calculated time. For the ancient Egyptians, the regnal year formed the basic framework in time, as the sun, earth and sky formed the parameters in space: the birth of the children of Nut marked the beginning of this regular cycle of time.

## Ra withdraws to the sky

Curiously for us, the creation of humankind does not seem to form a major episode in Egyptian creation myths, at least in the surviving record. Instead human beings make their first appearance in accounts of rebellion against Ra. The solar cycle in nature involves the darkening and setting, one might say the ageing, of the sun. In terms of a ruler, this evokes ideas of a loss of power, and the Egyptians did not hesitate to depict this 'eldest' of the gods as an aged being, leaning on a stick as in the hieroglyph denoting old age. Some compositions go so far as to paint the Ra of late evening, or late in rule, as a decrepit figure in advanced senility. From one narrative first attested in the reign of Tutankhamun, we learn that the sun god ruled earth in the early phase of creation, only to face rebellion. In his anger he sent out

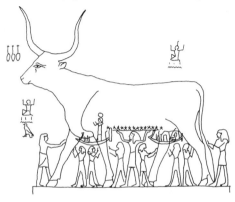

9 *The illustration of the Heavenly Cow held aloft by eight untiring gods, as found with one narrative on creation. Beside the cow is inscribed the word neferu, 'perfection', and under her passes the barque of the sun. Tomb of Sety I, Valley of the Kings, Thebes. 19th Dynasty.*

10 *A depiction of the cosmos on a funerary papyrus, showing the sky Nut arched over the earth Geb, set between solar symbols of winged disk and scarab. The figure to the right is 'the West', where the dead were buried and would be reborn. From Thebes West. Third Intermediate Period.*

his eye, emblem of all-seeing divine power (*cf. ill. 8*). In the Egyptian language, the word for eye is feminine, and the despatched eye could accordingly be perceived as a 'daughter of the sun', a raging goddess. One of the most widely used names for this force was Sekhmet, meaning simply 'the Mighty Goddess', the righteous Fury in the world of the gods. Sekhmet set about annihilating all life on earth, including all human beings, with such ferocity that the sun god relented. The hieroglyphic inscriptions relating this tale show that the goddess could not be dissuaded from her bloodthirsty destruction, and the gods resorted to a ruse: at the instigation of Thoth, god of wisdom, they coloured a lake of beer with red ochre, to make it look like human blood. Sekhmet came upon the lake, drank herself into a stupour, and relaxed from hatred into the benign intoxicated force of love in creation – effectively turning from Sekhmet the fury into Hathor the creative feminine principle. Despite this happy outcome, the sun withdrew from his direct rule on earth, and from that time began his distant journey through the heavens around the earth. This immense voyage appears in Egyptian imagery as a journey by river boat, typically enough for the civilization of the Nile (*ill. 9*). In the morning he appeared on a boat named Mandjet; in the evening the boat was named Mesketet. His retinue included the supreme mechanisms of power, Sia 'farsightedness' and Hu 'command'. A third companion enabling the sun to oversee the created world from a distance was Heka, for which the conventional translation 'magic' fails to capture the essential meaning, the genius of creation.

The failed rebellion against Ra and his consequent withdrawal to the sky accounted for the essential structure of the earth as viewed by men. This is encapsulated in an image among the most frequently reproduced in modern books on Egypt, in which Nut bears the boat of the sun god as she arches over the prostrate Geb, held aloft by Shu (*cf. ill. 10*). The scene offers a mythic dimension to the visible world as it appeared along the Nile in the 2nd and 1st millennia before Christ. Beyond the horizon of this world of gods and men, the endless nothingness might at any moment attempt to reclaim this precious space, suspended as an air bubble of time and space within anti-matter. The day and night journeys of the sun kept the structure of the earth and sky intact, but he and his crew had to resist and overcome every night the inherent hostility of the outer darkness. From the Middle Kingdom the Egyptians gave the name Aapep to its nightly manifestation, depicted as a giant serpent, threatening to capsize the solar boat on hidden sands, like a river boat in low waters. Imbued with the experience of valley-dwellers bordered by the desert, the ancient Egyptian account of creation carries a strong negative undercurrent, a belief that all life remains exposed to the peril not so much of death as of more final annihilation, being returned to nothing. The living strive to maintain just the possibility of life within a universe of anti-matter, and this is the principal task of the sun god and his agents of order.

## Divine rebels

Threats to divine order did not come only from beyond its confines. Strife within creation did not end with the rebellion which resulted in the withdrawal of Ra to the heavens. Later texts paint a picture of continuous jealousies and rebellions in the following reigns of his firstborn Shu, and then of his male offspring in turn, Geb. However, the conflicts most prominent in the sources from the Old Kingdom to the Roman Period are those in the following generation of Ra's family – the tales surrounding Osiris, Seth and Horus. In these tales, the sun god continues to act as the supreme authority, despite his withdrawal to the heavens. Osiris as eldest son becomes the next king of the world, but his perfect rule rouses the jealousy of his anarchic younger brother Seth. For Seth, Egyptian formal art delivered one of its most brilliant compositions, an amalgam of a series of features as they do not occur in nature. This creature has long ears like those of a donkey, but straight-topped, a long tail, but forked rather than tufted, and a curving snout not quite like that of any creature. Several scholars have tried to identify the Seth-animal, but it seems more likely that this is a sort of anti-animal, a creature deliberately constructed to express the violation of natural laws. If the ancient Egyptian artist excelled in one area, it was animal art, the concise and evocative depiction of animal figures. Such an art would not have been likely to produce an unrecognizable animal form without good reason. This anarchic force struck out at perfect order: Seth murdered Osiris. The exact details rarely surface even as an echo in Egyptian sources, and we rely on the Greek historian Plutarch for one series of grisly details about the methods used by Seth. Common to both sets of sources, however, are the theme of dismemberment and the role of Isis in bringing the corpse back to life to the point where she could conceive be impregnated by it. After the murder, Osiris retired to the underworld, mirroring the retreat of Ra to the heavens, leaving earth to become a battleground between Seth and his new nephew, the adolescent Horus, child of Isis and Osiris. In the early days after the birth, Isis fled with the child into the most inaccessible marshes of the Nile Valley, deep in the western Delta. The terrain becomes so deceptive there that the Greek historian Herodotus speaks of the place, Akhbit (later written Kheby, and rendered Chemmis in Greek versions), as a floating island. Here the child would be safe from his dangerous uncle, but must still survive the noxious forces of chaos ever present in Egypt as the serpents and scorpions lurking among the fields and rocks. Isis had repeatedly to use all her powers to protect her child, until he was old enough to challenge his uncle in a series of physical and legal duels. Finally the sun god and the company of the gods around him brought themselves to arbitrate, at first delivering one part of Egypt to Horus and another to Seth, but eventually handing the kingship entirely to Horus. Seth continued to embody the forces ranged against life in the desert, and his anarchic physical power was even harnessed to the cause of good, as he wielded his sceptre on the prow of the sun god's boat against the ultimate enemies of order, the chaos beyond creation.

## The family of Ra in Egyptian life

These episodes form the framework not only for the cult of the sun god, but in a sense for all ancient Egyptian life. Each episode or 'constellation', each grouping of deities, provided the prototype for personal experience. We might more tellingly reverse this formulation, and recognize that each challenge in life takes on the form of words and illustrations in the mythic episodes. Isis is the great healer: she corresponds to the experience of being healed. Horus as child is the experience of being vulnerable to ill health (*ill. 12*). Horus the adult champion expresses the prowess of the young man at the peak of his physical abilities, again a human experience that the ancient Egyptians lived no less vividly than our generations today. Seth is the mythic form of disorder in society, in the family, and in the individual. Osiris is the body surviving death, corresponding to the practice of mummification. In their various combinations, each finds its meaning. There

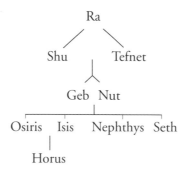

11 *The unfurling of creation as a sequence of generations from Ra to Horus.*

12 *Horus as child, mastering the creatures threatening order and health, on a miniature healing stela. Excavated by Flinders Petrie at Iunu. Late Period.*

could be no Osiris without Seth, no Horus without Isis, just as within their pairings order and disorder, good and bad health, must mutually define each other. The surviving manuscripts and inscriptions contain relatively few examples where different episodes combine to form narrative sequences. Where this is attested in manuscript, the source is more literary than religious, that is to say, it carries no liturgical or cultic function, no role in healing, but is written for a more reflexive social function, that of being read.

The most elaborate surviving literary tale about the gods is also one of the most beautifully crafted books (scrolls) from ancient Egypt. This masterpiece in the art of the book is known today as Papyrus Chester Beatty I, taking its name from its first modern owner, an industrialist who retired to Dublin, where the great work is preserved. Thanks to the detective work of scholars such as Georges Posener, we know in some considerable detail the social-historical background to the copying of this composition. It belonged to a man named Qenherkhepshef, who was the secretary to a very particular workshop of artists, at the end of the 13th century BC. These were the draughtsmen and workers responsible for the cutting and decoration of the king's tomb in the Valley of the Kings. During the 19th and 20th Dynasties the team lived in a government-built and – supplied settlement at the edge of the desert, on the Theban West Bank. This demarcated group of houses appears in the ancient manuscript sources simply as 'the village'; in Egyptology it carries the more recent Arabic name Deir el-Medina ('monastery of the town'). As royal draughtsmen the artists needed to know the principles of the hieroglyphic script, and more could read and write than would have been usual in an average village of the day. Working on the edge of the desert, alongside the crews cutting the Ramesside royal corridor tombs, they lived on an abundance of a rather unusual writing material, the clean, white limestone chippings. Limestone survives better than the ancient paper made from the papyrus plant, and so it is that we inherit from the colony of Ramesside royal tomb artists one of the greatest treasuries of written information about any ancient community. From these chippings and from the manuscripts buried at the dry desert edge, we learn that many regarded Qenherkhepshef as disagreeable, even corrupt. We learn that he married late in life a young widow, and that her children inherited his wealth – presumably including his library. For, despite his questionable personality, this clerk of works was a learned man with a good range of literary manuscripts, from technical prescriptions and incantations to secure good health, to copies of fine hymns, to the great manuscript here mentioned. On one side of the scroll runs a series of love songs, one of the most beautiful lyrical cycles to survive from Egypt. On the other we read the tale of the battles between Horus and Seth.

The narrative draws from the detailed episodes in religious literature recording all manner of legal and physical contests. In this sense it is a myth, a tale of the gods. Yet the social context indicates what we might see as a secular motivation uniting all these episodes. For it is difficult to read the tales as written here, with a knowledge of Egyptian myth, without laughing. The repetition of the episodes (the very feature absent in religious contexts) makes the gods, or rather the procedures described, look ridiculous. Most ludicrous of all is the behaviour of the sun god, who assumes the role of judge in the tale. This is a tale of the justification of Horus, the long- drawn-out procedure to the point where the tribunal declares him 'true of voice', vindicating his claim to inherit the kingship from the murdered Osiris. Yet the literary strategy of uniting all the mythic episodes in one long sequence obtains a quite specific effect: the tale of justice becomes a satirical commentary on the slow delivery of justice. You have to read this in the light of the litigious wranglings, the petty disputes, the accusations between neighbours, the divorce suits, even the bitter will of Qenherkhepshef's widow, who, long after his death, disinherits the children who failed to help her in her old age. This is a darkly comic tale from a very human setting. Egyptologists have often branded the Ramesside period, to which this manuscript dates, as an age of corruption. They overlook the special survival of the sources: there seems to me no more, or less, corruption in this time and place than in any other. The difference lies rather in the survival of all these details from this singular community. Possibly it was a uniquely quarrelsome community, but it seems not very different from societies small and large elsewhere. The tale provides us with numerous episodes confirmed from other, often much later sources, and can be mined as a rich store of religious-historical information. Yet it demonstrates also a familiarity with the gods that was felt by at least this outpost of relatively elite living. Ra, Horus and Seth made possible this special means of criticizing Ramesside village tribunals, much as Osiris 'meant' embalming, or Isis 'meant' healing. These names express human relations in life and death not only at a theological level of thinking, but also and more vitally in the lives lived throughout the Egyptian Nile Valley over these 3,000 years.

# CHAPTER TWO
# THE SUN CULT AND THE MEASUREMENT OF TIME

## Offerings of words

It would be wrong to imagine that ancient religious practice involved only mechanical actions. The danger in this underlying assumption is that these might then be set in opposition to the words privileged in the modern religious experiences of prayer and hymn. The sun cult presents a challenge to such an opposition in the understanding of cult, because the central action is performed by cosmic bodies rather than humans on earth, also because it is not hidden to the population at large, and, perhaps most importantly, because their participation can almost be reduced to words and writings. Instead of inhabiting a closed, restricted, dark sanctuary, the drama necessary to cult takes place in the open sky: it involves the daily movement of the solar sphere from the eastern to the western horizon. The active engagement of the participants on earth consisted in large part of the correct enunciation of words. It was the words of the ritual that ultimately ensured the smooth continuation of the sun in its cosmic journey. These words were doubtless uttered in the company of ritual actions, and required prescribed material ingredients such as incense to sanctify the ritual environment. Nevertheless, the primary offering to the sun god was not the great table of food and drink offerings, which he also received, but the word, and above all the deified Egyptian word Maat 'What is Right'.

The Egyptians inscribed in a variety of select and more or less inaccessible contexts the words offered to the sun. Thanks largely to the detective work of Jan Assmann, we can now distinguish an outer (or more widely accessible) and an inner (or more restricted) cycle of these word offerings. These enable us to recover an extraordinary amount of the detail for a cult even though its epicentre, the city of Iunu, has long since disappeared (see Chapter Three). We can follow from the hieroglyphic record the hymns sung as a litany of hours. There are 12 of these each night and 12 each day, the origin of our own 24-hour clock. No treatise explains the reason for selecting 12, but this may be deduced from the movements of earth and moon in relation to each other and to the sun. The moon completes its cycle of waxing and waning roughly 12 times, the 12 months, in relation to each

13 *The finest surviving ancient Egyptian time-keeper, a water-clock depicting Amenhotep III and the deities of the northern skies. From Karnak (Thebes). 18th Dynasty.*

greater cycle of the sun in its year of seasons. In Egypt these seasons are late-summer flood, winter sowing (as the Nile waters recede), and early-summer drought (with the river at its lowest level, before the next flood). The 12 cycles of the moon in relation to the one cycle of the sun provided one framework of time, at the level of the farming year. On the shorter level of daily life, the 12 segments were presumably transferred by analogy from year to day, creating 12 day-sections and 12 night-sections.

These hours were not measured into equal sections of minutes: before the refinement of time-measuring in the late Middle Ages, there were no precise minutes, and even the hours were relatively rough and ready divisions of time. Yet the framework provided a reasonable operating base for a complex society, and for the religious tasks of maintaining the fragile fabric of the universe, the cosmic daily journey of the sun. The scattered sources cover only the second half of ancient Egyptian history, the earliest appearing about 1450 BC in the tombs and temples of kings and the tombs of a few high officials. The more sacred liturgical texts appear also in a handful of manuscripts on papyrus, and were used again for hieroglyphic tomb inscriptions for the most important officials of the king in the Late Period, during the 7th and 6th centuries BC. In theory, these formed an innermost core of mystery, the knowledge of the universe available only to the sun king. In practice, as with all cult in Egypt, the sun received worship throughout the Nile Valley, and the king therefore had to delegate the recitation of the correct texts to deputies at each locality. Without this pragmatic devolution of the most sacred cosmic knowledge, our circle of sources would be restricted even more drastically to the direct evidence for ritual actions performed by and words recited by the king.

# PART ONE

# Innermost Circle: the King accompanies Ra

## The Underworld Books from the tombs of kings

Hieroglyphic inscriptions and great tableaux of images reveal both the words recited by the king, and the object of the cult, the daily and nightly voyage of the sun in his boat as perceived and expressed by the ancient Egyptians. The images appear first in the mid-18th Dynasty, laid out around the Hidden Chamber or sarcophagus hall of the king's tomb in the Valley of the Kings. The title 'Writings of the Hidden Chamber which is in the Underworld' introduces the earliest cycle of images and extensive accompanying cursive hieroglyphic inscription, emulating manuscript. In later periods this heading was abbreviated to 'that which is in the Underworld', Egyptian Imyduat, and this is the name by which the cycle is generally known today (usually in the older Egyptological reading 'Amduat', which is followed here for ease of recognition). The cycle follows the nocturnal sailing of the sun on his boat across the 12 segments of the night hours. At the end of the 18th Dynasty, a revised version appeared in the king's tomb, without a heading but known since the last century as the Book of Gates – a reference to the fact that the sun enters each night hour through a spectacular portal, enveloped in fire-spitting serpents. Other compositions in the later New Kingdom royal tombs develop the themes of the night journey, and some include other aspects of solar creation. In perhaps the best-known example, the image of the sky goddess as celestial cow becomes the illustration to a

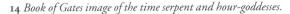

14 *Book of Gates image of the time serpent and hour-goddesses.*

Tale of the Destruction of Humankind, explaining the withdrawal of the sun god to heaven as the result of rebellions on earth (*ill. 9*). Alexandre Piankoff edited with great sensitivity several of these cycles and compositions, among which perhaps the most important for the understanding of the sun cult is the group which he labelled the Book of the Day and of the Night. This gives an outline of the entire circuit, through the day and night, where most other recorded cycles concentrate, in this underworld setting of the tomb, on the night journey alone. After the 20th Dynasty, when the king no longer sited his tomb at Thebes, the cycles did not fall out of use. Excerpts appear in the few surviving inscriptions from the 21st and 22nd Dynasty royal tombs at Tanis, in the Delta, but the weight of later evidence comes from Thebes. Here it is likely that the archaeological record for the 1st millennium BC may be distorted in favour of the southern city. The drier desert ground of the Theban West Bank cemeteries has preserved organic materials such as wood and papyrus, which quickly perish in the damp soil near the river in the Delta. At Thebes, the nobility of the 21st and 22nd Dynasties drew extensively on the vast repertoire of imagery and inscription in the Valley of the Kings. The royal motifs swarmed into a new medium, no longer the walls and ceilings of corridors and chambers in a rock-cut tomb, but over the brightly decorated wooden coffins and the magnificent funerary papyri that make this one of the peaks in the history of Egyptian art. If the royal Delta cities ever produced any coffins or papyri of their own, such organic material could not have survived in the damp soil. Nevertheless, it seems clear that at least within Upper Egypt the artistic output at Thebes was indeed unparalleled. The superb quality of the Theban burial equipment points to royal origins. Most probably the royal artists of Deir el-Medina continued their fine draughtsmanship beyond the closing and dismantling of the Valley of the Kings, and served a new, local Theban elite with their mastery of the formal canon of proportions and the forms of the hieroglyphic script.

## The sailings of the sun god

The Underworld Books of the kings' tombs in the Valley of the Kings provide us with a visual and written accompaniment to the journey of the sun. They show us how Egyptian kingship envisaged the object of its cult, the solar journey. A religious geography opens up before our eyes, with a richness of detail presaged only by the Book of Two Ways in the coffins of the early Middle Kingdom, some six centuries earlier. A central feature in the solar journey is the density and variety of its population. This applies both to the hordes of figures on all levels of the journey and to the immediate surrounds of the sun god. The sun does not travel alone, but sails on a

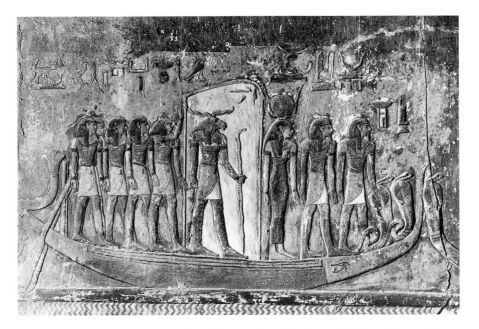

*15 The night journey of the sun, depicted as a ram-headed god named Flesh, with boat and crew of deities: from right to left, Isis and Nephthys as serpents, Wepwawet and Sia, a goddess 'Lady of the barque' (Hathor?), and behind the sun god, falcon-headed Horus, and four other gods including Hu.*

boat with a full crew (*ill. 15*). Each member on board offers a quality indispensable to safe passage and effective rule. Sovereignty in the sky depends as much on movement as political power on earth must still depend, in the Bronze Age and Iron Age, on speed and ease of communication. It would take a fortnight for news in the south to reach the north, another fortnight for a reply, longer for the mustering of a military force in the event of trouble. These conditions make rule a continuous movement: the king can never rest. The day–night–day circuit of the sun echoes and confirms the kingly progress. Just as the king needed to sail to all parts of Egypt to maintain his presence there, for the sake of stability, the sun god steers his course through the sky by both night and day. Movement is not taken for granted: it involves struggle both at midday, when the boat may run aground on the sandbank of Aapep, the enemy of Ra, and in the middle of the night, as it passes the sandy terrain of the earth god Seker. In the mid-hours of the night, a mystery must unfurl, to enable the sun to rise again in the morning. This mystery of regeneration is expressed as a reunion of the sun god, in his mobile form or *ba*, with his static form, his 'corpse', presented in the New Kingdom cycles as Osiris. The reunion reanimates the sun and provides the force leading to dawn resurrection. In all of this activity, the sun remains the source of authority, but does not actively participate: it is the retinue that

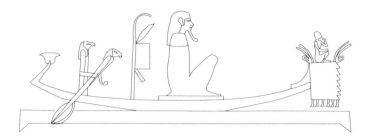

**16** *The sun god as a seated human mummiform figure, on the Morning Barque, with a child symbolizing rebirth on the prow. East wall of the Tomb of Panehsy, Iunu. 26th Dynasty.*

mans the boat, drags it through sections of the circuit, and provides the necessary accompaniment in paeans of praise, as Ra moves through night and day. The crew itself comprises a group of divine qualities necessary to creation and rule, and a select number of important deities. Each of the qualities of the cosmic ruler stands in the boat personified as a rather anonymous standing man with long braided beard (reserved in Egyptian art for divine beings). Their names are Sia 'farsightedness', Hu 'command' (specifically the command that brings sustenance, so also a word for food offerings), and Heka 'creative force', a neutral primeval energy essential to creation, often translated as 'magic' by Egyptologists. Some cult hymns to the sun list by name the deities accompanying the sun in the depictions. Other listings can be gleaned from the depictions themselves, where the names are generally inscribed beside the figures. The principal members of the retinue are Shu, Tefnet, Geb, Isis, Horus, Thoth and the goddess Hathor, as well as the all-important personification of the order established by the sun, his daughter Maat 'What is Right'. Seth appears more rarely, and where he does so he defends the boat against the enemy Aapep.

The sun god travel does not travel in one boat alone. He uses two to complete his daily circuit. The night boat took the name Mesketet, from the root *sek* 'to perish', as the boat for the period of disappearance of light from the earth (*ill. 17*). In contrast, the day boat was called Mandjet, from the root andj 'to grow fat', for the time of day when light swells to fill the world (*ill. 16*). The method of transfer from one boat to the other does not figure either in the pictorial images or in the writings on the sun. Yet the two often take different forms, distinguished in the late New Kingdom for example by an emblem set at the prow – Mandjet for the day has a swallow, while Mesketet for the night has a child, image of the rebirth of the sun god to come at dawn. By setting the sun on a pair of boats, the Egyptians gave dramatic expression to the complementary of day and night. As so often in

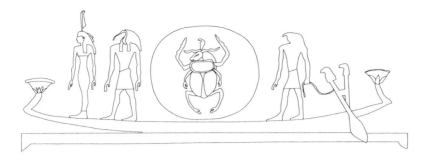

17 *The sun god as a ram-headed scarab in the solar disk, on the Evening Barque, accompanied by Maat, Thoth and Horus. West wall of the Tomb of Panehsy, Iunu. 26th Dynasty.*

ancient Egyptian symmetry, visual and written, the duality of opposing units is a careful strategy to reinforce control over the whole. From this non-analytical vantage point, the line of divide between the two is not a theme requiring discussion. The importance of pairing lies in the combination, in the greater unity that the oppositions demarcate and emphasize. In this case the two boats complement one another to secure the unity of the solar circuit through both the day sky, visible to the human eye, and the night sky, unseen and so potentially not covered.

## The hours portrayed in the Amduat

The 12 hour-sections of the Amduat provide a detailed chart of the under-world journey of the sun. In practice this distributes the various motifs of the voyage across the walls of the king's tomb, and the composition in its surviving form owes much to the specific requirements of that architectural space. Nevertheless, it is worth summarizing the passage in this form, as it covers the principal aspects of solar rule above as well as below ground. Each hour receives a distinguishing name. In the first hour, named 'smiter of the foreheads of the enemies of Ra', the sun meets the baboons of the horizon, a group familiar to any visitor to the tomb of Tutankhamun, where the restricted space allows for only one or two excerpts from the whole composition. The decision to include the baboons in preference to so many other details of the Amduat indicates their importance to the Egyptians. Continuously through history the religious literature on the sun concentrates on the dawn response of nature, the moment demonstrating how life depends on the celestial source of energy. In the area around the Nile, before human settlement crowded out the original fauna, the shrieks of baboons would have given most piercing voice to each sunrise. It is small wonder, then, that the various Nilotic species of large ape became symbols of not cacophony, but a living mystery, the link between sun and life. These morning baboons become by reflection the divine creatures welcoming the sun into any new phase of its passage (*cf. ill. 25*). This explains why we find them also at sunset, in the first hour of the night, labelled in hieroglyphs as 'those who open to the great *ba*-soul', and 'those who make music for Ra when he enters the Underworld'. The sun god in his boat takes the form of a ram-headed man, labelled 'Flesh', to emphasize that this is the aged evening body in need of regeneration (*ill. 15*). The short descriptive passage refers to the 'distribution of fields to the deities who are in his retinue', and names the district as 'waterway of Ra'. This administrative act takes the title 'decree'. Ra is here the literal king of the cosmos, providing his followers with the physical means of sustenance, the fields from which crops supply the barley for bread and beer, and the flax for clothing.

In the second hour, 'the wise one who protects her lord', the Amduat has the sun rowed through the Field of Reeds in the waterway of Ra, 'spending time in Wernes'. Here the fields are allotted to the divine beings in the underworld, with the recommendation 'Know the Underworld-dwellers – whoever knows their names will be with them.' This instruction and gloss provide a rationale for recording all the features with labels, as the secret knowledge guaranteeing the solar king rule and eternal life. The hybrid forms of deities in the upper register for this hour receive a similar accompanying caption, 'whoever knows them can emerge by day', in other words receive resurrection. The boat of the sun moves through the hour together with no fewer than four other sacred boats. One of these bears the moon, while another, named 'carrier of Wernes', supports a Hathor-sistrum, anticipating the cult object on a plan of the Iunu temple of the goddess, to be described in Chapter Four. One of the most striking features of these accounts of the unknowable is the mathematical precision, both in the naming and in actual measurements. Thus the second and third hours specify the area covered as 309 *iteru* in length, and 120 in width. The third hour, 'she who cuts *ba*-souls', sees the sun resting in 'the Field of the Riverbank-dwellers'. Thereafter the terrain changes from water to sand, with paths shifting abruptly from horizontal to diagonal, and the boat of the sun-god becomes a serpent in order to pass this 'cavern of Sokar'. The god Sokar belongs to the creative forces of the earth and is similar to Ptah as a god of the crafts using materials from the earth. The fourth hour captions identify the sandy route as 'the secret way which Anubis entered to hide the corpse of Osiris' (*ill. 18*). We are coming close to the heart of the midnight mystery. These two hours leading up to the critical moment of midnight both refer to the region as Imhet. The fourth bears the name 'Great in her powers', or 'Great one in the Underworld', and the fifth is 'the guide who is in the midst of her boat'. In the fifth an oval shape lies

18 *The angular path through the sandy domain of Sokar, in the journey of the sun through the fourth hour of the night, as depicted in the Amduat. Sarcophagus chamber, Tomb of Thutmose III, in the Valley of the Kings, Thebes West. 18th Dynasty.*

between two outward-facing bearded heads, denoting another, rather more primeval earth god Aker.

In the sixth hour the Amduat reaches its first climax, spending time in 'the watery depths, lady of the Underworld-dwellers'. The many inhabitants of the underworld here include the lines of earlier kings and the blessed dead. From this moment on, in a sign of its successful regeneration, the sun appears beneath a winding serpent named Mehen 'the coiled', symbol of eternity. At the end of this hour, moving into the seventh, the decisive battle over Aapep passes to completion, affording the hour the name 'she who repels the forces of chaos, and decapitates the savage-faced'. Here the sun

**19** *The damned and the saved, as depicted in the Amduat. To the left, lion-headed goddesses pour fire on the bodies of the evil in sand pits. To the right floats the body of someone who has drowned, and thus been claimed by the gods as a blessed being. Detail from an early 22nd Dynasty papyrus, as recorded by the French Revolutionary Expedition of 1798–1801. From Thebes West.*

god rests in the cavern of Osiris, and his foes receive punishment on the lower register in the presence of Osiris himself. The central scene presents the slaying of Aapep at the foot of the solar boat. Twelve star gods and 12 star goddesses are among the divine host, indicating the control over time throughout every moment of the day and night. The eighth hour, 'the coffer of her deities', introduces the Cavern-dwellers, a term for the most secret gods buried since the earliest phase of creation. In the ninth and tenth hours too, the sun rests 'in this cavern'. Like the second hour, the ninth bears the name 'protector of her lord', while the tenth is 'the raging one, who boils alive the rebel'. As the name suggests, the damned receive their final punishment here, from eight lion-headed aspects of Sekhmet '(Divine) Fury' who have to 'allot the eye of Horus to the one in the Underworld' (*ill. 19*). There follow eight 'images made by Horus' to destroy the bodies of the foe. A more peaceful image acts as counterweight to the last judgment: the bodies of the drowned appear floating in the underworld waters. This forms primary evidence for the belief that the gods had claimed as their own those who died by drowning. The idea finds one of its latest and most famous expressions in the deification of Antinous, the lover of Hadrian, after his death in the Nile in Middle Egypt. The punishment of the damned continues through the 11th hour, named 'the instructor, lady of the sacred boat, at whose emergence the rebels are punished'. The night voyage is drawing to its close, and already 12 gods bear a coiled serpent, with the caption specifying that their task is to place Mehen on his course towards the eastern gateway of the sky. Finally the 12th hour, 'who sees the perfection of Ra', bears witness to the miracle of rebirth, as the gods physically drag the sun on his boat through the body of the coiled serpent, renamed in this scene as 'Life of the Gods' (*ill. 20*).

In order to understand the poetic force of the underworld imagery, it is useful to look at the differences between the Amduat and its first major revision, the Book of Gates, attested in the restoration of traditional religion after the reign of Akhenaten (see Chapter Five). A summary of the features in both brings out some of these differences.

| Hour of Night | Amduat motifs | Book of Gates motifs |
|---|---|---|
| 1st | Entry to underworld | Entry to underworld |
| | Journey of 120 iteru to Wernes | |
| 2nd | Time in Wernes/Field of Reeds | |
| | Distribution of fields | |
| 3rd | Field of Riverbank-dwellers | Boat of the Earth |
| | Waterway of Osiris | |
| 4th | Sand way, Cavern of West | Time serpent |
| 5th | Sand way, Cavern of West | Gods measuring fields |
| | | with cord, after this |
| | | hour the Judgment Hall |
| 6th | Watery depths | |
| 7th | Cavern of Osiris | |
| | Felling of Aapep | Enemies bound |
| 8th | Cavern-dwellers | |
| | Cloth (for embalming) | Mummified dead rise |
| | | to see sun |
| 9th | Cavern | Depiction of the drowned |
| 10th | Depiction of the drowned | Netting the enemies |
| | | of the sun |
| | Punishment of the damned | Felling of Aapep |
| 11th | Cavern | |
| | Decapitation and burning | Destruction of Aapep |
| 12th | Sun god passes through snake | Destruction of Aapep |

20 *The rebirth of the sun at the end of the night, when the solar boat is drawn through the body of a serpent named 'Life of the Gods', as depicted in the twelfth hour of the night, in the Amduat. Sarcophagus chamber, Tomb of Thutmose III, in the Valley of the Kings, Thebes West. 18th Dynasty.*

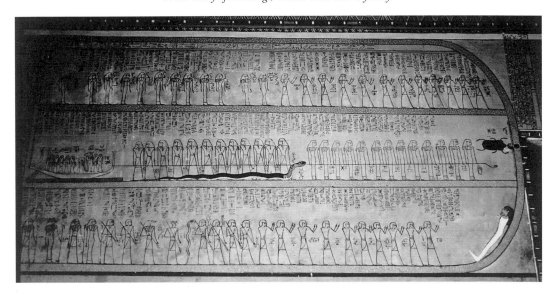

The table shows that the features and events of the journey overlap, though they do not entirely coincide. The comparison becomes a little more complicated thanks to a scholarly debate on the Book of Gates, over whether the first gate marks the beginning of the first hour, or whether the introductory scene depicts the first hour. Despite the differences, the themes of passage, rule and judgment are common to both compositions. If we understand the motifs as elements in two or more great collages, we need not expect them at exactly the same place. Instead, they may draw from a central stock of imagery relating to the entire journey, or perhaps more plausibly to each of the three broader sections of the night identified by the Egyptian language and used in the inscriptions – early night, middle night, and the 'end of the darkness'.

## The arcane knowledge of kingship

Accompanying the rich imagery of the depictions, the Underworld Books and the Book of the Day provide captions and phrases, incorporating some of the finest and most extended religious literature surviving from ancient Egypt. These are more than embellishment of the illustrations: they combine to form a seamless description of the solar journey. Even the first word of the Amduat, *seshu* 'writings', refers in fact, in the Egyptian language, both to the outline black and red drawings by the draughtsmen (Egyptian *seshu qedut*, literally 'writers of outlines') and to the cursive hieroglyphs accompanying them. The full title of the Amduat explains the need for both: both are forms of knowledge, complementing and completing one another.

> *The writings of the Hidden Chamber. The positions of the Powers, Gods, Shades, Transfigured Dead, Created Forms. The beginning is the Opening of the West, door of the Eastern Horizon. The end is outer darkness, door of the Western Horizon.*
> *Knowing the Powers of the Underworld. Knowing [their] created forms. Knowing their transfigurations for Ra.*
> *Knowing the Secret Powers. Knowing what is the hours and their gods. Knowing his apportioning to them.*
> *Knowing the doors and the road upon which the great god moves.*
> *Knowing the course of the hours and their gods.*
> *Knowing those who adore [i.e. the good] and those who belong to destruction [i.e. the evil].*

These opening words for the most detailed Underworld Book insist above all that the composition contains knowledge. The secrecy of this special cosmic knowledge can be seen in the restriction of the sources, in the New Kingdom confined almost exclusively to the king's tomb. The theme of secret knowledge recurs throughout these illustrated accounts of the solar journey, but also in a number of compositions of equally restricted distribution. Most important of these are the Morning and Evening Accompaniments to the sun worship by the king. The words of these may have been recited, but they are not exactly hymns. Rather, they serve to explain, almost to justify the cult of the sun. The Morning Accompaniment includes the passage already cited on the King as Priest of the Sun, one of the most explicit and eloquent ancient Egyptian accounts of kingship. The phrases before the cited passage first describe the occasion for the recital, and then develop the theme of arcane knowledge. These lines ascribe the secrets quite explicitly to the king: the secrets themselves define kingship, and make the king something more divine, more solar, than human.

[THE TIME FOR THE RECITATION]
The King worships Ra at daybreak, in his emergence as he opens his disk,
    As he rises to the sky as Khepri
Entering the mouth, emerging from the thighs, in his birth at the East of the
    sky,
When his father Osiris raises him, when Hehu and Hehut receive him,
And he rests in the Morning Barque.

[THE KNOWLEDGE OF THE KING]
The king knows this secret speech, which the Easterners say
When they chant the song for Ra at his rising, at his appearance on the
    horizon,
When they open for him the double door in the gateway of the Eastern
    horizon,
And he sails on the paths of the sky.
He knows their initiations and their forms,
Their settlements which are in the God's Land.
He knows the place of their positions there, at receiving Ra upon the way.
He knows the speech, spoken by the crew, as they drag forward the Barque
    of the Horizon.
He knows the birth of Ra and his forms that are in the Floodwater.
He knows this secret gate by which the great god emerges.
He knows those who are in the Morning Barque, and the great Image who is
    in the Evening Barque.
He knows your mooring posts in the horizon, and your steered paths in the
    sky.

There follow the reasons for which Ra placed the king on earth (see the Introduction). After this the concluding line reads simply 'Emergence of Ra as Khepri'. It is possible that this outline of kingly cosmic knowledge existed first as an inscription. Only the address to Ra at the end of the section ('your mooring posts... your steered paths') indicates that the lines may have been intended for recital. This may have applied only to this portion of the composition. The Evening Accompaniment has not survived in full, yet this too has a structure incorporating at least one section suitable for recitation. This is an address to Ra, also positioned in the central part of the composition.

## Hymns of the hours

The preceding compositions concentrate on visual and written imagery to describe the solar journey, whether or not the written elements were intended for recitation in accompaniment to the cult. If we are looking for the focal cult words and actions by which the king used this cosmic knowledge, Jan Assmann has provided the entry point through the select hymns inscribed in the same restricted contexts as the cosmographies (the Underworld Books) and Accompaniments. Foremost among these are the hymns in the Ritual of Hours. This follows the same twelvefold divisions as a key liturgy in the cult of Osiris, the so-called Hourly Vigil (*Stundenwachen*). The Austrian scholar Father Junker published those Osirian compositions from temple inscriptions of the Ptolemaic and Roman Period in 1910, and they correspond to fragments in earlier monuments, attesting to their existence at least by the Middle Kingdom. For the sun cult, the divisions of time carry more immediate significance, as the movement of the sun determines the degree of light and therefore the intensity of presence or absence of the divine power, the source of life. Clearly of extreme importance, their relation to the core solar cult becomes evident in the pattern of their distribution over the surviving monuments. Shadowing the Sun Cult Accompaniments, they survive first in the solar shrine on the upper terrace, in the temple to the cult of Hatshepsut at Deir el-Bahri. Excerpts then reappear in the same select environments: the tomb of Ramesses VI, the Theban tomb of a Ramesside sun priest named Nebsumenu, and the overwhelming temple-tombs of the most important officials at Thebes and Saqqara in the 7th century BC. Day and night at the transition from each hour to the next, the king sang a hymn of double purpose. At one level the words mark the passage of time, and at another, more creative, level they safeguard that passage. In these secretly transmitted inscriptions we meet the core of, not only the sun cult, but the kingship. The king is there to ensure that the precarious journey of the sun survives the midday and midnight encounters with Aapep, with evil.

Only broken fragments survive from the earliest version of the Hours of the Day in the cult of Ra, inscribed in the Hatshepsut temple at Deir el-Bahri (*ill. 21*). The Polish archaeological mission on the site is working on the reconstruction, aided by later versions, though these often contain variants. For example, the closest parallel for the Hatshepsut version Sixth Hour occurs in the Ptolemaic temple of Horus at Edfu, inscribed over 12 centuries

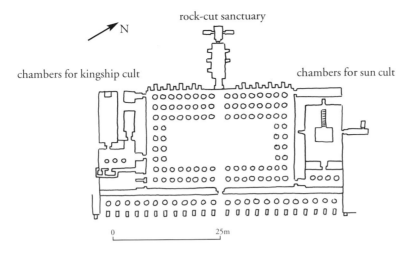

rock-cut sanctuary

N

chambers for kingship cult

chambers for sun cult

0       25m

**21** *One of the earliest surviving repositories of the kernel of sacred compositions of kingship: the upper terrace of the Hatshepsut temple at Deir el-Bahri, Thebes West.*

later, in modified form and used instead for the Eighth Hour. In the Hatshepsut temple, Hours 9 to 12 are more substantially preserved, and are worth citing here, as our closest guide to the original royal cult of the sun.

NINTH HOUR OF THE DAY, NAMED 'MISTRESS OF LIFE,...
OF THE LORD OF THE TWO LANDS...
WORDS TO BE RECITED:

Rise, rise: shine, shine. Ascend, O he who emerges from his egg,
Lord of Appearances, Primeval God of the Two Lands, the bull of Iunu,
He who traverses the islands in the fields of reeds,
Whom the turquoise gods acclaim, their oars dipping into the river.
You sail your two skies, you are arrived in peace,
...your... You have crossed your two skies, Ra, in peace.
The inhabitants of Tjehenu [the 'gleaming' western desert] praise you,
Your enemy, driven back before you, lies fallen.
The King...your beauty, your enemy is struck down.
May you smite the enemies of the King in all their places,
And grant that she breathes the sweet air of the north wind.
Install her as a follower among the just, who are in your following forever.

TENTH HOUR OF THE DAY, NAMED 'SHE WHO COOLS THE STEERING OAR'.
IT RISES UP FOR HEKA.
WORDS TO BE RECITED:

Hail, Gold at the brow, at whom the crew of the Evening Barque rejoice.
Hail to those your rising cobras, who bring you what heaven and earth
contain,
And burn your enemies with the great flame that comes from their jaws.

55

How high you are, Ra, overlord of powers,
You distribute to those in your following,
And you have repelled those that are in the turbulence of Shu.
You sail south, and are given praise,
You sail north, and are received with the cry 'on guard, earth'.
The immortal powers announce Truth to you.
The King has invoked you for your transfiguration,
And has appeased the face of your rising cobras.
Come, then, sail to the King,
Granting food daily, and elation in the marsh of the wild birds.
May the King drink water on the banks of the river,
As befits a follower among the peaceful.
May the King come and go with Ra,
and be called [to eat] with the ancestors.

ELEVENTH HOUR OF THE DAY, NAMED 'BEAUTIFUL TO BEHOLD'.
IT RISES UP FOR THE GOD ENTRUSTED WITH THE TOW-ROPE.
THIS IS THE HOUR OF DIRECTING THE TOW-ROPE TO THE HORIZON, AND OF
THE DESCENT OF THE SUN BOAT TO THE WEST.
WORDS TO BE RECITED:

Hail, Ra, Hail O you gods ahead of Ra and in his following on the Great
    Barque,
Who accompany him in peace in his hour of the one entrusted with the
    tow-rope.
The journey comes to pass, for him who emerges in his perfection,
Who unites the primeval waters with his mother by morning,
Lord of the festivals of the 6th day and the 15th day [of each month].
King for the western gods, sovereign of the eastern gods,
'Welcome in peace', say the gods of the western horizon,
'Rejoice', say the gods with the tow-rope, who keep steady your places in the
    West, who cast their protection for you as lord of the western mountain.
The King greets you, uniting with Ra in life,
Like [your] union with your mother, her arms around you.
May you join the King in life, that he be justified before Atum.

TWELFTH HOUR OF THE DAY, NAMED
'SHE WHO UNITES WITH THE LIVING ONE'.
IT RISES UP FOR THE GOD GIVING PROTECTION IN THE TWILIGHT.
WORDS TO BE RECITED:

Praise to you, Ra-Atum, going to rest in the sacred fields in the western
    horizon,
Joining your fields in the western mountain, with your rising cobras around
    you.
Hail, in peace, Ra, the eye of Atum has joined you, and you have hidden in
    its coils.
It repels strife from you, and makes you well for full life.
It unites your protection around your body.

O you gods rejoicing over the All-Lord, raising jubilation at his approach,
Until he descends to his seat in the West,
Seize your weapons to repel the rebels,
Fell the foe for Ra.
The western gods rejoice, taking up the tow-rope in the Evening Barque.
They come in joy: 'in peace, in peace, Ra-Horakhty', say the gods in the
    secret place.
Those in the West [say] 'on guard, earth', as they escort in peace, in the
    West.
You descend, Ra, to your place, your seat that is in the West.
You judge the inhabitants of the underworld,
You cast the forms of those who are in the underworld.
You count as the one [bringing] health to those of the western mountain.
Hail, as you enter the earth that you created,
And rest in the interior of your solar disk.
The King appeases the sight of those jubilant beings
That emerge from the earth at your approach,
And over whom those in the Evening Barque rejoice.
Grant me nourishment, fashion my life, elate me among the followers of Ra,
And repel all my enemies among the dead and the living.

In the ritual, each hour (in Egyptian a feminine word, wenut) stood person-ified with its own name, but Ramesside and later sources indicate that each daytime hour also stood aligned with a god or goddess. As time moves round in the daily cycle, each hour in turn 'rises up' (or 'stands') for its deity. Some of these gods and goddesses are the very same beings so often depicted on the boat of the sun god (*cf. ill. 15*). Others rarely occur elsewhere, or even have general descriptive phrases in place of names, as in the case of the last two hours. The full list runs as follows:

| Day Hour | Deity |
| --- | --- |
| 1 | Maat |
| 2 | Hu |
| 3 | Sia |
| 4 | Asbet (a serpent deity) |
| 5 | Igeret |
| 6 | Seth |
| 7 | Horus |
| 8 | Khons |
| 9 | Isis |
| 10 | Heka |
| 11 | the god entrusted with the tow-rope |
| 12 | the god who gives protection in the twilight |

The night hours too could be personified as goddesses, as we have seen in the Amduat scenes. Just as for the Day Hours, the earliest version of the hourly hymns for the night survives only imperfectly, in the Hatshepsut

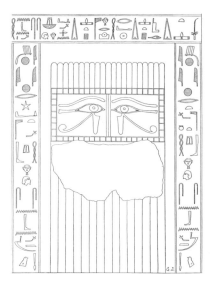

22 *Detail of the east outer face of the coffin of the chief lector Sesenebnef, the earliest surviving source with part of the Hour Ritual. Note the deliberately incomplete hieroglyphs for snakes and birds. Lisht. 13th Dynasty.*

temple at Deir el-Bahri. The surviving portion covers the words to be pronounced in the ritual for the first four night hours, and, interestingly, in each case the inscriptions are paralleled in the Book of the Dead. Although funerary papyri are far more numerous than sources for the Hour Ritual of the sun god, it would be wrong to assume from this that the Hour Ritual used excerpts from funerary literature. The reverse seems more plausible – that the compilers of the Book of the Dead 'chapters' drew on the most potent religious compositions known to them, the hourly royal cult of the sun. The first night hour incorporates passages found in 'chapters' 22 and 59 (the numbering system for these is modern), while the second to fourth hours include parts of what became 'chapters' 42 and 71. Intriguingly, the earliest source for two of these 'chapters' (59 and 71) is the burial of a late Middle Kingdom chief lector-priest named Sesenebnef (labelled as Coffin Text 222 and 691, respectively, in the modern corpus of Middle Kingdom funerary literature). His coffins were found in the cemeteries for the 12th Dynasty residence city Itjtawy, on the border between Upper and Lower Egypt (*ill. 22*). His title may have denoted the most important man for the transmission of sacred learning, including the hieroglyphic script. This would have given Sesenebnef special access to such otherwise regal religious compositions as the hymns to the sun. The other two 'chapters' are not known before they appear on New Kingdom Books of the Dead.

## Rites to be performed with the hymns

The words of the cult mysteries constitute the core of the ritual, but the Egyptians did not leave it to the word alone to secure the continued motion of the sun, and so the survival of the creation. They added ritual actions to be performed alongside the knowledge and words, and presumably intended to be carried out first and foremost by the king himself. In another field of life, that of healing, we see a similar triple strategy of action, combining knowledge (diagnosis/prognosis), materials (prescriptions) and incantations (in modern terms, resocialization and rehabilitation as a member of the community of the healthy). Cult did not differ in its approach; indeed it used in part the same terminology, applying the term *re* 'formula' (literally 'mouth', so 'what the mouth pronounces', 'utterance') to the separate sections of the ritual. This word was used in the technical sense only in healing, ritual and funerary literature. A healer would diagnose his patient, apply any prescribed remedy, correctly prepared from the particular proportions of ingredients, and recite from a manuscript the exact words required for that instance. Often, as we have seen, he cast himself as the great healer of heaven, the goddess Isis, in her role of healing her child, the vulnerable young Horus. This united the strategies of mind, touch and word to secure that most precarious of possessions, good health. The strategy in the sun cult follows a similar pattern. The great cosmographies provide the knowledge, corresponding to the diagnosis and prognosis of the healer. The secret hymns transfer that knowledge on to the plane of speech, the words linking heaven and earth. This leaves the third aspect, like the physical remedy, the use of materials to accompany and underwrite the cosmic cycle. Here Jan Assmann has identified the places in the written record that can provide evidence for what the king did, while he was saying or singing the sacred words. These all-important sources consist of written instructions or descriptions of activities, and are found appended to the end of the same restricted group of sun hymns that provide the words to be recited. The thematic pattern inferred from these closing 'instructions' matches the pattern of the daily cycle itself, and together they suggest that the hourly sun worship amounted to a ritual re-enactment of the sun journey through the day and night skies. The various ritual actions implied by these glosses to the hymns can be summarized as follows:

> Purification
> Raising Maat ('What is Right') to the sky
> Securing free passage for the sun
> Protecting the sun
> Destruction of enemies
> Placing insignia of rule

The king (or his substitute) has undergone purification, both by cleansing the body ('has come to worship you with pure arms') and by the use of aromatic substances ('has chewed myrrh on the banks of the Two Knives lake').

23 *A unique painting on a funerary papyrus, showing Ra falcon-headed in his barque, over the mutilated serpent Aapep. The scribe Ramose stands on the prow facing Osiris. Papyrus of Khnumemheb, from Sedment. 19th Dynasty.*

He must raise the image of Maat to her father Ra, perhaps especially at dawn, given the name of the first hour of the day as the one that 'raises What is Right to her lord'. The themes of free passage for the solar boat and destruction of enemies are closely connected. There may be a series of ritual acts to protect the sun on his boat, and to achieve this by destroying images of any obstacles or enemies. The sources imply the burning of images of Aapep and other figures, echoing the cosmographic illustrations in the Underworld Books (*ill. 23*). These may have been of wood, or, as suggested in one passage from the funerary literature, of wax. The closing instructions to one secret hymn reveal that the officiant 'has read to you the 77 scrolls on the slaughterhouse of Aapep every day: his *ba*-soul is cast to the fire, his corpse to the flames, his power to the Eye of Horus'. The king or deputy also placed emblems of power on the deity, again indicating an enactment of the heavenly drama in the sacred replica space within the sun shrine on earth. One poetic closing statement alludes to the foremost symbol of solar rule, the fire-spitting cobra rising on the brow of the ruler, recording that the officiant 'gives you [i.e. the sun] your two eyes, your two sisters who have emerged from your head, so that you may live'.

In many of the closing statements, the king or officiant does not seem to do very much more than look on, while actions take place around him. In this he mirrors the impassive stance of the sun god in the cosmographies and in myth: the sun moves forward, while the other divine forces around him combat evil and steer the solar boat in safety. In the closing statement for one of these mystery hymns, the person reciting makes the following declaration:

'I have destroyed Aapep in his onslaught, I have seen the *abdju*-fish as its moment fell, I have seen the *inet*-fish in its transformations, when it guided the boat on its waterway. I have seen Horus at the steering oar, Thoth and Maat ['What is Right'] upon his arms, the front rope in the Evening Barque, and the back rope in the Morning Barque.'

Here destruction is one act, but the remainder of the passage involves witness and contemplation. There is then a tension between the ruler as protector and the ruler as protected. Both active and impassive roles apply to the sun god and to his representative directing the cult, his mirror image on earth below. Another closing statement reads: 'I have steered the Evening Barque clear of the sandbank of the Two Knives Lake in a fair wind.' Here the officiant steers, where in the preceding citation he watched the god Horus steering. This need not be seen as self-contradictory. The combination of doing and looking, the active and the contemplative, fits the model of a parallel ritual enactment of the solar circuit within the sun shrine. Here, the king or his deputizing officiant would both perform the rite and, in the open court, see at least the daytime passage of the sun. In the terms of the divine, he would be doing and seeing the deeds at once: steering the sun god in the model version on the ground below, and seeing the sun 'steered' through the sky above. This is the sun cult in its double earth–sky movement.

## Thebes as a treasury of solar hymns

From the preceding paragraphs it should be clear how greatly we depend on the exceptional breadth of sources from New Kingdom Thebes, compensating for the dearth of information from Iunu itself (for which see Chapter Three). There may be a specific reason for this. In the joint reign of Thutmose III with his aunt, Hatshepsut, solar features flooded into the temples of king and gods at the moment that the Valley of the Kings became fully established as the royal burial place. Perhaps then Thebes became a solar city precisely when the decision was taken to bury the sun king in the Valley of the Kings. The first ruler of the 18th Dynasty, Ahmose, seems to have been buried originally at Abydos, where his largest royal cult complex lies to the south of the city and cemeteries of Osiris. His son Amenhotep I may have been the king who took the decision to use Thebes as the royal cemetery, and perhaps the full effect was felt first under the successors of this king. Already the first successor of Amenhotep I, Hatshepsut's father, Thutmose I, had introduced the obelisk and perhaps also the pylon to Karnak. The pylon, or massive temple gateway, is today one of the most familiar features in ancient Egyptian architecture, but none of the examples now standing dates earlier than the New Kingdom and its origins remain obscure. The pyramid complex of Amenemhat II at Dahshur includes two great solid rectangular structures at its gateway, a slight hint at possible solar origins for the later pylons in temples to the gods. Towers beside temple entrances appear around the same time, during the early Middle Kingdom, at various sites. Otherwise, the earliest certain survivors are those of the 18th Dynasty at Thebes. When the gateway was aligned east–west, with the sanctuary behind at the east, a pylon could be read as the Egyptian hieroglyph for 'horizon' each time the sun disk emerged between the pylon towers over the gateway itself. It is not entirely certain whether or not the Egyptians intended this, as north–south oriented temples, such as the temple at Luxor, also have pylons, and the Egyptian word for pylon, *bekhenet*, does not seem to allude to the sun. Whatever the precise significance of the pylon, the obelisk is certainly a symbol for the sun god, and throughout the remainder of the dynasty architecture at Thebes became steadily more solar. At Deir el-Bahri the Hatshepsut cult complex includes its own royal sun chapel, on the upper terrace. In the tombs of both Hatshepsut and Thutmose III, and even of the highest officials of Hatshepsut, the Amduat and other compositions of secret kingly knowledge appear for the first time. At the eastern end of the Amun temple at Karnak, Thutmose III set up his unique 'sed temple', with a solar shrine at the northeastern corner. Fronting the enclosure wall on this side of the complex, previously the back end of the temple, he and his successors raised a new style of sun shrine, its focus a remarkable single obelisk. Egyptian inscriptions lay particular emphasis on its singularity, using the phrase tekhen waty 'solitary obelisk'. Perhaps this was intended to evoke the single benben stone of Iunu. Certainly it brought the sun cult in force to what had apparently been nothing more than the rear wall of the Karnak complex. Today, it stands outside the basilica of San Giovanni in Laterano in Rome, the city where it has now been for most of its existence. It is the tallest surviving monolithic obelisk, at 36 m (118 ft). These various spaces in the architecture of gods and kings were designed to provide a setting for the cult, and this finds its indirect expression in the scattered compositions reunited to such effect in the research by Assmann. The New Kingdom Theban sun cult may have undergone some change in its transfer from the north, though it may have remained as close as possible to its model. From this time there was also a 'Greatest of Seers' in Karnak, and Thebes itself became known as 'the Iunu of Upper Egypt'. As will be seen in Chapter Four, only two other cities in Egypt acquired the same solar colouring, the successive foundations of Piramesse and Tanis in the Delta northeast of Iunu. Neither survives to anything near the extent of the Theban temples, but by any standards the solar transformation of Thebes is an astonishing accomplishment in the history of both religion and architecture.

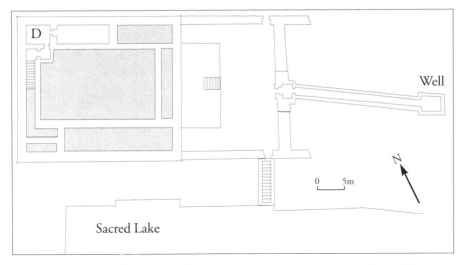

24 *Lower level of the building of Taharqo beside the Sacred Lake at Karnak (Thebes).*

## A solar cult chamber beside the Sacred Lake at Karnak

We are fortunate that the surviving record, so often inimical to our knowledge of Egyptian religion, includes one structure that brings together the different strands of the sun cult, again at Thebes. The cycle of words and images upon its four walls encapsulates the cult in its mysterious inner core, at one decisive point in the history of the civilization. The moment is the reign of Taharqo, king of Napata in what is now Sudan, and ruler of the largest empire in the Nile Valley, the Napatan realm during its 50 years in control of Egypt (about 715 to 664 BC). The reign of Taharqo built on the 8th-century BC renewal of Egyptian art, religion and literature. At Karnak beside the Sacred Lake for the Amun temple, Taharqo had a building constructed for certain rituals of kingship (*ill. 24*). This includes a chamber assigned the letter D in the modern publication of the edifice by Richard Parker and Jean-Claude Goyon. Here we find in effect a summary of the secret rites and knowledge, the preserve of the king, mapped out on the walls like a manual guide to the worship of Ra (*ill. 25*). As indicated by the other sources, the sun cult can be recognized from its unusual combination of the pictorial guide, or cosmography, with its Accompaniments, and the more directly recitational, liturgical compositions.

The cult chamber by the Sacred Lake raises the question of the practicalities in the inner circle of solar cult. Most of these questions cannot be answered, but it is important to ask them. Above all, we should consider whether the king himself had to rise every hour for the rites of accompanying the sun through the hours of day and night. The idea is not impossible,

25 *King Taharqo and the 'souls of the east' in the form of baboons, their arms raised in adoration of the rising sun. Chamber D of the crypts beside the Sacred Lake, Karnak (Thebes). 25th Dynasty.*

and would indicate how heavily the position of cosmic kingship lay under ritual duties. Nevertheless, there remains the possibility that select persons substituted for the king, sometimes or often, if not always, as suggested by the regular practice of appointing deputies ('priests') for daily rituals in cult centres throughout Egypt. Without such deputies, it becomes harder to understand how many of our sources for the inner circle of the sun cult could have come into existence, let alone survived. If only the king pronounced the words of accompaniment, we would need to explain how and why other select Egyptians such as the chief archivist Khay of the 19th Dynasty could include the most sacred compositions in their tombs. With the question of practical access and performance we turn to the outer circles of the Egyptian sun cult.

PART TWO

# The Outer Circle: the chorus of the sun cult

## Degrees of participation in ancient Egyptian religion

In addition to this innermost regal kernel of religious practice, the sun cult, probably along with all other cults, displayed a less closed aspect, whereby a larger number of worshippers would participate in hymns sung in some less restricted area of the temple. In the surviving temples, undoubtedly rather different from the solar shrines, at least this demarcation of different levels of access appears with dramatic clarity. According to a scheme repeated from the New Kingdom to the Roman Period, the least accessible area comprises the innermost halls, on a slightly raised floor level, like the first mound of creation, with lower ceilings, and little or no light. Here the secret

**26** *Stelophorous statue of Tury, head of the provisioning-sector of Amun, inscribed with a 'hymn to Ra when he rises till the moment he sets in life'. The name of Amun in the title of Tury, in line 3, was erased under Akhenaten. Athens L 76. 18th Dynasty.*

rites of the cult were performed in the presence of the image of the deity. This is the principal difference from the sun cult, which had a cosmic icon in the visible world, the sun disk itself. Therefore, the demarcated chamber for the rites of the sun took the form of an open court, from which the person conducting the ritual could see the solar icon. Yet the other cults also had, closer to the principal entrance, slightly more accessible areas. These did not amount to public halls for congregations of the faithful, in the manner of the sanctuaries for the religions of scripture – Judaism, Christianity and Islam. Nevertheless, expanded access seems implied by the grand columned halls, where the decoration on the mass of pillars evoked the primeval marshes around the first dry land. Here clerestory windows admitted a controlled level of daylight, and royal favour might permit the placement of statuary of officials, securing for eternity a position as close to the sanctuary as possible. The broadest level of access would have been at the open court nearest the entrance gateway, where the difference between sun worship and other cults was least evident. In these broad courts open to the sky we can imagine less hidden material offerings, and the chanting of hymns. This then would have been the most likely setting for the outer circle of sun hymns. Whether the broad courts were used by large numbers every day or, as seems more likely, only at festivals, they would have set a scene for the spread of participation in, and therefore knowledge of, the offering of words to the gods. The hymns of this broader liturgy to the sun god survive in two principal contexts. First are the rare ritual manuscripts of the New Kingdom and the 1st millennium BC. Far more widespread are hieroglyphic inscriptions of the New Kingdom, on tomb-chapel stelae and statues depicting men holding stelae ('stelophorous statues' – *ill. 26*), and on the sides of doorways to tomb-chapels. The great bulk of the surviving evidence comes from Thebes, the best-preserved elite cemetery of Egypt from these later periods, as the Memphite cemeteries are for the earlier. Throughout the New Kingdom, and most especially in the mid- to late 18th Dynasty, the siting of the royal tomb in the Valley of the Kings at Thebes acted as a magnet to the court in plans for obtaining an afterlife. Eventually the West Bank at Thebes became home to hundreds of magnificent decorated tomb-chapels, over the burial places of higher officials and their families. This is the broadly elite court circle to which we owe the survival of the hymns from the sun liturgy in such abundance. In contrast to the secret tradition of cosmic knowledge in the Underworld Books and Hour Ritual, these hymns adorn tomb entrances, with images of the lord of the tomb, facing the rising sun, hands raised in adoration. With the more open corpus of sun songs from the open court, we can begin to reconstruct another, looser daily cycle in which the wider population acclaimed the central task of kingship, keeping the sun on its course against the threat of shipwreck.

## The words of the chorus for the sun

Jan Assmann notes seven hymns repeated over a number of different monuments, four of them known already in the 18th Dynasty. This repetition in the most accessible funerary contexts allows us to identify them as the standardized core of a repeated practice, the liturgy of singing to the sun. The opening phrases specify that they apply to praise of the sun at sunrise and sunset. We cannot be sure that these were sung at special occasions, for particular festivals, rather than every day. However, their phrasing makes them suitable for daily repetition, and this is certainly how they function in their architectural setting, at the eastern doorway of the tombs on the West Bank at Thebes. The contents of the hymns reveal a solar belief embedded in the constellations of deities, characteristic of ancient Egyptian religion before and after the reign of Akhenaten.

### Assmann Hymn A

Hail Ra in your rising, Atum in your perfect setting.
You rise, you shine on the back of your mother,
Risen as king of the Nine Gods.
Nut performs the water-ritual at your face [i.e. at the sight of you],
Maat contents you at each end of each season.
You travel the sky, your heart elated [after battle]
– the Waterway of the Two Knives is become still
– the enemy is felled, his arms bound,
the blade has severed his neck.
Ra is indeed in fair sailing.
The Evening Barque has destroyed her assailant.
The southerners and the northerners draw you forward.
The westerners and the easterners are in adoration of you.

Hymn A occurs in various forms on the walls of Theban tombs from the 18th to the 20th Dynasty. The relatively high number of sources suggests long usage and accessibility to a broad circle of the elite. This may well then be the standard hymn used in the daily ritual at different points, though it could have been compiled from hymns sung at different times of the day and reconfigured as a separate new product for the funerary context from which it survives with such frequency. However, in the doorway to the chapel of the courtier Kheref (Theban Tomb 192) it faces Hymn B, for which the manuscript sources demonstrate use in daily cult. It seems plausible, then, that they belong together as morning and evening songs to the sun.

### Assmann Hymn B

Hail Ra, as you set in life,
When you have merged with the horizon of the sky.
You are appeared on the western side as Atum who is in the dusk,
Arrived in your might, without flinching,
You have taken sovereignty over the heavens as Ra.
You tread the two skies as the sweet-hearted.
You dispel rainclouds and tempest.
You have descended into the body of your mother Nunet
As your father Nun is performing the water-ritual.
The gods of Manu [the horizon land] are jubilant,
Those who are in the underworld are rejoicing
As they see their lord who extends the ways,
Amun-Ra lord of all humankind.

Like Hymn A, Hymn B occurs in a wide number of tombs, but these are more restricted in range, suggesting slightly narrower circulation. Besides the tomb of Kheref, dating to the reign of Amenhotep III, it appears in a series of tombs of royal draughtsmen at Deir el-Medina, from the Ramesside period. It may have become part of the decoration of the latter thanks to its inclusion in the ritual for King Amenhotep I, who received worship at shrines popular with the royal draughtsmen. This manuscript liturgy at least demonstrates that it was used as a sun hymn in that daily cult.

### Assmann Hymn C

Hail Ra in your rising,
Amun, the Might of the Gods.
You rise and you have lit the Two Lands.
You cross the sky in peace, your heart elated [after battle] in the Morning
    Barque.
You pass by the sandbank of the waving water, and your enemies are felled.
You are arisen in the Temple of Shu, you are set in the western horizon.
Your Active Person has received the condition of 'revered'.

The arms of your mother close after you in the course of every full day.
May I see you in your beautiful festival at your sailing of Djeserdjeseru.
May your radiance come to be upon my breast
As I adore you, your perfection in my face [in my sight].
May you grant that I rest in the Temple I have made [= the tomb-chapel]
by favour of the Perfect God [= the King].
May you grant that I be among your followers, and rest in the chamber of
    your gift,
As is done for a good man on earth.

The second half of Hymn C refers to the annual Theban festival at which
the image of Amun of Karnak travelled in procession across the Nile to the
temple of Hathor at Djeserdjeseru (modern Deir el-Bahri). Therefore, this
part of the hymn would not have carried the same resonance in other parts
of Egypt. Local Theban reference also seems likely in the naming of Amun
near the start, though the 'Hidden God' was already worshipped across
Egypt as a form of the creator by the mid-18th Dynasty. Despite the Theban
colouring, the hymn may be related in part to Hymn D, forming with that a
possible matching pair for the cult of the sun at dawn and at evening. There
is a variant to Hymn C, which does not include the Theban phrases. It is
tempting to see this as the core liturgical hymn, from which Hymn C was
adapted for Theban use, though the adaptation could have occurred in the
other direction. This 'Hymn C'' reads as follows:

> Hail Ra in your rising,
> Atum Ra-Horakhty.
> I adore you, your perfection in my eyes.
> May your radiance come to be upon my breast.
> You proceed, you set in the Evening Barque,
> your heart elated [after battle] in the Morning Barque.
> You traverse the sky in peace, all your enemies are felled.
> The Unwearying stars rejoice for you,
> The Indestructible stars adore you.
> You set in the horizon of the Horizon Mountain,
> Perfect as Ra every full day,
> Living and stable as my lord,
> Ra the true of voice.

### ASSMANN HYMN D

Hail overlord of circling time, Atum the great one of the line of eternity.
You are come in peace, you have landed, and joined the arms of the Horizon
    Mountain.
You have received the condition of 'revered', moored at your place of
    yesterday.
The arms of your mother close after you, the rebellious [Seth?] fells your
    enemies.

The Powers of the west draw you forward along any road that is in the
    Sacred Land.
You illuminate the faces of those who are in the Underworld,
You raise up those who lie asleep.
May you grant me transfiguration among your followers,
That I may receive the tow-rope of the Evening Barque,
And the mooring rope of the Morning Barque.
I am come before me, my arms bearing Maat ['What is Right'], 'What is
    Right' written on my fingers.
I have rowed the Active Person of the Thousand-footed god [of embalming].
I have performed the ritual of transfiguration in the embalming tent
In the course of every full day.

The Theban tombs with Hymn D all date to the reign of Amenhotep III,
but the same phrases occur later in the north at Giza and Saqqara. An 18th-
Dynasty stelophorous statue preserved in Moscow combines Hymns C and
D, as if they form complementary sunrise and sunset hymns as part of the
same daily service. This could give us the core of the daily ritual in different
parts of Egypt, albeit largely through the prism of their inscription within
Theban funerary architecture.

In addition to these hymns, two other compositions occur on a variety of
monuments, all dated later than the 18th Dynasty. By the dates of these
sources, we may speculate that they were both added to the liturgy after
the reign of Akhenaten. They may even form a part of the reshaping of the
liturgy in reaction to his own rejected cult hymns to the sun as Aten.

### ASSMANN HYMN E

Hail He who rises from Nun,
He who lights the Two Lands after he emerges.
The assembled Nine Gods praise you,
The Two Goddesses, the two Meret [chantresses] nurse you.
Perfect child of love,
Whose rising is the life of the populace,
At the sight of whom the Nine Gods rejoice,
For whom the Powers of Iunu dance in joy,
Whom the Powers of Pe and Nekhen exalt.
'Obeisance to you', say the horizon-baboons.
'Adoration to you', say all creatures.
Your rebellious one [Seth?] fells your enemies,
You rejoice upon your sacred boat,
Your crew is at peace.
The Morning Barque has absorbed you, your heart elated [after battle].
Lord of the gods whom you created,
They give you praise.
Nut gleams lapis-blue beside you,

You have mingled with Nun with the rays for him.
[There follows a prayer perhaps added for the funerary contexts]
May you shine for me, that I may see your perfection.
I am a healthy being upon earth,
I give praise to your perfect face,
As you rise in the horizon of heaven.
May I glorify the sun disk at its setting
On that mountain of the Life of the Two Lands [name for the Saqqara
 cemeteries]

## ASSMANN HYMN F

Hail Amun Ra-Horakhty, Atum Khepri,
Horus who ferries across the sky,
Great falcon, breast decorated for festival,
Perfect of face with the Great Double Plume.
May you awake perfect upon daybreak
At what the assembled Nine Gods tell you.
Jubilation resounds for you in the evening,
Kenmut glorifies you,
One who sleeps conceived, you at whose birth dawn breaks.
Your mother absorbs you every full day.
[Refrain or separate chorus?]
May Ra live and the enemy die.
[Continuation of main hymn?]
You are set firm, your opponent is felled.
You cross the sky in life and power,
You make the sky festive in the Morning Barque.
You pass the day in your sacred boat, your heart sweet.
Maat ['What is Right'] is appeared at your brow.
Rise, Ra,
Shine as the Akhty [horizon god],
Dark god light of form,
The crew of Ra is in joy,
Heaven and earth are in rejoicing,
The Great 'Nine Gods' are making jubilation for you,
Amun Ra-Horakhty is emerged true of voice.

The hymn ends with the instruction that it is to be spoken four times, pre-sumably once for each of the four cardinal points. Hymn F is the only example found in original papyrus manuscripts used for the daily liturgy, from the temples at Karnak, on the East Bank at Thebes. Its practical use in the temple is also clear from its occurrence on the walls of the Khons temple at Karnak and at the Hibis temple, a Persian Period (5th century BC) monu-ment in the western oases. This composition at least, then, we can imagine being sung in the middle and/or outer courts of these temples for sunrise and/or other key moments in the daily drama of the solar journey.

Looking back over the seven hymns, we may tentatively assign each to a precise physical setting in time and space within the cult of the sun. All would be, if not the only, then a prominent or continuously used part of the repertoire for the chorus singing in the outer courtyard of the sun shrines (and other sanctuaries) at Thebes. This would render them accessible to the wider circle of all those attested in the written record, while leaving the level of communication, if any, to the outer circles, the mass of the population that did not use writing. The three principal pairings would be the following:

> Hymn C` and D: sunrise and sunset hymns from the 18th Dynasty
> (Hymn C may be a Theban variant for the sunrise hymn)
> Hymns A and B: sunrise and sunset hymns, paired at least in the reign of
> Amenhotep III
> Hymns E and F: sunrise and sunset hymns produced after the reign of
> Akhenaten

The principal songs for morning and evening service would then be Hymns C` and D. As recorded on the surviving funerary monuments, they may have been abbreviated or adapted in detail from longer hymns or from a whole series of hymns to the sun during the day. This applies even more to Hymns A and B, where A is the most widely attested hymn in tombs, but paired with B only in the tomb of Kheref. Possibly Hymn A was the sun hymn used on the widest variety of occasions, or the most popular condensation of the general corpus of hymns. It may have been tied to Hymn B only secondarily, perhaps as part of the sweeping changes that took place under Amenhotep III. By the date of their first appearance in the surviving record, the Ramesside Hymns E and F took shape in the very specific acts of restoration after Akhenaten. Under Akhenaten there is no cosmic knowledge, or at least none is expressed. Instead, as we see in the final chapter of this book, the solar journey is reduced to the phenomena witnessed in the sky by the human eye. The night journey of the sun disappears completely, and so does its boat. In their place remains simply the solar sphere moving across the sky during the daylight hours. The special status of the king is now ensured not by a separate body of secret hymns, the inner core of the sun cult, but by the restriction of the sun hymn to the king alone. In practice, the great hymns to the sun occur also on the monuments of the highest officials. However, this relaxation of royal control is not very different from the slippage of cosmic knowledge into a restricted number of elite contexts in the case of the traditional Underworld Books, Accompaniments and Hour Hymns. When Akhenaten died, his successors oversaw the return to the traditional sun cult. The depictions of the solar journey again used the motifs of boat and retinue, and here the contrast between inner (esoteric) and outer (exoteric) hymns and cult would have been the first item for renewal. The act of reviving the inner–outer boundary of cult might have been the moment to revise the cosmographies of the inner, kingly and secret cult: here we see for example the appearance of the Book of Gates beside, and initially replacing, the Amduat. It would also have been an occasion for rewording the outer zone of the cult, in the broad courts of the shrines. The echo for this would have been the appearance of new standard sun songs such as Hymns E and F. As with the earlier hymns, the practical pairing may be misleading. Possibly the hymns present adaptations for tomb-chapel entrances. Yet they bring us relatively close, in this indirect record, to the substance of sun worship as it was practised at Thebes during the New Kingdom.

For all the uncertainty, and the underlying absence of a direct source in manuscript or inscription, the research by Jan Assmann has brought us deep into the practical procedures and activities of the sun cult. The cult follows a structure recognizable elsewhere, of inner and outer circles of access. Only here, the inner circle seems more tightly drawn around the person of the king, and its knowledge seems more intricately woven into the fabric, and the physical survival, of creation. With this conceptual framework comprising outer chorus of hymns around inner mysteries of the sun, we may turn now to the epicentre of the cult, the home of the creator, Iunu.

# Chapter Three

# Iunu – Lost City of Ra-Atum

## In the shadow of modern Cairo

Across three millennia of ancient Egyptian history, the cult of the sun was centred on the city named in Egyptian as Iunu, and known to the Greeks as Heliopolis 'city of the sun'. Its name recurs more frequently than that of any other earthly place in the religious literature of ancient Egypt, and it became the model for New Kingdom Thebes, and probably too for Amarna (see Chapter Five). Yet few now know its ancient name, or its importance in pharaonic civilization, for history has not been gentle with the place where time was once so assiduously measured for the worship of the sun. Today the main enclosure of the Ra temple is an uncharted field containing few visible remains, and hemmed in on all sides by the urban and industrial expanse of the northeastern Cairo districts Ain Shams and Matariya. This and the very scale of the site have so far prevented any systematic modern survey to underpin our study of the solar city. History has deprived us of the kernel of the ancient civilization. Already at the time of Strabo, writing about 24 BC, the great temples were ruined, ready to be quarried of any remaining stone to embellish shining new cities, above all Alexandria, Rome itself and then the later imperial capital Constantinople. After the Arab conquest, its monuments fell prey to yet another generation of governing centres, including eventually the Fatimid foundation al-Qahira, Cairo. Nevertheless, the aura of this forgotten solar city did not entirely disappear. Throughout the Middle Ages, pilgrims visited the church near the site to view the tree in whose shade, according to the Christian texts, the Holy Family rested on their flight from King Herod. Today the numerous busloads of Western tourists do not venture as far as this corner of Greater Cairo, to the enclosure protecting the one substantial monument still standing at the temple of the sun, the obelisk set up by Senusret I in the 20th century before Christ (*ill. 70*). Those few hardier travellers who undertake the journey to Iunu may use their imagination, but they face a remarkably blank surface. Without a survey the intermittent excavations around the site cannot answer many of our questions about its history. Nevertheless, enough has emerged to provide some idea of its brilliance and form.

## Two centuries of excavating Iunu

There had been a promising start to the study of the site. The French Revolutionary Expedition produced a map with characteristic military precision, at the cutting edge of the art in the period, during their occupation of Egypt, 1798–1801. Four decades later a purely scientific expedition led by Richard Lepsius for the ruler of Brandenburg added detail and the new benefits of being able to read the inscriptions, following the brilliant decipherment and first grammar of the Egyptian hieroglyphic script by Jean-François Champollion in 1822 and 1824 (*ill. 27*). Official and unofficial digging took place throughout this period, but the most important work has been largely forgotten. In the early 1850s an Armenian engineer named Joseph Hekekyan conducted a series of test digs to a standard unparalleled in world archaeology prior to the Second World War, thanks to his surveying and recording of the different levels of finds. The quality of his work can be set in context when we consider that a full 60 years later at Iunu even the great archaeologist Flinders Petrie recorded none of the stratigraphic information, and published no accurate general survey of the site (*ill. 37*). Hekekyan carried out these works not to reconstruct the history of the ancient site, but to gather data on the geology of the Nile Valley, for an enthusiastic entrepreneur, Leonard Horner. His industrial training in England served better than any of the historical and philological schooling benefiting other early archaeologists. Sadly, the work did not receive the attention it deserved, partly perhaps following unfavourable reviews of the limited published accounts. Whatever the reasons, the work never produced any offspring, and science lost the potential for a Hekekyan school of Egyptology. Perhaps the motivation was too firmly labelled in the minds of contemporaries as geological, rather than historical. More simply, Horner published only a limited proportion of the information gathered, and a full appreciation is difficult without consulting the original manuscripts, largely unpublished and housed in two separate institutions, the British Museum and the British Library. These are now being brought back to life through the work of David Jeffreys, director of the Egypt Exploration Society archaeological operations at a second key ancient site, Mennefer (Memphis in the Greek texts), under and around the expanding modern village of Mit Rahina. Hekekyan concentrated on the two ruinfields, Mit Rahina, ancient Memphis, and Matariya, ancient Iunu. For both sites the contribution of the early recorder remains invaluable. His work also opens up the question of the links between the two sites, one the centre of the sun cult, the other the node of government throughout ancient Egyptian history. The importance of these links can be seen in the paragraph on the pyramid fields later in this chapter. The list of later excavators at Iunu forms an illustrious

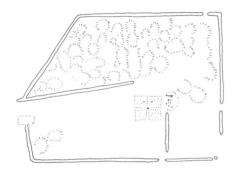

27 *The enclosure walls of Iunu as planned by the Lepsius expedition to Egypt in 1846–8. The square to right of centre appears to represent a garden area around the obelisk of Senusret I.*

sequence of Egyptologists. They include Edouard Naville and Frances Llewellyn Griffith, hunting for the mighty stone monuments that had largely disappeared a thousand years before, but concentrate on the untiring efforts of the Egyptian Antiquities Service to preserve monuments threatened by urban development. In an early example of interpreting complex urban archaeology, in 1896 Ahmed Kamal published his account of rescue archaeology during 1892–3, in the cemetery zone near the then Ard el-Naam, 'the ostrich farm', to the east of the main temple enclosure. Other crucial interventions have been reported more often in short articles or reports, such as those documenting the find of Ramesside sacred bull tombs in 1902 and 1918. In 1903–4 Ernesto Schiaparelli retrieved an array of sculptural fragments in the main temple area, and presented an architectural model of the structural remains from his experience of digging the site. During March and April 1912 Flinders Petrie targeted the site on one of his rapid forays into several sites per season (that same year he dug two sites well south of Cairo, the vast cemeteries at Kafr Ammar and the late Roman fort, town and tombs at Shurafa). During the First World War, M.A. Barsanti reported on the discovery of an Old Kingdom cemetery in Matariya-East, of which he published a brief account. In this way the single finds have continued, in virtually unbroken series as Cairo grows. The Egyptian archaeological services are still staging a heroic defence of the heritage of the area, one of the most difficult in the world for excavation (*ills 2, 28, 36*). They rarely win international attention, even when their finds are as spectacular and important as the 1986–7 retrieval of an intact wooden ship from an ancient canal zone, reported in a 1996 article on recent finds at Iunu by M. Abd al-Gelil and others. Only the series of university excavations in the 1970s and 1980s have so far produced a more substantial publication, from A. Saleh in his 1981 and 1983 reports. In 1935, Herbert Ricke sought to draw together the then available strands of archaeology, combined with the numerous references in text. Still today we can only confess our ignorance on such essential points as the origins and the last days of the city, and even the exact location of the

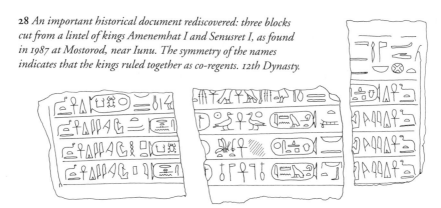

*28 An important historical document rediscovered: three blocks cut from a lintel of kings Amenemhat I and Senusret I, as found in 1987 at Mostorod, near Iunu. The symmetry of the names indicates that the kings ruled together as co-regents. 12th Dynasty.*

main sun temple and the direction it faced. The following outline of the city over the ages can serve as an impressionistic sketch, in anticipation of the general survey we need to anchor our knowledge before localized excavations can be planned and keyed in to the wider questions of history.

## The location of Iunu: quarries of quartzite

To the southeast of Iunu rises a great desert mountain, named in Arabic Gebel Ahmar 'the Red Mountain', after the ruddy hue of its stone. Here the shining limestone of the Upper Egyptian valley, most perfect just to the south at Tura, gives way to sandstone and the silicified version of sandstone, quartzite. Quartzite might justly be called most solar of the stones of Egypt. Over the different veins its colour ranges through golden and white to purple-red, covering all the variations in the spectrum of the sunlit sky, and its sparkling texture is derived from the gradual metamorphosis of the grains over time. The solar interpretation does not rest on modern imagination: the Egyptians quarried this hard stone as specifically as they mined for gold, using the blocks for only the highest quality of sculpture in the round and in relief. In several inscriptions, the king himself is credited with particular knowledge of the stone vein, notably in a royal stela set up in year 8 of King Ramesses II for a shrine on the road to the quartzite quarries. The stela, itself of quartzite and 2.11 m (6 ft 10 in) in height, came to light in 1907 during construction work at Manshiet es-Sadr. In the scene over the inscription, Ra-Horakhty offers sceptres of power to the king, watched by a goddess identified as 'Hathor, lady of the Red Mountain, lady of heaven, mistress of the Two Lands [i.e. of Egypt]'. The inscription below records how 'His Majesty was wandering over the desert of Iunu, to the south of the House of Ra, north of the House of the Ennead, by [the shrine of] Hathor, lady of the Red Mountain.' There he found a striking purple vein of quartzite, perfect for quarrying, and ordered specialist stonecutters to hew a statue: the work took a full year, resulting in a colossus named 'Ramesses the god', designed to stand in the main temple of the king's new city at Piramesse, northeast of Iunu. According to the inscription, Ramesses went on to find a series of other fine veins of quartzite at Iunu and in the Beautiful Mountain of Elephantine, on the southern border of Egypt with Nubia. Over half the inscription on the stela records the correct payment of the skilled stoneworkers engaged in the quarrying and sculpting of monuments from these veins, a reminder that Egyptian kingship regarded social justice as great a duty as the dedication of statues.

Whatever the skills of Ramesses II in prospecting, kings were not alone among the elite in scouring the rocky surface. Among Schiaparelli's more remarkable finds is a fossil inscribed in hieroglyphs with this line: 'found on the south of the quarry of Soped by the god's father Tjanefer' (*ill. 30*). God's father denotes a member of a particular group of priests who had to care for the divine image, as it were paternally. Tjanefer may have been involved in a quarrying expedition, and perhaps deposited his rare prize at the main Ra temple, where Schiaparelli discovered it. There may have been a particular connection between the personnel in the Ra temple and the intimate knowledge of materials for its adornment. In the 18th Dynasty, another 'god's father of Iunu' named Hatra bore the non-priestly title 'overseer of goldsmiths of the Ra domain'. He is known from a block statue (Louvre E 25520) bearing the cartouche of Amenhotep II and a hieroglyphic inscription including the declaration 'I am a skilled craftsman of Upper and Lower Egypt', to emphasize the national scope of his commissions for the king. The crafts of metalwork and sculpture are more closely associated with Ptah, the god of earthly creativity, and his city Mennefer (Memphis), but the cult of Ra and the city of Iunu also acted as powerhouses for the formal art and

29 *Rock inscription at Gebel Ahmar, depicting an obelisk identified in hieroglyphs as 'a work from the hand of the master of works Penamun'. New Kingdom.*

30 *A fossil inscribed in hieroglyphs to record its discovery by a priest named Tjanefer. From Iunu, Schiaparelli excavations 1903. Turin, Egyptian Museum. Late New Kingdom or Late Period.*

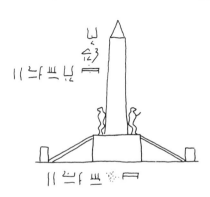

sacred knowledge at the core of Egyptian civilization. There may have been a strong current of hieroglyphic learning at the solar city, and this would account for such sources as the reference to workmen from Iunu, cited on an ostracon at the Theban temple of Hatshepsut at Deir el-Bahri.

## The quartzite lintels of Senusret III

An outstanding example of the careful selection of stone is the pair of quartzite lintels of Senusret III, which may come from Iunu. Both were known in the 18th century, but the second re-emerged to public view in the British Museum only a few years ago. Each had been cut down in size already in antiquity and, to judge from the grooves and chisel marks on the back, clamped back to back to form a building block. By the time they were fastened together in this way and used as part of the foundations for the triumphal column raised at Alexandria for the Roman emperor Diocletian, they may have moved from one site to another more than once over the centuries. They were exposed only in the early 18th century, when a religious fanatic attempted to dynamite the pagan classical monument, by then christened Pompey's Pillar, and the first great antiquity seen by the traveller arriving from Europe by ship. The explosion succeeded only in clearing a space at its foot. Here in 1737 one of the hardiest of early travellers, the Danish captain Frederik Norden, not only saw but took the time and effort to draw the inscriptions on one rather worn, golden-brown quartzite block. Other drawings were also made, but, in these days before the invention of lithography, none of the printed copies give more than an impression of the block. At the end of that century, it became detached from the foundations of the pillar, probably marked out by the French Revolutionary Expedition of 1798–1801 as a piece deserving public view in a museum. When the Ottoman Turkish and British forces expelled the French, the discarded inscription arrived in London, perhaps simply as ballast. In 1805 the then Minister of War, the Earl Spencer, presented it among other substantial hard stone antiquities to the British Museum, where it has been on display to all ever since. In 1989 Marie-Louise Buhl published the notes and original drawings made by Norden over 260 years earlier. For the first time the quality of his copies could be admired, including his fine reproduction of the worn quartzite relief block, and the attached note could be read, where he observed that the reverse side of the block bore a similar depiction to the outer face (*ills 31–32*). This was curious, as the reverse of the quartzite block in the British Museum is rough-hewn and bears no trace of decoration. There seemed no solution to this puzzle until a few years later, when an entirely forgotten quartzite twin appeared in a southern English garden. Presumably this had been removed after Norden had visited and gone, and

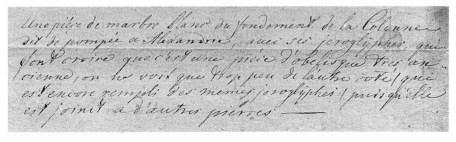

31 *Drawing by Frederik Norden of a quartzite lintel beneath the Pillar of Diocletian at Alexandria in 1737.*

32 *The manuscript note by Norden referring to an inscription on the reverse of the block: this is the principal evidence for two lintels being joined back to back as a foundation block.*

it too may have been shipped to England more as ballast than ancient relic. Today an international public can appreciate the two blocks side by side in the Egyptian Sculpture Gallery of the British Museum. The long-lost block is of the whitest vein of quartzite, in dramatic contrast to the golden block. Where the worn, golden block is broken off halfway through the throne name of the king in whose reign it was carved, the white block preserves enough for us to be able to read the name, Khakaura, and thereby identify the ruler as Senusret III, one of the great kings of the 12th Dynasty. The gods included in the relief are solar, as befits the stone: Atum, Ra and the Powers of Iunu, the anonymous troupe summarizing the genius of the place. Yet the original provenance of the two blocks remains a mystery. Hard stone blocks were moved all over Lower Egypt from the Second Intermediate Period onwards, and the Memphite area suffered as much from this continual antiquities' road show as did Iunu. The pyramid complex of Senusret III stands near the modern village of Dahshur, on the southern end of the sequence of cemeteries running from Abusir and Saqqara. The wreckage of the sacred structures at both Dahshur and Iunu leaves their internal ground plans blank, and the blocks could have fitted a slender doorway equally easily on either site. Despite this uncertainty, the solar connection seems firmly established here between the deities mentioned and depicted and the choice of building stone.

## Quarries and trade

Quartzite can be seen to be supremely solar and kingly in another respect, the rarity of non-royal sculpture in the stone. Several officials of the court of Amenhotep III were privileged to have sculpture in this material, yet this only emphasizes its select and solar aspect, as no reign sees such monumental focus on the identification of king with sun god. If the connection between this stone and the sun is well grounded, the quarry provides one reason for the location of the sun's city. The apparently universal cult of the sun has a sharply local Egyptian reason for existence. There is no place on earth where the sun imposes on human life more than the Sahara. Further, the cult of the sun flourishes in a specific time span, the 3,000 years of the developed nation-state, from the 3rd Dynasty to the Roman Period. There is no obviously solar symbolism in the funerary arts of the predynastic periods, and even the formative years of the Egyptian state, under the 1st and 2nd Dynasties, seem to concentrate rather on the balance of divine powers, Horus and Seth. The sun takes hold as creator when the state itself imposes monolithic form, and raises its impossible scale of monumental self-expression. The sun cult is oriented in effect to its source, the stones and mineral and metallic wealth of the desert. When life in the valley masters even partially the surrounding desert, the sun cult expresses that overriding sovereignty to the limits or horizon of that society's experience. When Seth, desert and anarchy lose to Horus, fields and settled life, Horus too in effect loses his pre-eminence as a new dominance arises over both desert and fields. The relation of the sun to the veins in the earth can be detected in the location of Iunu near the Red Mountain of quartzite. It may equally account for the role of the city in more distant expeditions, those to the turquoise and copper ore sources in the Sinai peninsula. These in turn present a second, perhaps the main reason for the importance of the city in ancient times: trade routes.

The mountains east of Iunu include desert valleys that provide natural roads out of Egypt to the borders of Asia. These ancient routes doubtless contributed more than any other single factor to the growth of a settlement at the crossroads of land and river trade. The turquoise of Hathor and the gold of Ra are merely the exotic colouring for more substantive contacts between regions, between the earliest settlers in the Nile Valley and the inhabitants of neighbouring Asia. The role of these trade routes can be appreciated when we turn to the first traces of human life in the area, from the 4th millennium BC. These are tombs positioned exactly at the Nile Valley end of the main mountainous roads through the eastern desert to the Bitter Lakes and the Red Sea. As Upper Egypt meets Lower Egypt at Mennefer (Memphis), here at Iunu Asia meets Africa.

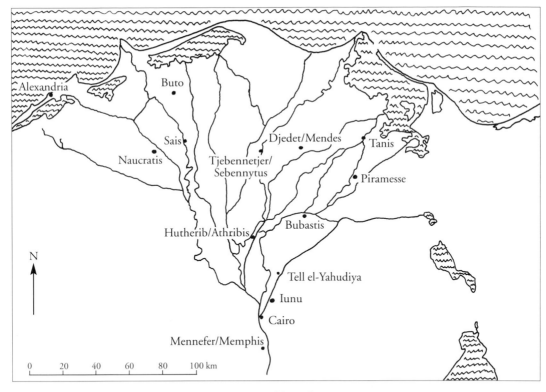

**33** *Map of the Delta.*

## Beginnings – Iunu in the prehistory of Egypt

In the centuries before the first recorded unification of Egypt, before 3000 BC, there existed already a settlement with richer and poorer levels of society. The houses of the living have not yet been found, but we can see the social structure reflected in the predynastic tombs unearthed in the desert margin area southeast of the main temple and cemeteries of Iunu. The grave goods included a distinctive style of pottery that differs in detail from the contemporary wares of Upper Egypt and even the nearby site of Maadi, a trading emporium on the routes from the Nile Valley to Western Asia. Despite these finds from 1950s excavations, we remain ignorant of the size of the settlement, or its relative importance within the Nile Delta. Of the beliefs of these people, the tombs reveal only that they, like their Upper Egyptian contemporaries, believed in a material life after death, sustained by food and drink. By the end of the 4th millennium BC all the separate lifestyles in the area between the First Cataract and the Mediterranean had yielded to a single material culture, that of Upper Egypt, named by archaeologists after one of its most important settlements and cemeteries, Naqada. This marks the beginning of the Egyptian state, an era of rule by one king, and Iunu was to find itself at the centre of this new world. It is worth summarizing the formative phase of the kingdom, the four centuries of the Early Dynastic Period (*c*.3100–2696 BC), when the sun had not yet risen to the status of supreme god in the Egyptian pantheon. The struggles of the period may contain clues as to why Egyptian kingship adopted, at the dawn of the pyramid age (after 2696 BC), so strong a belief in one overriding celestial power, the sun.

At the time that Naqada pottery and other goods are finally found throughout Egypt, hieroglyphic writing and formal Egyptian art appear, about a century after the invention of the cuneiform script in Western Asia. The first, laconic inscriptions reveal the existence of a single king ruling the entire area of the Egyptian Nile Valley and Delta. The first eight kings were buried at Abydos, in Upper Egypt, and these eight enter later histories of Egypt as the 1st Dynasty. Only a few years ago new excavations at the royal tombs at Abydos by the German Institute in Cairo retrieved mud seal impressions from a seal of the necropolis listing, in one case the first five, but in the other the first eight kings from Narmer to Qaa. The group does seem to exist then in the contemporary record, as the first eight rulers of Egypt buried at Abydos. There followed an unknown number of kings apparently buried at Saqqara, and then two further kings, Peribsen and Khasekhem(wy), buried at Abydos. Together these correspond to the 2nd Dynasty of later histories. The reasons for the change in burial place are obscure, and there are inscriptions relating to war at the end of this period. The titles taken by the kings tie them to the later mythic records of the battles between the gods Horus and Seth. From the first inscriptions until the end of hieroglyphic writing under Roman rule, the king of Egypt took a first accession name when he ascended the throne, with the title Horus. The name was written in a rectangle with partial segmented panel, echoing the protective niched-brick wall of First Dynasty royal tomb and palace architecture. Thus each king is Horus, in later myth the embodiment of order and good. However, Peribsen alone of all the kings of Egypt took the title Seth over the rectangle for his name. His successor reverted to the Horus title over his name Khasekhem (meaning 'the Power rises') with the alternative name Khasekhemwy (meaning 'the two Powers rise') written beneath a unique combination of Horus and Seth, facing one another atop the rectangle. These unique names and the changes in the location of the king's tomb have encouraged a good deal of historical speculation, allied with later Egyptian tales of the gods. The cult centre of Seth was Nubyt, the modern village of Naqada after which Egyptologists have named, as we have seen, the ascendant predynastic culture of the Valley. Egyptian myth casts Seth as the god of disorder, an anarchic trickster spreading confusion and undermining the perfect order of the gods, though

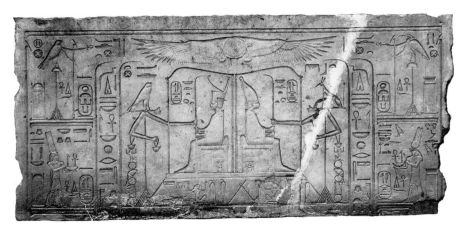

34 *Horus and Seth beneath the winged sun disk, offering on each side to King Senusret III, enthroned and wearing, on the left, the Red Crown, on the right, the White Crown. 12th Dynasty lintel.*
*Egyptian Museum, Cairo.*

still within creation. Does myth reflect history? Did there take place some gargantuan political power struggle between Nubyt (Seth) and the early cult centre of Horus, Nekhen? Modern commentators sometimes favour a political-historical interpretation of such tales of the gods, but in truth we have few sources for either religious or political history during this period. There are no manuscripts from these reigns, and the inscriptions limit themselves to names and numbers. We ought not to imagine that we might reconstruct out of late myth, as the Egyptologist Kurt Sethe once attempted, an early history of Egypt. Yet the early Seth and Horus names do illustrate for us a strong tendency to use pairings, possibly reflecting the binary composition of the early state in Egypt. This united kingdom comprised Valley and Delta, and could also be viewed as fertile fields within the arid desert, or within the home territory of the Naqada culture, in Upper Egypt, as a combination of the two river banks both united and separated from each other by the river. All of these pairings figure explicitly in later Egyptian inscriptions of kingship, and the duality of Egypt as the 'Two Lands' of hieroglyphic inscription survives into Hebrew scripture in the direct translation Mizraim. The dualism of the Early Dynastic does not disappear in later kingship and administration, yet it does cede on the religious plane to a more singular vision, that of the sun. From the 3rd Dynasty we have the evidence for a new emphasis on a single creator, eclipsing the balance between the good Horus and the anarchic Seth. The battles of Horus and Seth do not disappear in the new, classic Egyptian arrangement of divine powers, but they become a smaller part within the general scheme of a single all-powerful creator. After King Khasekhemwy, Horus and Seth are to live in the shadow of Ra (*ill. 34*).

35 *Fragment of relief from a shrine, with a depiction of the god Geb. From Iunu, excavations of Schiaparelli, 1903–4. Turin, Egyptian Museum 2761/20. 3rd Dynasty.*

36 *The inscription of King Teti on an obelisk fragment, found at Iunu. 6th Dynasty.*

## The city of Ra in the Pyramid Age

The rise of the sun in Egyptian kingship seems reflected in the ruinously broken inscriptional record on the ground of his cult centre at Iunu. The historical profile of the city of the sun emerged perhaps most graphically from a dumping ground discovered by Schiaparelli in 1903–4. This pit, presumably a pious burial of sacred material, was full of fragments of royal sculpture and hieroglyphic reliefs. The kings named on these range in date from Netjerkhet (Djoser in later Egyptian tradition), builder of the Step Pyramid at Saqqara in the 27th century BC, to Nakhthorhebyt, last indigenous ruler of Egypt before the Persians ousted him in 343 BC. The name of Netjerkhet appears in a group of limestone chippings from a shrine of unknown size, possibly quite small (*ill. 35*). It is even conceivable that the Netjerkhet shrine had been moved in antiquity from some other site, such as the cult complex at his burial place. Nevertheless, it is tempting to link the find of his chapel at the city of the sun with the shape chosen for the superstructure over his tomb at Saqqara, opening the way to the final smooth-sided form of the classic Old Kingdom pyramids. Other Old Kingdom evidence on the ground at Iunu itself is sparse, and, intriguingly, the record seems to pick up again only after the period when royal pyramid complexes were built within sight of Iunu (see below). In 1972 the Antiquities Service recovered fragments of a shrine and an obelisk inscribed with the name of King Teti, first king of the 6th Dynasty (*ill. 36*). The obelisk provides the first surviving example of that form of royal solar monument.

From an inscription cut for the governor of the southern frontier, Sabni, we know that obelisks were set up in pairs no later than the reign of Pepy II, about a century later. Sabni refers to his work in preparing the two transport barges to carry them from one end of the country to the other. If each obelisk needed its own barge, they must have been on the same colossal scale as Middle and New Kingdom examples. The original obelisks of Pepy II, though, have not been found. The same period, towards the end of the Old Kingdom, found an echo in the small, roughly obelisk-shaped limestone funerary monuments for officials of middle rank at various key cemetery sites such as Abydos and Memphis, but above all at Iunu. At this time, the end of the Old Kingdom and the First Intermediate Period, the area to the southeast of the great temple enclosure became the burial ground for men with the title 'Greatest of Seers', perhaps already used to denote the high priest at the Ra temple.

## The great platform of the Ra temple – questions of date and structure

In the central area of the Iunu site Flinders Petrie spent part of his four weeks there in 1912 tracing the outline of a great roughly round-edged square of rubble that had acted as the platform for raising some long-vanished building or activity (*ill. 37*). He identified the structure as a fortification, and dated it to the Second Intermediate Period, about 1650–1550 BC, when military advances were introduced under new Asiatic masters of northern Egypt, the heqau-khasut 'kings of hill-lands' (rendered

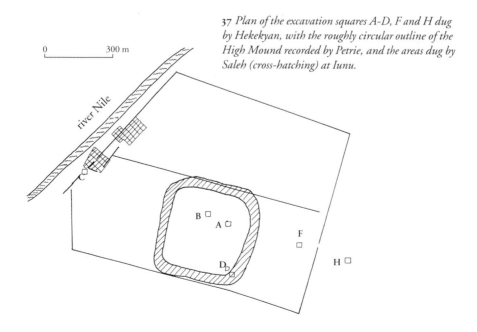

0        300 m

river Nile

37 *Plan of the excavation squares A-D, F and H dug by Hekekyan, with the roughly circular outline of the High Mound recorded by Petrie, and the areas dug by Saleh (cross-hatching) at Iunu.*

Hyksos in Greek in later histories). However, another, more peaceful, interpretation is possible. Higher ground makes for better sightings, and the cult of the sun revolves around the observation of the heavens. It seems suitable then for the ground on which the temples of the sun should rise, an architectural echo of the dry ground that first emerged from creation. Had Petrie found the original primeval mound of Egyptian myth? And, if so, when did the Egyptians construct it? Dietrich Raue has pointed out that the Petrie platform must be the same structure as the casemate foundations uncovered a decade earlier by Schiaparelli, who gave them the term 'labyrinth'. Such compartmental basement structure is best known from structures later than 700 BC, such as the fortified palace of Apries at Memphis, or the Greek mercenary forts at Daphnae and Balamun. However, earlier works also make use of internal segment walls, as at the 17th Dynasty palace at Deir el-Ballas south of Dendera, in Upper Egypt, or indeed the 12th Dynasty royal pyramids. Until further investigation the date of the great artificial platform remains as obscure as the rise of the city of Iunu. Nevertheless, its very form presents an instructive contrast to the trend in other temple sites. Often in the 1st millennium BC, earlier buildings were removed and the foundations for a new temple would rest on a great lake of sand cut deep to keep the shrine at its ancient level. At Esna or Edfu, for example, the visitor looks up from the Ptolemaic and Roman Period temple floor to the houses of the town, built up on centuries of accumulated rubble. Nothing like this seems to have happened at Iunu. Here, at the heart of the city of the sun, the temples stood raised high on a great platform. No wonder Petrie saw this as alien to his concept of Egyptian religious architecture, and identified the feature as a fort of the invading Asiatic rulers. Ricke interpreted it as far more ancient, and indeed it would find parallels in the non-geometric squared mounds beneath Middle Kingdom temple levels at Upper Egyptian sites such as Medamud. However, excavation by the Egyptian Antiquities Service in 1990 brought to light a number of inscribed limestone blocks, prised from tombs of officials of the First Intermediate Period or early Middle Kingdom. If these dismantled reliefs were built into the support of the mound, the mound itself in its surviving form must have been either built or extensively reshaped no earlier than the 12th Dynasty.

At this point the soundings by Hekekyan reveal their great value, as David Jeffreys has demonstrated. The Armenian engineer uncovered a monumental pedestal 20 m (66 ft) south of the sole surviving royal monument to be seen today, the obelisk inscribed with the names of Senusret I. Evidently the survivor was the more northerly of a pair. This contradicts the evidence of its inscriptions, oriented to face the other way: hieroglyphic texts are arranged to lead the reader towards a focus, here the innermost sanctuary, and the east and south faces should face inwards, not outwards. However, the obelisk seems to have been moved more than once both in antiquity and in modern times, and the present east and west faces may originally have been north and south. Whatever the explanation, the stand- ing obelisk and the second obelisk implied by Hekekyan's pedestal would form an entrance to a temple. If this were on their western side, it would stand precisely over the centre of Petrie's great mound. Rather than facing west, the temple of the sun would possess an east-facing monumental gateway flanked by obelisks, at least as striking as any west-facing gateway. In the enclosure wall itself, there was a great gateway, inscribed with the name of Ramesses II, but perhaps aligned on a more ancient processional way. Why should the sun face the desert? Why would anyone enter from that direction? David Jeffreys points to the hieroglyphic inscription record- ing the conquest of Egypt by the Sudanese king Piy, at the end of the 8th century BC. There the victorious king moved from Kheraha (somewhere in the vicinity of modern south Cairo) up to the Red Mountain, the quartzite quarries inland from Iunu, and then proceeded west into the temple of Ra. One approach must have been by river, from the west, but another was by land, from the Saharan mountains offering the most golden stone of Egypt (*ill. 41*). The practical approach to the quarries would have received sym- bolic reinforcement in the meaning of the east for the sun cult. The temple would have faced sunrise, as the single obelisk and its shrine did on the rear wall of the Amun temple at Karnak. This must evidently have been a temple not quite like any other, but leaving clues to itself as echoes around the country. As to the date of the structure, the blocks incorporated into the great platform seem to provide the only published evidence available to the historian. As mentioned above, they come in part from dismantled build- ings that had been set up in the First Intermediate Period, a century before the reign of Senusret I, whose obelisk stands over the area of the platform. Is he then the king who created the first great temple of Ra? There is some indirect evidence that his construction work at Iunu made an impression on ancient posterity. A leather manuscript now preserved in Berlin bears a text purporting to be a copy of a literary inscription in which Senusret I decrees the founding of a new temple structure for the sun god at Iunu. The copy dates to the mid-18th Dynasty, some five centuries after the death of Senus- ret I, when another great monument-maker ruled Egypt, Thutmose III. Some historians have seen the 'copy' as a literary fiction, but the elegant phrasing of the text sits well with other royal inscriptions of the 12th Dynasty, such as the imperfectly preserved temple narrative at Tod in Upper Egypt, or the famous boundary stelae of Senusret III from Nubia. The com- position opens with the date of the occasion at which Senusret I declared his intentions to create a new monumental structure at Iunu:

YEAR 3, INUNDATION MONTH 3, DAY 8 UNDER THE MAJESTY OF
KING KHEPERKARA SON OF RA SENUSRET [I]…
APPEARANCE OF THE KING WITH THE DOUBLE CROWN. THERE TOOK PLACE
A SITTING IN THE AUDIENCE-HALL.
COUNCIL OF THE RETINUE, THE COURTIERS OF THE PROTECTIVE PALACE –
MAY (THE KING) LIVE, PROSPER AND BE WELL!
THE WORDS OF THE KING TO HIS COURTIERS FOLLOW THIS SETTING:

See, My Majesty is planning works to be remembered as potent for posterity,
I will make monuments to establish my decrees for Horakhty…
I will build my temple in his precinct, that my goodness be remembered in
    his House.
The benben shrine will be my name, the [sacred] waterway will be my
    monument.

Senusret I may then have restructured the temple of the sun, giving it its
later contours as perhaps found by the 18th Dynasty copyist of this text,
500 years after his death. Nevertheless, this does not remove the possibility
that the temple he found on the site was already of considerable size. The
builders of the great mound supporting the temple platform and the 12th
Dynasty obelisk would have obliterated any earlier structure, unless traces
survive somehow within the core of the mound, yet to be uncovered by
more meticulous archaeological labour.

## Iunu and the sight-lines to the pyramids

There are a couple of hints that an imposing religious structure stood at
Iunu long before Senusret I. First, there are the 6th Dynasty obelisks, both
the large royal monoliths and the small-scale non-royal tomb-chapel monuments in the form of squat obelisks, inscribed in hieroglyphs with the name
and title of the official buried beneath the chapel. Perhaps the focus of the
cult here, the original *benben* stone, was a slender obelisk of the classic proportions with which we associate the word, perhaps some squatter structure
like the core monuments of the 5th Dynasty sun shrines across the river at
Abusir. Whatever its form, we have at least a hint that some substantial
sacred and solar feature stood on the site of Iunu in the Old Kingdom. The
second clue to the existence of a great solar temple at Iunu before the Middle
Kingdom comes at the other end of the scale in what survives: the pyramids
of the Old Kingdom royal tombs. David Jeffreys has drawn attention to the
location of all tombs of kings from the 2nd Dynasty to the 6th, as they
would have been seen from Iunu. By the curve of the cliffs around modern
Cairo and the outcrop transformed by Saladin into his great Citadel, the
Old Kingdom royal tombs divide into two groups. In the centuries and
millennia before our industrial smog, the northern series would have been

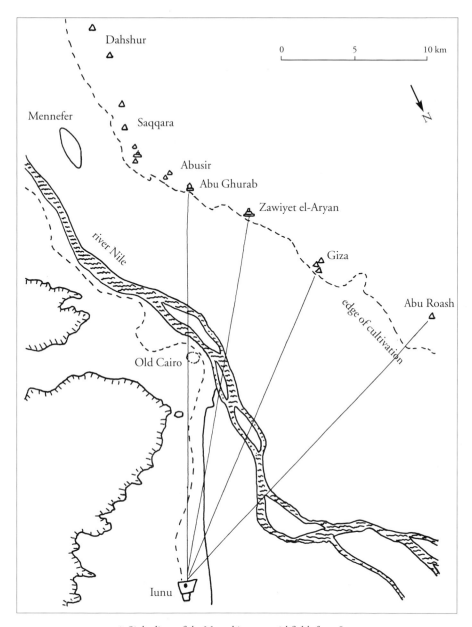

**38** *Sight-lines of the Memphite pyramid fields from Iunu.*

clearly visible from Iunu. To put it the other way around, Iunu would have been clearly visible from those tombs at the northern end of the Old Kingdom pyramid fields: this may have been the original motivation – to locate the royal burial place within sight of Iunu (*ill. 38*). These comprise the 4th Dynasty tombs of the kings at Abu Roash and Giza and, only just visible before the Citadel blocks the sight-line, the 5th Dynasty sun temples at Abusir. Any more southerly royal tomb would not have had a view of, or been visible from, Iunu: this covers the pyramid field of Abusir–Saqqara–Dahshur, all the monuments south of the sun temple of Niuserra at Abu Ghurab. The implications of these sight- lines are dramatic. The enigmatic sun temples of the 5th Dynasty kings around Abu Ghurab would have maintained an eternal solar link necessary to the cult complex of each king (*ill. 62*). Without such a link, the 5th Dynasty kings would have lost sight of the sun cult after death. We might ask why they did not simply continue to build within the northerly zone, but here it is important to remember the practicalities of monumental stone architecture. Giza and Abu Roash provide stable natural plateau surfaces suitable for building on this scale in these materials. After Menkaura had his, the third king's, pyramid built on the Giza plateau, there remained no space there for a further full pyramid complex. Later kings would be forced by the geology of the West Bank of the Nile Valley to move further south. This is not to deny the input of other powerful ideological factors in the decision to locate the later Old Kingdom royal tombs around Saqqara. A new Early Dynastic city at Inebhedj 'the White Walls' (probably near Abusir) seems to have acted as centre of the administration, and was drifting southwards as the river Nile gradually altered its course to flow further east. Eventually it lay at the latitude of the Saqqara South pyramid field, and thereby acquired the name Mennefer (the Memphis of the Greek historians), from the 6th Dynasty pyramid complex. This must have helped to draw the presence of the king to the area in death, as in life. There were also strong religious magnets to tomb-building on the Saqqara plateau: the first great stone complex stands there, the Step Pyramid of King Netjerkhet (Djoser), and at the northern end of the site the Abusir desert valley led to the tombs of the Apis or sacred bull of Ptah. During the Old Kingdom, then, there seems to have been a variable pattern of royal activity oscillating between the two force fields of Iunu (Heliopolis), city of the solar creator Ra, and Mennefer (Memphis), city of the earthly god of creativity, Ptah. In this permanently changing relationship, the 4th Dynasty located the king's tomb within sight of Iunu across the Nile, while the early kings of the 5th Dynasty each added a second complex to provide a solar channel for their tombs, because they themselves lay out of sight of the sun centre. What did they see at Iunu from across the river? Do we imagine an early focus of the sun cult, on the same immense scale as the royal cult at the height of the Old Kingdom? Or would the sacred character of the site have sufficed, without any colossal architectural feature to view? We can only hope for an answer from future archaeological investigation on the site, or from the discovery of a more explicit reference in Old Kingdom sources.

## The scale and form of the sun temple at Iunu – the Great Shrine

On the site itself, for all the utter destruction one point does emerge with force – the sheer scale of the surviving precinct. The ancient Egyptians named the sun temple at Iunu Hut aat 'the Great Shrine', or main sanctuary in the land. The great platform in the area of the obelisks lies within a larger enclosure wall, over a kilometre east to west. The entire enclosure follows a roughly rectangular line, cut across at the northwest corner, along the line that the canalized river branch runs today. An internal wall running roughly east–west divided this space. North of this wall may have been an area less sacred to the sun, but just the acreage to the south covers an extent exceptional even by ancient Egyptian standards. It is possible to gauge the massive scope from the monuments surviving in Upper Egypt, and familiar to visitors to the modern country (*ill. 39*).

Another indication comes from the height of the obelisks on the site. Only that of Senusret I can still be seen there today, but others can be identified from classical authors and by their inscriptions as coming from Iunu. These can be compared in size with the obelisks at Thebes, where the ancient architecture has substantially survived (*ills 71–72*). Two obelisks set up by Thutmose III measure 20.88 and 21.21 m (68.5 ft and 69.5 ft): these were moved to Alexandria to adorn a new temple to Caesar, and in the 19th

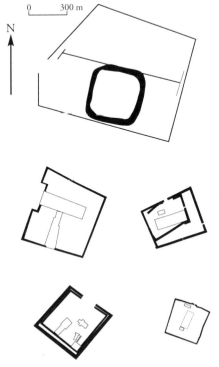

0    300 m

N

**39** *Scale comparison of major temple precincts.*
*Uppermost: Iunu. Centre left: Karnak.*
*Centre right: Tanis. Lower left: Balamun.*
*Lower right: Dendera.*

century moved on, one to London, the other to New York. Though not a single monument of this great king survives at Iunu, the obelisks belong to the select group of 'super-obelisks', cut in ancient Egyptian times only for Iunu and Thebes. They testify to the scale on which Thutmose III must have built there, confirming an autobiographical passage in the tomb of his high official Iamunedjeh. Iamunedjeh relates the establishment of three pairs of obelisks, stating 'I saw the erection of the great obelisks made by His Majesty for his father Atum lord of Iunu, at the gate of the great double pylon made by His Majesty anew.' Whatever the date of the temple entrance 'renewed' by Thutmose III, its height called for monolithic granite obelisks over 20 m (66 ft) tall. The lost architecture at least matched, and perhaps surpassed, anything surviving at Thebes.

## The reach of Iunu across Egypt and its territories

Another index of the importance of Iunu may be found in mentions of the city in administration outside its immediate territories. The evidence post-dates the reign of Akhenaten (for which see Chapter Five), and the estates may be a residue of state fields assigned in that revolutionary time to the sun cult. One fragment of accountancy manuscript (British Museum EA 10447) records deliveries of grain for offerings to 'the great statue [i.e. colossus] Ramesses-beloved-of-Amun may he live, prosper and be well, beloved of Atum'. The fields supplying this harvest lay in the 15th province of Upper Egypt, the area where Akhenaten had built his city to the sun god, modern Amarna. The greatest surviving ancient Egyptian accountancy manuscript, Papyrus Wilbour, includes numerous entries referring to the institutions and personnel of the Ra domain or Iunu, as part of a land assessment carried out in year 4 of Ramesses V. From the preceding reign another lengthy manuscript, Papyrus Harris, recorded all the good deeds of the deceased Ramesses III in a prayer to the gods on behalf of the new king Ramesses IV. These included pious donations to the sun god of some 441 sq. km (274 sq. miles) across Egypt. The donation lists of Papyrus Harris have often been interpreted as a cession of royal land and power to the temples. However, the Egyptian context does not support this: most of the fields went, not directly to the gods, but rather to the cult of the king within the domain of a god. Ramesses III established estates throughout Egypt to support his own cult in new temples such as those at Karnak and Medinet Habu in Thebes, and the now-vanished structure he had built at Iunu. In this he was follow-ing standard practice for an ancient Egyptian king, and might expect his successors to divert resources from his cult when they finally needed the land for another purpose, such as the establishment of their own cults. The major overhauls in the nationwide accountancy of land were marked by a

40 *Upper part of the inscription decreed by Sety I, at Nauri in Nubia, showing the king before the three principal gods of late New Kingdom Egypt: Amun, Ra and Ptah. 19th Dynasty.*

*sipty wer* 'Great Revision', such as that launched in year 15 of Ramesses III. The particular estates associated with supporting the temple for Ramesses III in Iunu, and the location of this temple within the city, are discussed below in the section on the great northern extension to the Ra precinct.

Like the estates of Amun and Ptah, the Ra domain reached beyond the borders of Egypt into Nubia, at least in the Ramesside Period. The 67-year reign of Ramesses II saw a series of remarkable temple buildings constructed or sculpted out of the rock along the Nile Valley in Egyptian-occupied Nubia. The rock-temple at Derr was attached to the Ra domain. Hieroglyphic inscriptions in the temple refer to its principal deity as 'Ra-Horakhty lord of heaven, amid the temple of Ramesses-beloved-of-Amun in the Ra domain'. Along similar lines the temple at Gerf Hussein was incorporated into the Ptah domain, while the other Nubian temples of the period seem to fall within the Amun domain. In Ramesside theology the three deities together expressed the fundamental aspects of creation, as formulated in the great hymn to the creator on the literary manuscript Papyrus Leiden I 350:

> All gods are three, Amun, Ra and Ptah, incomparable,
> His name is hidden [Egyptian *amen*] as Amun,
> He is Ra in sight,
> His physical body is Ptah.

In this triad, the creator has an invisible aspect, Amun, the visible aspect of the sun, Ra, and a material or tangible aspect, that of the earth and created things, Ptah (*ill. 40*). This theological formula receives in the Nubian temples an extraordinary administrative expression that extended the reach of the Ra domain far into the south. This administrative expression of theology depended on Egyptian control of Nubia, which did not survive beyond the end of the 20th Dynasty (about 1070 BC).

## A visit by the Sudanese conqueror King Piy in the 8th century BC

There survives not a single ancient Egyptian description specific enough to reconstruct in detail the principal temple of the sun god at Iunu. Instead we must search for echoes of the layout and contents. One of the most useful passages referring to Iunu comes in the inscription describing the triumph of Piy, king of Napata, over his Egyptian enemies in the late 8th century BC. From deep in what is now Sudan, Piy and his armies pushed past the Theban domain first into Middle Egypt, and then to the edges of the Delta, the home of his principal foe, Tefnakht, ruler of Sais on the western branch of the Nile. When he arrived at the sacred city of the solar creator from the south, he followed an itinerary recorded on the triumphal stela in some detail. First there was a ritual purification to the west of the Ity canal. This waterway appears in other sources as the principal thoroughfare for river traffic to the city, and probably followed roughly the course of the modern canalized Nile branch passing north to northeast, along the western side of the site. From here he proceeded to the 'high sand' in Iunu, facing the rising of the sun god. He moved into the temple precinct of Ra, for the ritual of repelling the enemies of the king, of order. The inscription refers to the establishment of the 'morning house', for ritual cleansing and sung worship. As the *sedeb* garment was tied, incense burned, and then branches were brought from the Domain of the *Benben*. In a motif recalling the art of Akhenaten, hieroglyphic signs of life were offered, much as the sun disk extended the same sign to king and queen in the temples of Akhetaten (Akhenaten's city at Amarna). Now the king ascended the stairway to see Ra in the Domain of the *Benben*. Unexpectedly, in order to see his father Ra in this house, he broke a seal and opened the doors. Does this imply a shrine with doors closed upon a relatively small image, as in the cults of other deities? Perhaps, but the inscription does not exclude the possibility that the king moved through the doors into a broader space, hidden by a screen-wall from the eyes of all others. In that case, the (open?) platform might bear some more substantial feature. In either case, it seems that the procedure did not differ in its individual acts from cults involving small sacred images in dark sanctuaries. The Piy stela also refers here to the morning barque of Ra and the evening barque of Atum. Again, the scale is not given. Only after resealing the Domain of the *Benben* did the king proceed to the Atum temple, to offer incense to his father Atum-Khepri 'the eldest in Iunu'. This form of the creator features in an inscription of an earlier ruler, Osorkon I, in the 10th century BC, discovered at Bubastis. The question arises whether Piy was visiting one complex of the sun god, or two, a Ra temple and an Atum temple. The stela places the initial activity in the temple of Ra, moving to the domain of the sacred benben stone, and then to the precinct

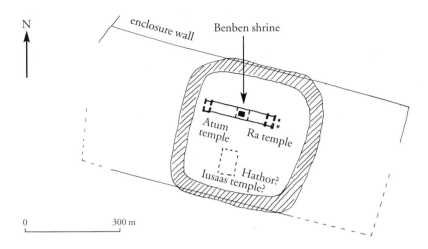

**41** *Hypothetical plan of the sun temple at Iunu, proposing a double-entry sanctuary to Ra-Atum, with a separate temple for Hathor to the south.*

of Atum. However, other evidence points to a single administrative entity. The gifts of Ramesses III, posthumously recorded in a single great papyrus, refer to personnel in the one 'temple of Atum lord of the two lands, the god of Iunu, Ra-Horakhty'. The High Priest of Ra may be qualified as 'of Ra-Atum', as may the women with the position of cult musician. There are various possibilities, of which perhaps the most radical would be a double temple, not on a parallel axis like that of Sobek and Horus at Kom Ombo (and Shedyt in the Fayum?), but back to back. In this scenario, the Ra temple would be the part facing the east, the rising sun and the desert hills, while the Atum temple would face the west, the setting sun and the river, the source of fertile life from the hidden underworld. One might even speculate further that the Domain of the *Benben,* also cast as early as the Pyramid Texts as the Domain of the *Benu* Bird, formed some kind of linking sanctuary between the Ra and Atum zones (*ill. 41*). At the core of the temple, we might imagine a particularly potent shrine, where the *benben* stone stood in order to pinpoint the earthly worship of the solar creator. Here we have no ground plan from Iunu itself, but we do find clues among the monuments at other sites, suggesting a leading role for platforms concealed by balustrades.

## The balustrade as a feature of architecture and of royal cult

The Egyptian Museum in Cairo preserves a massive quartzite block, 2.5 m (8 ft 2 in) in height, found built into a mosque near the citadel in Cairo (CG 34175). The royal reliefs on both sides indicate that it once adorned the

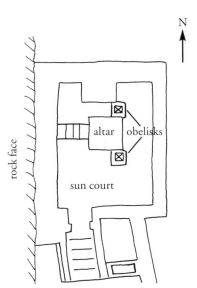

N

rock face

altar | obelisks

sun court

42 *Plan of the sun shrine at Abu Simbel. 19th Dynasty.*

temple at Iunu. On one side a scene shows King Akhenaten, his wife Nefertiti and one of their daughters worshipping the sun disk, the special form of the sun god promulgated by this one king (see Chapter Five). The sun disk is identified here as the god 'amid Wetjes-Ra-m-Iunu [meaning the temple Which Raises Ra in Iunu]'. The other side shows the later King Horemheb before the more traditional form of the sun god as Khepri, evidently having turned the original Akhenaten block into a royal stela. Here the original Akhenaten relief is of greater importance. It records the name of a sun shrine established at Iunu by Akhenaten, but it also reveals the special form which such a shrine took, as Ian Shaw has shown. For this great quartzite block, well over human stature, can best be explained as part of the wall enclosing an open-air shrine, with an altar at the centre. The king could move into this private space to commune with the sun god, otherwise available in the sky indiscriminately to all. The walled sun shrine finds parallels both at Akhenaten's residence city, Amarna, but also in traditional royal temples both before and after his reign. The clearest early example has been reconstructed from fragments by the Polish Egyptological mission restoring the upper terrace in the temple of Hatshepsut at Deir el-Bahri. A more remote example lay at the foot of the colossal images of Ramesses II cut from the living rock to form the façade of his temple at Abu Simbel, deep into Nubia (*ill. 42*). The Akhenaten block from Iunu seems to confirm that the royal worship of the sun involved a specially delimited space, screened from view, and perhaps ideally, on the evidence of Deir el-Bahri, at the highest level available. Possibly this most sacred and kingly space took at Iunu the name of Domain of the *Benben*.

## A model shrine for the sun god

The observations on the sun shrines in New Kingdom temples to kings, and on balustrades in Amarna, may find corroboration in one of the most extraordinary antiquities from Egypt, the base for a model of a temple entrance cut into a quartzite block preserved in the Brooklyn Museum (inv.no. 49.183). The block measures 87.5 by 112 cm (34.5 x 44 in), and is only 28 cm (11 in) at its tallest point when laid flat (*ill. 43*). A band of hieroglyphs accompanies images of the king, kneeling in offering, around the thickness. This indicates the correct orientation of the block, as a thin slab lying flat on the ground, and reveals in part the purpose of the monument. At the centre of one narrower side two short columns of hieroglyphs record the names of the gods to whom the block was dedicated. On the left we read 'Ra-Horakhty, the great god, lord of heaven, amid the Great Temple', and on the right 'Atum lord of the Two Lands, of Iunu, the great god, lord of heaven'. The better-preserved line inscribed over the figure of the king on the right reads 'King Menmaatra-image-of Ra [throne-name of Sety I] has come before you [singular], Atum Khepri Ra-Horakhty, and has fulfilled you [plural] with the oils emerged from the eye of Horus.' This indicates the offering of oil, confirmed by the items in front of the king: green and black eye paint, and oil (the names of the eye paints are added in hieroglyphs beside them, that for the oil does not need to be repeated from the line of inscription). On the other side the offerings in front of the kneeling figure of Sety I comprise food and drink. Evidently the offering ritual for the sun god did not differ greatly in substance from the offerings in the daily cult of other gods.

Yet the upper face of the slab contains a quite exceptional feature, a series of neat depressions cut into the quartzite, either side of a gently sloping series of steps, rising to the centre. Four of the depressions are long and rectangular with a rounded outer end, two are small circles, two are thicker and larger rectangles, two are square, and two are smaller rectangles. Alexandre Badawy worked ingeniously from the limited information along the right side of the base to produce an interpretation of their possible significance (*ill. 44*). He recognized that the long rectangles with rounded ends would make perfect anchors for inset figures of a recumbent statue, most probably a sphinx. In this case the quartzite block would have been the base of a model of the entrance to a temple of the sun. The other shapes could accommodate obelisks, statues and, at the back, gateway towers, though not an Upper Egyptian-style pylon. The small circles might each indicate the position of a flagstaff, as mentioned in the inscription on the base, though their location between the gateway jambs suggests rather the pivot-hole for the fixing of two great door-leaves.

**43** *Quartzite base for a model temple gateway inscribed for King Sety I. Brooklyn Museum of Art 49.183. From Tell el-Yehudiya. 19th Dynasty.*

The model itself was acquired at Tell el-Yahudiya, over 10 km (6.25 miles) north of Iunu. Here there had been a large Asiatic settlement during the Second Intermediate Period, and later Ramesses III had a magnificent palace laid out, famous today for the superb multi-coloured glazed floor-tiles shaped as foreign enemies, upon which the king could tread. The site of Tell el-Yahudiya might have been a solar outpost, but at all events the Brooklyn model clearly refers in its inscription to the sun god in his various forms, and the Great Temple ought to refer directly to the main temple of Ra at Iunu. Is this then the addition made by Sety I to the centre of the sun cult? If so, the model presents the structure as it would have been visible to all but the king and the closest circle of participants in royal ritual. If we restore high slabs either side of a doorway at the top of the steps, with sphinxes, obelisks and colossal statues at the front, we have the entrance perhaps specifically to a raised platform in which the open court contained a screened sun altar. The name of the king is significant: Sety I was a great restorer following the heretical reign of Akhenaten. Perhaps at Iunu he forti-fied the cult with its hymns in all their mysteries, and made this restoration of words tangible and visible in great architecture. The Brooklyn model would have served to underpin that monumental sculpture. It has achieved its aim to an unexpected extent, for it has survived where Sety's great temple building has irretrievably disappeared. Perhaps a future survey might recover enough of the temple plan to date individual sections of the complex and relate them to one another. In the meantime, the quartzite model-base of Sety I indicates how much was constructed on the site, and how different it may have been from Upper Egyptian temple pylons. If we have lost the orig-inal emplacement, at least one of the obelisks of Sety I survives, transported

**44** *Plaster reconstruction of model temple gateway. Brooklyn Museum of Art 49.183.*

in 10 BC to adorn the Circus Maximus at Rome, and since 1589 the centre-point to the Piazza del Popolo. At 23.2 m (76 ft) in height, it gives some idea of the scale of the great temple entrance in the New Kingdom (*ills 72–73*). Its inscriptions immortalize the project intended by the king, 'he who fills Iunu with obelisks, for the shining of sun-rays, with the house of Ra flooded by his beauty, and the gods of the Great Shrine united in joy'.

## The northern extension to the main temple – space for the cults of kings?

At some point in the New Kingdom, a new enclosure wall added a second vast area to the Ra precinct, extending north of the main temple enclosure. Cairo university excavations in the western sector of this area during 1976–80 have shed some light on its contents, though it is now largely buried beneath modern urban development. In the publications by A. Saleh, a series of sacred and other buildings appear together in a complex arrangement, within which at least one sacred precinct may be identified. At the end of the 20th Dynasty, one part of the complex became the house of a son of Ramesses IX who was a high priest of Ra. The other sections seem to involve one or more sanctuaries set up by Ramesses II, in part using blocks from earlier structures. Without further publication and excavation, the function or functions of the complex must remain unknown. However, it is worth speculating that the entire area might have contained a series of buildings attested in inscriptions and manuscripts of the New Kingdom: the temples established in turn to perpetuate the cult of each reigning king (*cf. ill. 45*). The kings of the 19th and 20th Dynasties were buried at Thebes, in the Valley of the Kings, and along the West Bank there they sited their principal cult temples. Running from north to south along the western edge of the fields lie the temple of Sety I at Gurna, the mighty Ramesseum for Ramesses II, a temple of Merenptah at the rear of the ruins of the Amenhotep III temple and, furthest south, best preserved of all, the temple of Ramesses III. Egyptologists often call them 'mortuary temples', but they began to be built, and probably to function, as soon as each reign began. The Egyptian term for them was 'Temple of Millions of Years', and those at Thebes were 'in the Amun domain'. At some point, perhaps under Amenhotep III, the kings began to establish equally massive temples to their own cult in other places, notably at Mennefer (Memphis) 'in the domain of Ptah', and at Iunu 'in the domain of Ra'. The exact location of the examples at Iunu remains unknown, but perhaps the great northern extension represented an additional enclosure whose purpose was to attach the regal cults to the Ra precinct. Possibly here should be sited the solar temple of Akhenaten 'which raises the Aten in the domain of Ra', cited in the quartzite balustrade. The structures of Akhenaten, and perhaps of his father Amenhotep III, would have been reused by the Ramesside kings, much as the ruined Theban temple of Amenhotep III was quarried to build the Merenptah temple behind it.

The plan and even the scale of the regal cult buildings at Iunu remains unknown, but perhaps included a focal open court, with a balustrade, like the sun shrine at Abu Simbel. A group of relatively small-scale obelisks would fit such a pattern of regal sun courts. Three granodiorite obelisk fragments now in Copenhagen and Avignon were inscribed for Ramesses I, and later, perhaps in a reuse of a shrine, for Ramesses IX. On a slightly larger scale at up to 6.34 m (20 ft 9 in) are four red granite obelisks inscribed for Ramesses II. The emperor Domitian had these transported to Rome during his great expansion of the temple to Isis on the Field of Mars there. However, an original emplacement in Iunu seems clear from the hieroglyphs describing Ramesses in terms such as 'monumental, rich in monuments in the House of Ra' and 'effective son of Ra, his sacred effigy'.

45 *Inscription on bronze offering-table of Ramesses II, referring to Ra in hwwt-sdw. This may denote the area outside the main sun temple, with cults of 19th Dynasty kings. The offering-table was found in secondary context, in the 21st Dynasty royal tombs at Tanis.*

**46** *The column of King Merenptah at Iunu, showing the gods Mont, Seth and Ra-Horakhty offering him kingship and victory over foreign enemies. 19th Dynasty.*

**47** *Detail from the column of King Merenptah at Iunu, showing a bound foreign captive in the lowest register. 19th Dynasty.*

His son and successor Merenptah also had at least one red granite obelisk, from which there survives a fragment almost 6 m (19 ft 8 in) in height. It was found at Qaha, some 20 km (12.5 m) northwest of Iunu, but such dispersal of monuments can be explained by the vagaries of reuse of stones and their transport across the Delta. On one side Merenptah receives the epithet 'he who founded Iunu anew for the one who created him' (i.e. for the sun god). The only institution that he is known to have founded in the city is the temple for his own cult 'in the Ra domain', still functioning a century later according to the accounts in Papyrus Wilbour (see above). If his cult temple lay within the great northern extension beside the Ra precinct, this would help to explain the location of one of the most remarkable monuments from the city, the monolithic red granite victory column of Merenptah (*ills 46–47*). The column stood on a quartzite plinth upon a limestone platform, just outside the northern entrance to the main precinct, not far from its western end. It came to light during excavation in 1970. The sides bear offering scenes and a hieroglyphic inscription recording the defeat inflicted on invading western nomads in year 5 of the king's reign. In one scene the sun god Ra-Horakhty declares to the offering king 'I have granted you strength against every foreign land.' The victory column is unique in ancient Egyptian art history. Possibly it was intended to act as a link between the cult of the king and the precinct of Ra. Yet it must be remembered that the location of the royal cult temples remains uncertain, and that the northern extension is only one possibility within a vast area of sacred land. The most recent and best-documented publication on the city, that by Dietrich Raue, would place the kingly cults within the main precinct. Such wide-open options indicate how much archaeological work the site still needs.

In the 20th Dynasty Ramesses III set up a monumental gateway at the southwest corner of the northern extension. Here too, it is possible that the gate, exposed in the 1976–80 Cairo University excavations, belonged to the temple for the cult of that king. This is well documented in Papyrus Harris, where the dead king addresses Ra with a list of good deeds including the following:

> I made for you my noble temple within your temple, like heaven,
> established under the Sun Disk, before you … as a great secret horizon for
> Horakhty.

The accompanying lists identify this temple as the 'Temple of Millions of Years for Ramesses-ruler-of-Iunu in the domain of Ra'.

The new temple required supporting estates, and Ramesses III made the governing centre for these a new royal palace at the next available town to the north, a site today named Tell el-Yahudiya. In Papyrus Harris this palatial economic centre appears in the following good deed:

> O made for you a noble domain north of Iunu, embellished with the work
> of eternity, inscribed in your name, [as] Estate of the Temple of Millions of
> Years for Ramesses-ruler-of-Iunu may he live, prosper and be well, in the
> domain of Ra, to the north of Iunu.

Little remains of the palace today, but still in the late 19th century there was a platform littered with brilliantly glazed polychrome tiles. Many were collected, a few excavated by Petrie, and today the tiles of Ramesses III in numerous museums testify to the continuing technical and artistic brilliance of Egypt at the end of the New Kingdom. The quality of these remnants from the palace of Ramesses III suggests that he may have resided here himself, and this gives weight to the epithet he added to his birth name, 'ruler of Iunu'.

## An ancient plan for the temple of Hathor at Iunu

Where the ground plan of the principal temple appears lost in detail, we do have an incomplete inventory of a lesser element in the complex of solar cult, a temple to the goddess Hathor. In the same ditch where Schiaparelli

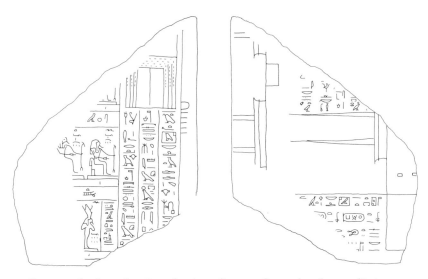

**48** *Fragment of a plaque from Iunu, bearing a diagram of a temple at Iunu and its inventory.*

uncovered the fragments of the oldest monument found at Iunu, the shrine of Netjerkhet, there survived the broken remnants of a slender siltstone panel, rather like a writing-tablet (*ill. 48*). This is incised on both sides with diagrams of the Hathor temple, together with hieroglyphic inscriptions of its contents. The reason for the existence of the stone panel can be gauged from the three columns of hieroglyphs written below a doorway: 'Decree of His Majesty to give command to the god's father and master of secrets Ra, true of voice, son of Amenemipet […] and the god's father and master of secrets Nebimes son of Amenemipet, of Ra-Horakhty, to carry out a review [of the temple?] of the mother of his father [?] Hathor Nebethetepet of Taded [perhaps to be translated as 'the grove'] …' At least four registers to the left record, according to the lowest line, 'what is in the secret store in this sanctuary'. There follows a series of images, the first of which depicts Atum, with arms folded, standing, wearing the Double Crown (*ill. 48, left*). The size of the Atum image is given as 'six cubits', about 3 m (9 ft 10 in) or twice life size, and its material is simply given as 'wood', unless this is an indication of condition. Statues of deities on this scale are rare, and it comes as something of a surprise that the sun cult needed an icon in addition to the solar disk. However, this is the image of the elder aspect of the sun, as primeval creator, and as the ageing evening sun, on its way towards renewal beneath the earth. Furthermore, the image stands not in the temple of the sun god himself, but as a supplement to one of the shrines for the feminine complement to creation. In the register above appear two seated gods, the first of *sekhem* 'the Image', and in wood (?), the other (name lost) of an undeciphered material (or condition). Both are about half the height of the Atum figure, thus somewhat smaller (not to be compared directly, as these are seated rather than standing). A fragment to be placed somewhere to the left includes the word for 'cult instrument', and a sistrum, the rattle-like device to measure the rhythm of chanting in cult. The sistrum incorporates the wigged head of Hathor, as often, from her role as goddess of the sensuous, including music. The uppermost register preserves to the right a part of the basket-hieroglyph reading 'neb', in which some have seen the remnants of the name of the goddess Nebethetep, 'Lady of the place of Offerings'. This would indeed be appropriate, as the aspect of the feminine complement to which this temple seems to have been dedicated. Further behind on the same row are Isis, Hathor 'Lady of Iunu', and two sceptre-like emblems named Power of Horus and Power of Seth. The last element discernible in the inventory is the emblem of Nefertem, embodiment of sweet smell and depicted as the lotus 'at the nostril of Atum'. Here, as with the goddesses of Iunu, we meet the mystery of life, a spark enabling creation at the beginning of time.

The other side of the plaque provides the plan of the temple, with massive rectangular gateways, depicted with sides more vertical than the sloping-sided temple pylons surviving in Upper Egypt. From the cavetto cornice atop each tower rise two slender and tapering poles, presumably the flagstaffs as seen from within the temple, looking out. To the bottom left a hieroglyphic caption reads 'the temple of Hathor Nebethetep ['Lady of the place of Offerings'] in the grove [?] [built by?] King Kheperkara and King... [...] the foundation at... [...] all [...] of all god's fathers [a priestly title]' (*ill. 48, right*). Two Egyptian kings took the throne name Kheperkara: Senusret I of the 12th Dynasty, and Nakhtnebef in the 30th Dynasty, 16 centuries later. The names of the priests mentioned in the plaque seem typical of the 8th to 7th centuries. Therefore, it is more likely that the Kheperkara of this inscription refers to the earlier ruler, Senusret I. This impression gains force from the presence of the obelisk of Senusret I on the site, and the fact that the 18th Dynasty manuscript copies an account of his building activity at Iunu.

Whatever the date of the foundation of this temple to a goddess at Iunu, in layout it presents a series of at least three open courts (*ill. 49*). The second has pillars at either side, and on at least one side a chapel, named as 'the chapel for the raising of the willow tree'. The third court has either pillars or offering tables, marked as squares across the width of the court, with a small chapel at the near left corner on entry. This second subsidiary chapel seems to be a platform approached by two short stairways, and bears the name 'house of Atum of the sycamore tree'. Above it a hieroglyph 'south' marks the orientation of the building, recalling the Memphite epithet of Hathor 'Lady of the Southern Sycamore'. If this was the innermost part of the structure, as the fragment to the right with the empty margin indicates, the third court may be an open sun court with altars. Where then would the image of

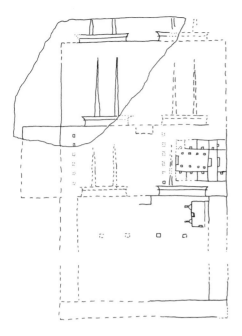

**49** *The temple plan on the Iunu plaque, as reconstructed by Ricke.*

Nebethetep rest? Was the goddess present here in any form other than the sacred trees themselves? It seems most likely that the sanctuary was a closed shrine, at the central axis, lost from the surviving fragments of the plaque. Yet the empty space on the far right fragment does not entirely seem to suit the original presence, in its expected position, of a holy-of-holies. Here, as so often, Iunu keeps its mysteries. Certainly we should not underestimate the role of flora in the cult, to be covered again below, in the case of the enigmatic *ished* tree of the sun god.

## The Greatest of Seers – high priest of Ra

At least in later periods, the high priest of the sun god bore the title Greatest of Seers, but the earlier significance and even the reading of this title remain subjects of controversy. In the 3rd millennium it is written with the hieroglyphs denoting 'great' and 'see'. In the hieroglyphic script, the more sacred word is often written first, even when it is pronounced second (compare the more prosaic practice in modern scripts where we place the currency sign before the numeral, even though we read unthinkingly £5 as 'five pounds'). The early writings might then be an example of this honorific transposition of signs, and be interpreted instead as 'He who Sees the Great One'. The Great One in question might be the king or a god. By the Middle Kingdom, after 2000 BC, we find the title written with the plural 'Seers', indicating that at least from this date the term should be interpreted as 'Greatest of Seers'.

These seers would have been, as discussed in the previous chapter, the men responsible for the observation of celestial movements, who charted the sun and stars in the sky in order to maintain the rhythm and rites of the kingly cult. Already in the Old Kingdom we find the title, albeit without the plural writing, combined with the name of the city of the sun god, Iunu. This suggests that the title may not have undergone any reinterpretation in the Middle Kingdom, though there is evidence for reinterpretation of other ancient titles at this date. On at least some occasions the holder of the title referring to Iunu acted as director of expeditions to Sinai and the Red Mountain. Whether the title denoted 'Greatest of Seers' or 'He who Sees the Great One', its link to Iunu suggests at least that 'sight' here, as so often in Egypt, involves the cult of the sun. However, this cultic aspect should not obscure one striking phenomenon in ancient Egyptian religion: there are no high priests in local cult centres before the Middle Kingdom. The titles later identifying the High Priest of Ptah at the city of Mennefer, or of Ra at Iunu, were used in the Old Kingdom for high officials at court. Since the royal court was itself a centre of cult, a specific sacred space, all high officials would have assumed some cultic functions, either individually in particular roles at the rites of court ceremony, or as groups of 'Companions', as recorded in depictions of the *sed* or epochal kingship festival. The Greatest of Seers became the title applied to the principal figure in any sun temple, but originally it denoted an official at court with responsibility for solar rites.

From the late 4th Dynasty the position indicated by 'Greatest of Seers/He who Sees the Great One' sometimes fell to the highest administrative official, the *tjaty* (loosely translated by Egyptologists as 'vizier'). One of the earliest more revealing references to the position occurs on the Palermo Stone, a fragment from an enigmatic basalt block inscribed with excerpts from royal annals (*ill. 50*). This annals monument apparently took the form of a free-standing block, inscribed on both faces, tapering towards the flat top, in other words shaped like a contemporary Mesopotamian mystery object, the Royal Standard of Ur. For the reign of King Neferirkara of the 5th Dynasty, the excerpts include a donation of land to the Powers of Iunu, placed under the charge of the Greatest of Seers/He who Sees the Great One. The shift from royal court to the temple itself may be mirrored in the surviving record, if the pattern reflects more than chance survival. During the early 6th Dynasty, holders of the title appear in the cemeteries around the royal pyramid complex. Isesikhaf is attested in the cult temple of King Teti, and Ibi is mentioned in the tomb-chapel of his father Khentika-Ikhekhi, also in the Saqqara royal necropolis. Tombs of the Greatest of Seers survive at Iunu itself only slightly later in the Old Kingdom and during the First Intermediate Period. The earliest in this series is a 6th Dynasty man

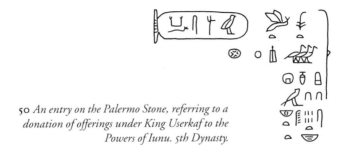

50 *An entry on the Palermo Stone, referring to a donation of offerings under King Userkaf to the Powers of Iunu. 5th Dynasty.*

named Khunhor, followed by Meru and two men named Sebeki. Other noble tombs of the same period seem to have served as quarries for the men who constructed the great platform beneath the Senusret I obelisk. When the 12th Dynasty re-established royal power, the Greatest of Seers may again have been buried at the royal pyramid complex. For this period the holders of the title are known only from scarabs or from references in contemporary papyrus manuscripts. Their names reveal the closeness of the links between the king and the sun cult. One papyrus refers to the Greatest of Seers Khakauraemhutaat, meaning 'Senusret III is in the Great Temple' (*hutaat* being the term for the central shrine at Iunu). A scarab preserves the name of another as Maakheruraemhutaat, 'Amenemhat IV is in the Great Temple'. The conjunction of solar high priestly title, accession name of the king and the Great Temple of the sun god's city is striking and unparalleled.

In the New Kingdom the shift from royal court to the location of the cult centre becomes decisive. From this moment the temples were used as the banking system of the royal administration. Their fortified enclosure walls and vast granary capacity became the secure food reservoir of a state, in which salaries at all levels were measured in grain. According to the summary of cult donations under Ramesses III, towards the end of the New Kingdom, the land of Egypt was effectively divided into three unequal parts, scattered in parcels along the Nile and its branches. The largest was the estate of Amun-Ra, centred on Karnak in ancient Thebes, with its 'First God's Servant of Amun', the high priestly title invented at the beginning of the 18th Dynasty, about 1550 BC. The second was the estate of Ptah, centred on Mennefer (Memphis), with its high priest taking the old courtly title 'Greatest of Directors of Crafts'. The third was the estate of Ra, its focus at Iunu, its highest authority the Greatest of Seers. We have seen this pattern on a smaller scale in Egyptian-occupied Nubia, with the estates of Amun, Ptah and Ra repeated between the 1st and 4th Cataracts. Despite this dramatic overhaul in the profile and interrelation of the different cult centres, the Greatest of Seers continued to play a specific role in kingly ritual. A Middle Kingdom papyrus includes the solar officiant in the Establishment of the *Djed* Pillar of Osiris at rites to cement the power of the king. Other sources show him accompanying the king at the *sed*, most important of all festivals of kingship. The funerary literature refers to him as a servant of Osiris, king of the dead, and he extends a leaf of the sacred *ished* tree on the day of filling the *wedjat* eye in Iunu.

## The ished – the tree of Ra and the ritual of naming the king

With the *ished* we return to the motif of gardens and flora, but in a very specific rite of kingship. The depictions of the *ished* resemble the persea tree, and accountancy papyri and inscriptions refer to *ished* fruit alongside figs and raisins, indicating that it did have a 'real' as well as a 'mythic' or symbolic presence (*ill. 51*). In the New Kingdom a special large-scale figurative composition in the repertoire of temple relief shows the king kneeling before the gods, in the shade of the tree, as Thoth, god of wisdom, and Seshat, goddess of the act of writing, record his name on the leaves. One of the most remarkable inscriptions concerning this motif survives imperfectly far to the south, in the court north of the 7th Pylon at Karnak. Here, over two inscriptions of his father Ramesses III, Ramesses IV recorded an episode in which he entered the temple of Ra to see the *ished* and found his name upon the leaves. It must be remembered that this reign probably followed the murder of his father Ramesses III in a palace conspiracy, and that the inheriting son may have felt exceptional pressure to legitimize his rule. The extent to which he felt it necessary to justify himself can be seen in the great papyrus recording the good deeds of Ramesses III, stated to have been done on condition that Ramesses IV succeeded to the throne. Here, then, the traditional New Kingdom motif of recording the name of the king on the *ished* tree becomes a miraculous episode in which the new king discovers his name already written on the leaves in acknowledgment of his accession.

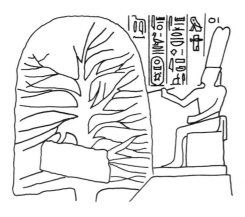

51 *The earliest depiction of the naming ritual at the* ished-*tree: Amun-Ra writes the name of Thutmose III 'on the noble* ished-*tree in the Great Shrine of Ra'. 18th Dynasty temple, south wall of sanctuary, Medinet Habu, Thebes West.*

52 *Stela depicting the king's son Ahmose, Greatest of Seers of Ra-Atum, offering incense to the Menwer bull, here styled 'herald of Ra, who raises maat (What is Right) to her lord'. Below stands the official Qen, who dedicated the stela, with his son Atumhotep. Egyptian Museum, Berlin 14200. 18th Dynasty.*

## The Menwer – sacred bull of Ra

Another feature in nature adopted in the cult complex of Ra is the Menwer bull (*ill. 52*). Ancient Egyptian religion allots considerable space to the imagery of bull and cattle herds, understandably in a land where animal husbandry played no less a role than the farming of plant crops. Already in the late Old Kingdom the Pyramid Texts refer to the 'bull of Iunu', distinguishing it in this way from the other sacred bull, the Apis, in the cult of Ptah at Mennefer (Memphis). In the funerary literature of the Middle Kingdom this single sacred animal at Iunu, named Meni or Menwer ('Meni the great', rendered in classical Greek texts as Mnevis), assisted the deceased in the process of regeneration for eternal life. During the 18th Dynasty, the bull received special estates for the pasture of its calves, by decree of Thutmose III. No burial of a Menwer earlier than the reign of Ramesses II, in the 19th Dynasty, has yet been found, though one canopic jar for a bull dates to Hatshepsut. The lack of other earlier evidence may be due to the high water level in the area where the bulls were buried during the New Kingdom. The humidity destroyed much of the funeral equipment placed with the Menwer buried in the 26th year of Ramesses II. Enough survived to indicate that the skin of the animal had been covered in gold at burial, emphasizing its role as 'herald of Ra' in Egyptian inscriptions. Nearby, Ahmed Kamal uncovered a slightly later and better-preserved burial, for the Menwer that lived under Ramesses VII. Although the evidence is slight at Iunu itself, we may look to the Late Period precinct for the Apis bull and its embalming at the Ptah temple in Memphis. The Apis too acted as 'herald' of the deity, and received a life of luxury and a burial on a royal scale at the Serapeum on the northwestern desert range of Saqqara. We may imagine the Menwer similarly housed like a living icon of the sun god during life, and receiving its sumptuous burial between temple precinct and river, between sun and Nile. A statue of the Menwer bull was set up early in the reign of Saptah and inscribed with the names of both the king and his influential treasurer, a Syrian named Bay. It is not clear whether this three-dimensional image once adorned a general shrine of the bull, or whether it comes from the chapel of a particular bull buried in that reign, but it was first noted by Frances Llewellyn Griffith in the area of the Menwer tombs, under the modern suburb Arab al-Tawil.

## Evidence for a concentration of healers in the city

For the cemeteries of the less divine inhabitants of Iunu, our information remains highly uneven. For the late Old Kingdom we have the burials of Greatest of Seers southeast of the temple precinct. At least one fine assemblage of the late Middle Kingdom derives from the general area of Iunu, according to the imprecise indications from collectors. This includes the only intact example of an implement used for incantations in healing, an ivory staff, rectangular in section. It comprises cuboid segments fitted together, with figures of marginal animals along the sides in relief and on the top in three dimensions, evoking the powers of creation. In the Western analytical tradition, such wands are denoted 'magical' in the degrading sense of 'inferior to science'. In Egypt, though, they had nothing to do with such a divide between superstition and exact science. Rather, they formed part of the single strategy for interpreting the world and warding off the danger of unwanted developments, from disease to the outright triumph of chaos. We have seen this strategy at work in the words and ritual acts for the cult of the sun. Iunu would have provided a natural setting for the men specializing in such branches of knowledge, which formed part of the same arena as medicine and astronomy. There must, though, remain some hesitation in ascribing such a delicate object to the terrain of Iunu, where the water table is generally high. Yet, there are occasional instances of localized preservation. Flinders Petrie excavated a house of the 8th century BC in the precinct of the sun temple, and found both a sealing naming a man with priestly title and a segment of a finely sculpted cosmetic spoon (*ill. 53*). The exquisite spoon, with its refined carving in the form of a goose head, proves both the quality of living in the city at that later date and the possibility for survival of such vulnerable goods in the ground. Possibly we should look to the same area for the site of the Middle Kingdom healer's tomb, though here a ground survey alone can determine the probabilities of preservation across the site.

*53 Cosmetic spoon handle carved in the form of a duck head. Excavated by Flinders Petrie in a house at the northwest of the temple enclosure at Iunu. UC 45671. Late Period.*

The anonymous healer of the Middle Kingdom is only one in a group of men of similar profession attested at the site. The archaeological and especially the textual record seem too slight for any very firm conclusions, but there are intriguing indications that Iunu acted as home to the early Egyptian healers, the forerunners of today's men of medicine. In Piramesse, the eastern Delta city of Ramesses II, a wall block preserves the identity of one house-owner there as a man named Yery, with the title 'pure-priest of Sekhmet'. This denotes a man involved in healing victims smitten by such invisible and apparently divine afflictions as plague (sometimes known in Egyptian as 'year of Sekhmet'). The religious formula in this inscription invokes 'Atum lord of the House of Life, lord of Heal[ing?...] in the House of Ra'. The House of Life was the ancient Egyptian institution for preserving the life of the king and country by keeping and extending the sacred arts. The block from the house of Yery could be taken to imply that healers at the residence city learned their craft in Iunu. One of the blocks from the building of Ramesses II in the great northern extension bears an inscription in which the names of the king are followed by the epithet 'beloved of the goddess Serqet': the 'conjuror of Serqet' was the specialist trained to heal victims of more obvious afflictions such as scorpion or snake bite. Here, then, perhaps in association with the temple to the cult of the king, we find another obscure hint that Iunu was a training ground for healers. Without further evidence, this can only be a suspicion, but the titles of several Late Period officials buried at Iunu seem to add weight to the idea.

## The New Kingdom and Late Period tombs

By the New Kingdom, to judge from the few blocks unearthed, the cemetery area at Iunu had extended further east, a good kilometre from the temple enclosure walls (*ill. 54*). This became the heart of the Late Period

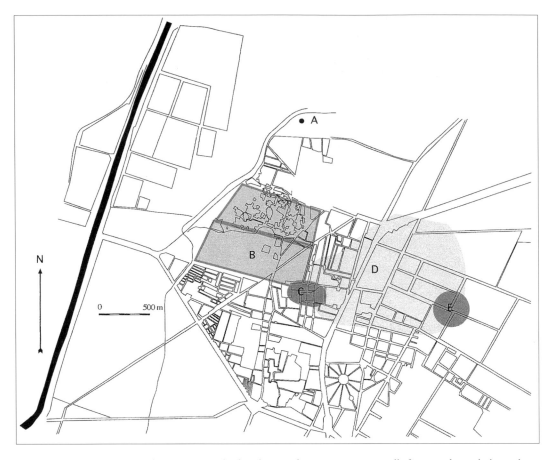

54 *Plan of Iunu showing the distribution of monuments, principally funerary, beneath the modern streets. **A** the Menwer bull tombs at Arab el-Tawil; **B** the main temple enclosures; **C** the Old and Middle Kingdom cemetery; **D** the full extent of New Kingdom and Late Period cemeteries; **E** the nucleus of the eastern necropolis at the desert edge.*

necropolis, including the tombs of healers such as Wedjahormehnet, chief physician of Upper and Lower Egypt, and Psamtekseneb, a conjuror of Serqet. However, some high officials selected sites among the earlier monuments, as if striving to return as near as possible to the area of the sun temples. In 1946, two blocks from the tomb of the 26th Dynasty vizier Horsmatawyemhat came to light near the eastern enclosure wall, within the precinct. These might have been reused, but the practice of burial within temple precincts occurs in the 1st millennium BC at other sites, from Thebes to Tanis. After this date there are relatively few elite burials in the area, and many of the Late Period tombs seem to have been dismantled and reused for more humble interments during the Ptolemaic and Roman Periods. Iunu seems to have lost its brilliance, not only in the cemeteries but more generally across the site. The 30th Dynasty kings continued to provide patronage, and one of the finest hieroglyphic monuments of the period, the so-called Metternich stela, drew its inscriptions from a decayed manuscript in the funerary complex of the Menwer bulls. The stela continues the theme of healing, for it is a 'Horus stela', a stone image of the child Horus in control of the dangerous forces of nature, standing on two crocodiles. This is one of the last pieces of evidence for high-quality or royal production at or for Iunu.

## The eclipse of the city

How did Iunu meet its demise? The signs of quarrying appear already under the Ptolemies, who had several great monuments removed to their great new cities at Alexandria and Canopus. Two great statues of Ptolemy II now in Rome refer to the sun god and are sometimes said to derive from a Ptolemaic temple building there. However, the solar aspect of the king could equally well be evoked at other shrines, and there is no other evidence for any Ptolemaic embellishment of Iunu. By the time that Strabo visited, in the early years of Roman rule, the local guides could show him the school where Plato had learned of Egypt, but the site already lay deserted. The emperors had already begun to relocate the obelisks in Alexandria and Rome, and later in Constantinople, following the example of the Ptolemies. Ironically, this wholesale dispersal carried on without any loss of prestige for the solar beliefs across the country, and despite the evident strength of devotion to Ra. The final flowering of funerary literature comes in a series of Theban compositions named Documents for Breathing. These often take an abbreviated form, and one of the favourite passages to open the pass to eternity begins 'I am Ra in his rising.' Perhaps, though, the position of Iunu undermined the destiny of the city itself, for all this strength in tradition, in depiction, manuscript and inscription. For Iunu lay on the route taken by armies moving from the Nile Valley into Asia or, increasingly, in the reverse direction. The Assyrian invasions of 671, 664 and 661 BC would have caused as much devastation in Iunu as in Thebes, and it is not clear from the Bible which city figures under the name 'On' in the lament of spectacular sackings. The Persian invasions too, from 525 to 343, can only have damaged the confidence and security of these wealthy precincts on the floodplain. Under Ptolemaic rule, the warring between Egypt and Asia continued unabated, with a series of 'Syrian wars' across the 3rd and 2nd centuries BC. Under these circumstances, it may have seemed prudent for the local elite to favour a sacred site at the southern end of the province of Iunu, at Kheraha, battleground of Horus and Seth. Increasingly, the higher officials of that town placed the ancient priestly titles from Iunu as mere supplements to their home positions.

Perhaps finally, too, the location and character of the solar king of Egypt had changed. The Ptolemies were Greek speakers, living at Alexandria. The Romans stood at two removes again, after their conquest of the country in 30 BC. Still, the survival of the solar traditions seems remarkable, even if the city itself became a ghost town. One final blow to the old configuration of kingship and sun cult came with the reign of Diocletian (AD 284–305). This forceful military emperor determined to become the sun king in his own manner. His legionary bases lay over ancient centres of cult, at Kheraha (the Roman 'Babylon of Egypt') south of Cairo, and at Luxor. There the entire Amun temple became a military Roman base centred on a chamber adapted with magnificent paintings of the imperial cult, preserved as late as the beginning of the 20th century. In his version of solarization Diocletian removed at a stroke the previous devices of Ra and Pharaoh. Ancient Egyptian kingship, and with it the religion, art and script, faded from the view and support of the state. The meeting with new faiths had already begun. Within half a century of Diocletian's death, reversing his ferocious persecution of the Church, the Roman empire had embraced Christianity.

# Chapter Four
# Solar Spires – Pyramids and Obelisks

PART ONE
## The solar and stellar significance of the pyramids

We have seen that the city of the sun has lost almost all of its ground plan and can only be sketched across the vast scope of its quarried terrain. Fortunately, much of its architecture survives scattered around the world in its dislocated monuments of hard stone. Equally, the original symbols of Iunu are mirrored in the most striking scale of surviving temples and tombs throughout Egypt and into Sudan. Most solar of all symbols is the pyramid, its tip named *benbenet* 'the (stone) of the *benben*'. The term refers us directly to the rock forming the primeval mound, the first dry land, at Iunu. It is connected with the root for several words in the Egyptian language, *weben* 'to shine'. Although it has become a commonplace in Egyptological writing, we ought not to take the solar character of the pyramids for granted. These are complex achievements in world architecture, and there are no explicit ancient Egyptian inscriptions to describe either the way in which they were created or the motivation behind their dramatic scale and shape, the purest geometric form attained in human architecture until modern times.

These monuments are not easily reduced to a single theme. Recently Kate Spence drew attention to the strong stellar significance of the pyramids. As she notes, this can be demonstrated in part by the probable method used to secure their orientation to the cardinal points. The only convincing explanations for the high accuracy of pyramid alignment involve sightings of particularly bright stars in the ancient night skies as a means of locating north. From observation of the stars, the Egyptians would have been able to mark on the ground the pyramid base lines oriented north–south and east–west. No document or inscription survives to reveal to us today the exact method employed, and this continues to stimulate great debate. Yet the various commentators agree on the role of the northern constellations, and the possibility of using specific stars with limited tools to achieve in particular the stunning accuracy of the Great Pyramid, uniquely aligned within two minutes of north. The importance of the starry sky also seems clear in the positioning of narrow shafts, through the massive masonry core, from

55 *Opening phrase of the inscription on the west face of the pyramidion of Amenemhat III from Dahshur, asserting that the king 'is higher than the heights of Orion'. Egyptian Museum, Cairo. 12th Dynasty.*

the inner chambers to the surface of the Great Pyramid. Whatever their practical application as air vents, these are far too carefully incorporated into the design to escape symbolic significance. Spence connects this star-oriented architecture with the names given to certain pyramids in the Old Kingdom. These names provide almost the only explicit contemporary statement by the Egyptians on the meaning of the pyramids, and require special attention. Here again the complexity of pyramid architecture presents obstacles to interpretation. The pyramid is the largest, but only one, element in a complex designed to secure eternal life and power for the king. It stood at the upper, desert end of a series of sacred buildings. The classic disposition was already established by the 4th Dynasty. It comprised a valley temple at the landing stage on the Nile, a causeway leading up from this into the desert, a pyramid temple at the foot of the pyramid itself, and then the pyramid over the king's burial chamber as the giant backdrop to the whole. In theory any of these might carry a specific name, as might the doorways, the statues, the particular chapels and the capstone of the pyramid. In some instances, it is not clear precisely which architectural feature belongs with which attested name. The following list of Old Kingdom pyramid names follows the interpretation by Wolfgang Helck: even if in some instances the name denotes a different part of the pyramid complex, it remains important to examine the general tendency in associations.

| NAME OF KING | LOCATION | NAME OF PYRAMID (COMPLEX) |
|---|---|---|
| *3rd Dynasty* | | |
| Netjerkhet | Step Pyramid, Saqqara | Horus is the star at the head of the sky |
| *4th Dynasty* | | |
| Sneferu | Meydum | Sneferu is firm |
| Sneferu | Dahshur [both] | Sneferu rises |
| Khufu | Giza | Horizon of Khufu |
| Djedefra | Abu Roash | Starry sky of Djedefra |
| Khafra | Giza | Khafra is great |
| Menkaura | Giza | Menkaura is divine |
| *5th Dynasty* | | |
| Userkaf | Saqqara | The [cult] places of Userkaf are pure |
| Sahura | Abusir | The power [*ba*] of Sahura rises |
| Neferirkara | Abusir | Neferirkara is a divine power [*ba*] |

| NAME OF KING | LOCATION | NAME OF PYRAMID (COMPLEX) |
|---|---|---|
| Neferefra | Abusir | The power [ba] of Neferefra is divine |
| Nyuserra | Abusir | The [cult] places of Nyuserra are enduring |
| Menkauhor | Saqqara | The [cult] places of Menkauhor are divine |
| Djedkara | Saqqara | Djedkara is perfect |
| *6th Dynasty* | | |
| Unis | Saqqara | The [cult] places of Unis are perfect |
| Teti | Saqqara | The [cult] places of Teti are firm |
| Pepy I | Saqqara | Pepy is enduring and perfect |
| Merenra | Saqqara | Arisen and perfect is Merenra |
| Pepy II | Saqqara | Enduring and alive is Neferkara (= Pepy II) |

In this list the Step Pyramid of Netjerkhet and the Abu Roash complex of Djedefra are explicitly stellar, in the one case using the word *seba* 'star', in the other *sehdu* 'firmament' or 'starry sky'. By contrast, there is not a single instance where the name of a pyramid refers explicitly to the sun. Admittedly, the solar interpretation receives support from the choice of the words *kha* 'rise' (used for sunrise) and *akhet* 'horizon' (using a word connected to *akh*, one of the terms for transfiguring sunlight). Nevertheless, the points raised by Spence combine to form a powerful corrective to any purely solar interpretation of the pyramids. This introduces a central question in the Egyptian conception of kingship: is the king the solitary celestial sphere, the sun, or should we consider him as just one member of a great celestial host? In the dearth of inscriptional evidence for the 3rd millennium BC, I would hesitate to choose between the two, but I feel that this is largely a matter of context. Within the reign of each king, he alone appears as the living representative of the sun god on earth, and enjoys a unique sovereignty in the practical exercise of power. Once he has died, however, he joins an already lengthy line of rulers, of past manifestations of the sun on earth. The living king is essentially singular; the dead king is a single link in a chain stretching back to the direct rule of the sun god. The single king is always an aspect of the one solar disk, whereas the many kings of history find a more persuasive celestial metaphor in the myriad stars, above all the circumpolar stars that never set – 'never perishing' as the inscriptions within the late Old Kingdom pyramids describe them. Each king is singular in space, plural across time. This reconciles the alignment of the greatest pyramids to the north star with the use of sunshine to name the pyramid capstone. The word for pyramidion, *benbenet*, seems unambiguous on this score: the root word from which it derives, *weben* 'to shine', refers specifically to sunshine, not to the glittering of stars. A double celestial identity awaits the king – single still, but not alone, as one star among many, but continuing like the stars to be an aspect of, and to reflect, the supreme celestial body, the sun (*cf. ill. 55*).

## Royal tombs earlier than the pyramids

The origins of the pyramidal form recede beyond our grasp in the surviving archaeological record. At Abydos, the earliest tombs of kings survive reasonably well for the part below the surface, but we can still only speculate on the form taken by any superstructure visible above the burial chamber. However, there are great rectangular brick enclosures at the edge of the fields, once interpreted as 'forts', but now identified as the spaces for the cult of kings. Two survive full height at Abydos itself, and another, of the late 2nd Dynasty, at the ancient southern centre of kingship, Nekhen (rendered in Greek Hierakonpolis). Additional enclosures at Abydos can be reconstructed from the vast empty rectangles delineated by small 'tombs of courtiers' of the 1st Dynasty. In the 3rd Dynasty the location of the king's tomb and cult complex moved decisively away from Abydos and northwards to the fulcrum of the two lands, Upper and Lower Egypt. On the West Bank southwest from modern Cairo, the 1st Dynasty kings established a focus for the new national government at Inebhedj 'the White Walls', destined to become ancient Mennefer (Memphis, in the Greek version of the name). On the desert plateau here, northwest of the modern village of Saqqara, there is already evidence for the substructure of royal tombs in the early 2nd Dynasty. However, the first great superstructure to survive is the Step Pyramid of Netjerkhet, of the 3rd Dynasty. In the Step Pyramid brick is discarded in favour of the earliest complex on such a great scale entirely built in stone (*ill. 56*).

Comparing Abydos and Saqqara, we can see how the architects of Netjerkhet brilliantly fused the kingly burial place with the enclosure for the cult. For the stone enclosure wall of the Step Pyramid complex matches exactly the niched brick architecture of the earlier brick enclosures at Abydos and Nekhen. Between the burial place and the enclosure wall the Step Pyramid contains a series of chapels and courts in stone. Many of the chapels are of solid masonry, but they may have evoked the appearance of pavilions in organic materials in the earlier enclosures for the king's cult. At Saqqara the significance is unambiguous: these are the settings for the *sed*, the principal kingship festival at which kingly power received renewal and confirmation for a new epoch. In the corridors around the burial chamber, magnificent relief limestone wall scenes reinforce the theme. These depict the king wearing the White Crown and running in the ritual ordeal required on his path to an ever more intensely divine sovereignty. Over the burial chamber rises the Step Pyramid, still one of the most impressive sights Egypt has to offer (*ill. 57*). In its final form, in six tiers the rectangular angled mountain rises to a height of 60 m (197 ft).

If the 3rd Dynasty enclosure casts a more ancient type of brick structure in stone, we might reasonably expect that the superstructure over the burial

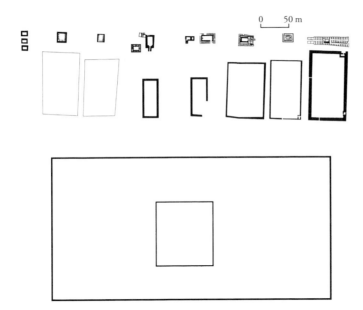

56 *Ground-plans of the tombs and cult enclosures of kings from the 1st to the 3rd Dynasties. Upper register, the 1st and 2nd Dynasty royal monuments at Abydos,* from left to right: *Aha, Djer, Djet, Merneit with Den, Semerkhet and Anedjib (one enclosure attested for the two reigns), Qaa, Peribsen, and Khasekhemwy. Lower register, the Step Pyramid enclosure of King Netjerkhet (Djoser) at Saqqara.*

place achieved the same, in other words that it emulated 1st and 2nd Dynasty royal tomb superstructures in other materials. In that case, we might expect that the first kingly tombs at Abydos also bore a pyramidal crown. However, nothing of the sort has been detected at surface level there, and any superstructure is therefore perhaps more likely to have been a low mound rather than an imposing proto-pyramid. Detailed investigation into the Step Pyramid has revealed that the first project for Netjerkhet provided for only a single tier of stone, a neat geometric refinement of the more organic circular shape of the earth or sand mound. Indeed, the perfection of the Step Pyramid can too easily lead us to underestimate the brilliance of its design, and to read too literally every motif as the literal petrification of a host of detail in perishable materials. If the long-lost matting, wooden beams and earthern mound of late predynastic structures provided the seed for the imagination of these architects, they did not merely copy, they transformed their inheritance into an entirely new concept. In the strictest sense, the Step Pyramid has no antecedents. It marks a revolution in architecture, and was received by later centuries as a stroke of divine inspiration, as we can witness in the veneration and cult of Imhotep, principal minister for the administration under King Netjerkhet. The religious idea driving this new construction is not recorded, but it seems that the Step Pyramid may be the

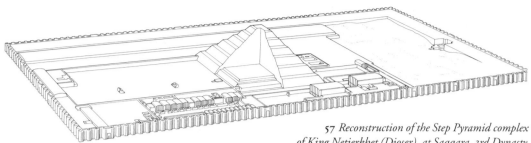

*57 Reconstruction of the Step Pyramid complex of King Netjerkhet (Djoser), at Saqqara. 3rd Dynasty.*

first great monument equating the single earthly king with a single power in heaven, the sun. There are two supporting, if circumstantial pieces of evidence. In the reign of Netjerkhet, for the first time Ra appears as not just the word for sun, but unequivocally as the name of a great god: one of the officials of the king bore the name Hesyra 'he whom Ra favours', with Ra written first as befits a deity. The second piece of evidence we have seen at Iunu itself, the fragments of a stone shrine inscribed with the name of Netjerkhet and images of the king and of gods associated with Iunu (*ill. 35*). Whether or not the shrine stood from the beginning in the Ra temple at Iunu, its combination of king and gods suffices to prove the new national importance of solar mythology. In the Step Pyramid the single divine ruler Ra has risen over the duelling Horus and Seth.

## The first and greatest true pyramids

After Netjerkhet the archaeological record breaks again, though it seems that the same kind of complex began to take shape for at least two other kings of the age, out on the desert margins at Saqqara. The later histories mark a break in dynasty, reflecting perhaps simply the next extraordinary revolution in the development of the king's cult complex. Whatever may have been happening on the political level, in architecture the stepped pyramid was replaced by the pyramid with smooth sides, the 'true pyramid'. Today the word pyramid conjures up ideas of inhuman scale, of the greatest single structures raised by humankind. We should, however, distinguish two types of pyramid (*ill. 58*). There are the dozens of kingly cult complexes in which the central feature takes the impressive form of a pyramid. Preceding these, and far surpassing them in scale, are the five giant pyramids, one at Meydum (A: height 93.5 m, 307 ft), two at Dahshur (B, C: height 104 and 105 m, 341 and 345 ft), and the larger two at Giza (D, F: height 146 and 143.5 m, 479 and 471 ft). These five are the monuments from which all later structures would be judged, the source of the inspiration of writers and artists down to our own day. For the perfect geometry of the Great Pyramid at Giza is only one aspect of its impact: it is also an impact of scale. Scale and perfection together guarantee the effect. When a visitor sees the pyramids at Giza during an inhospitable time of the day, they can lose their scale and become bleached in the heat of the midday sun, dwarfed by the modern explosion of Greater Cairo, lessened by the commercial drudgery of the over-hasty tour. Timing and preparation are essential to appreciate these structures as works of art. Slanting light, silence and the imagination bring back the scale and for the first time the geometry can make its impact. This power belongs above all to the Great Pyramid, but it has one successor beside it, and three forebears many miles to the south, all on the same implausible scale. The three earlier pyramids, at Meydum and Dahshur, seem to have been constructed for a single ruler, Sneferu. The Great Pyramid at Giza is the tomb for the son of Sneferu, Khufu (distorted into Cheops in Greek histories), and the Second Pyramid at Giza was constructed for his son in turn, Khafra (also distorted into Greek as Chephren). These three reigns transformed the civilization, introducing a scale of operation that required regular output and form. Although the proportions and shapes in Egyptian art and script took root at the end of the 4th millennium, the canon achieved its standard and consistency in the reign of Sneferu, towards the middle of the 3rd millennium. The pyramids (as opposed to the whole cult complex for each king) have remained ever since the symbol of Egypt. Since its discovery the painting of geese from the Meydum pyramid

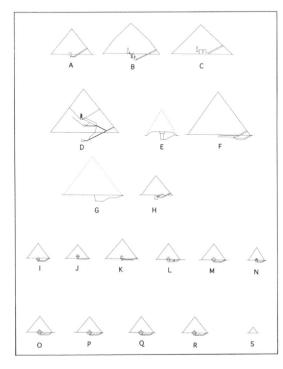

58 Sections, to scale, of the pyramids of Old Kingdom rulers in chronological order.

Pyramids of Sneferu:
A Meydum, B Dahshur,
C Dahshur North.

Pyramids from Khufu to Userkaf:
D Khufu, Giza.
E Djedefra, Abu Roash.
F Khafra, Giza.
G Nebka (?), Zawyet el-Aryan.
H Menkaura, Giza.
I Userkaf, Saqqara.

Pyramids at Abusir:
J Sahura, K Neferirkara,
L Nyuserra.

Late Old Kingdom pyramids at Saqqara:
M Isesi, N Unas, O Teti, P Pepy I,
Q Merenra, R Pepy II, S Ibi.

field has represented the classic perfection of Egyptian formal art in generations of art history books. After Khafra, the scale of the cult complex remained extensive, but the pyramid itself shrank to about a 'mere' 75 m (246 ft). The third king's pyramid at Giza, that of Khafra's son Menkaura, seems dwarfed by its two giant predecessors to the north.

The classic pyramid stood at the back of and above a great cult complex (*ill. 60*). This has generally survived less well than the pyramidal mountain of stone, and the imperfect preservation has caused the confusion over the purpose of the complex, including the pyramids. For these are only secondarily tombs: their first purpose is the cult of the king as a divine being, from the 4th Dynasty as son of the sun god. There is no reason why this cult should await the death of the king, though it was intended to continue in perpetuity. As soon as the last king died, and was buried in his cult complex, the next would begin his own cult complex. There were two spaces for the cult, one at the landing stage, down by the fields, the other up at the very foot of the pyramid itself. The landing-stage temple would have been the more accessible and was probably the usual site of the cult secretariat. However, it lay too close to the water to survive in most instances. The pyramid temple contained offering chambers and statues of the king, whereby he received the offerings for eternity. The pyramid behind acted as an external focus of cult, perhaps analogous to the great *benben* stone in the open courts of the sun temples. In this sense the pyramid itself is also an object of cult. This helps to explain why the pyramid is not always, even if primarily, the superstructure of a tomb. Sneferu may have planned the two Dahshur pyramids together, as they bore the same name, 'Sneferu rises' or 'sunrise of Sneferu', but only one could have been conceived as a literal tomb. The second is an extension of the cult for the king. Indeed, Sneferu seems to have diffused his cult throughout the land. Small stepped pyramids dotted along the Nile Valley have long aroused controversy and received various datings. The recent Brigham Young excavations at the small stepped pyramid at Seila, across the desert from Meydum, uncovered a stela inscribed with the name of Sneferu. This suggests that not only Meydum and Seila were built for the king, but possibly also other monuments of the same type. Here Sneferu may have been following a nationwide diffusion of cult, building on the 2nd Dynasty precedent set by Khasekhem(wy) with his two vast brick cult enclosures, one at Abydos and the other at Nekhen. The little-known predecessor of Sneferu, King Huni, may have been responsible for the stepped pyramidal structure on the island of Elephantine, at the southernmost border of Egypt. Here excavation in the early 20th century brought to light a block with Huni's name enclosed in an oval with a perpendicular line at one end, the 'cartouche' in Egyptological terms. With the exception of a possible but broken example on a mud seal impression from the reign of his

*59 The earliest surviving cartouches, one with the name lost, from Beit Khallaf, north of Abydos, and one of King Huni on a granite block found at Elephantine.*

predecessor, this is the earliest attested cartouche, and it confirms the solar-ization of kingship. In Middle and New Kingdom inscriptions, the cartouche or *shen* 'ring' reflects the phrase 'all that the sun disk circles (*shen*)'. The two innovations, pyramid complex and cartouche, inaugurate the 3,000 years of ancient Egyptian kingship in its classic form, as emanation of a solar creator.

## Pyramid ships

In yet another solar indicator in these complexes for the cult of the king, the Great Pyramid of Khufu incorporated into the south and east sides of the enclosure full-size royal boat burials. Only recently David O'Connor dis-covered a 2nd Dynasty precedent for these, in the cult enclosure area at the edge of the desert in the Abydos cemeteries. Yet the Giza boats exceed these in scale, and can be said to match the ambition of the giant pyramids. The Egyptian conservation expert Ahmed Youssef Moustafa extracted one sur-viving boat with miraculous dexterity, and reassembled over 1,200 timbers in a labour of ingenuity over many years. The boat continues a somewhat precarious existence inside its modern glass cage at the foot of the Great Pyramid, and should be ranked among the Wonders of the World, a superb cedarwood craft to sail the Nile and, perhaps, even the high seas. From any age this would be an astonishing feat in ship-building, and its survival from the 26th century BC makes it one of the most important archaeological treasures in world heritage. As reconstructed, it measures over 43 m (141 ft) in length. The displacement would be 45 tons. The planks were held together by ropes, rather as if sewn, a technique no longer used in Egypt today, but typical of seafaring technology around the Arabian peninsula until modern times. Whether or not the boats had been used in life, they provide the perfected means of travel for the eternal cycle that the king aimed to join more intimately after death.

## The Great Sphinx

Where Khufu concentrated his power in scale on one spot, the Great Pyramid, his son Khafra used to very slightly more diffuse effect the next available space. The plateau at Giza provides an earthquake-proof platform for colossal architecture, but its area restricts building operations. In order to retain a clear sight-line to the polar star for the entire north face of the pyramid, the Second Pyramid for Khafra moves back towards the desert. Its valley temple also could not lie aligned directly east of the pyramid, because

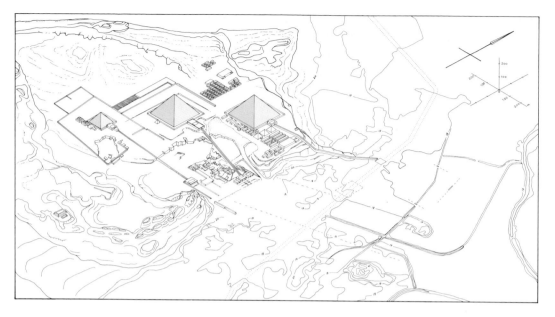

60 *The pyramid as part of a complex: the example of the Giza plateau, reconstructed after the work of Mark Lehner.*

a great outcrop of weathered rock juts into the east–west axis at the edge of the floodplain below. The architects could have used this as a quarry for the pyramid-building project, but something in the shape of the rock seems to have presented a different, and inspirational, solution. They carved the entire obstacle into the Great Sphinx, the largest man-made natural sculpture in Egypt, rather as the architects of Ramesses II would adapt the Nubian cliff-face at Abu Simbel some 13 centuries later. The form suited the elongated outline of a resting animal, and they shaped this as a recumbent lion, its tail coiled elegantly over its back. As with the superstructure over the royal tomb, the lion statue already carried a long history in the 26th century BC. Three of the earliest colossal figurative sculptures from Egypt are limestone lions of the late 4th or very early 3rd millennium BC, unearthed on the temple site at Coptos, in Upper Egypt. Yet the imagination of the 4th Dynasty artists did not stop at the sculpting of the lion body. They chose for the head, on a basic principle of Egyptian art, a different identity, the direct image of the king. If the lion represents an incarnation, we might have to say today an analogy, of sovereign power, the head here identifies the divine power quite directly. If we set the face beside the numerous surviving examples of royal sculpture, it can most plausibly be identified as a 4th Dynasty king, most probably Khafra. It is possible that the face might represent his father Khufu, for whom the only parallel images in three dimensions are on a far smaller scale and in different material, complicating comparison. However, the current consensus, and the view of this author, prefers the identification with Khafra. The combination of lion body and human head to depict the divine power of kingship proved a success rarely surpassed in art history. The motif continued in use to the end of Egyptian art, and became one of the most widely used images in the world beyond. We use for the hybrid form the name in Greek, sphinx. In Egypt it became an image appropriate above all to the entrances of temples, and in the New Kingdom to the sides of chariots, where the king used leonine force to repel and destroy the enemies of order. Throughout this long history for the image, the Great Sphinx of Giza never found a rival, and its impact on later observers can be seen in the treatment it received. From the New Kingdom it could figure as a form of the sun god, as Horus on the horizon (Horemakhet), to whom the Egyptians assimilated a god from Western Asia, Hauron. The kings of the 18th Dynasty even constructed a temple at its paws. One of them, Thutmose IV, left an extraordinary inscription narrating his pious care for the monument. While a prince, at a desert hunt, the future king took shelter in the shade of the mighty head, and dreamed that Horemakhet appeared to him. The deity promised him kingship if he would restore, that is clear the sand from, the Sphinx. This the prince duly did, and left the inscription as a mark of his divine kingship, the moment when the god identified the youth as not a man, but the direct offspring of the sun. Now the father of Thutmose IV, King Amenhotep II, had already set up a stela recording his might in archery and chariotry, at the foot of the sphinx. There was, then, already a focus of interest on the monument, and a temple for its cult. Thutmose IV seems to have adopted this episode as one part of his legitimation. The Sphinx here already plays the role of Fate, and at the kingly level, as later in the Greek myth of the riddle set by the

**61** *An ancient Egyptian view of the Giza pyramids and sphinx, as depicted on the stela of the scribes Mentuher and Kanakht. New Kingdom.*

female sphinx for Oedipus. The New Kingdom story of the Sphinx reminds us that the Giza pyramid field began to make its impact long before the Greeks came to Egypt, long before the birth of the West. It left a deep impression on the ancient Egyptians themselves (*cf. ill. 61*). In the Middle and New Kingdoms they cited the pyramids in literary reflections on monument-making and the nature of eternity, or at least survival into posterity. And in the Late Period Giza, and specifically the Sphinx, became again a religious magnet enticing the elite to site their tombs in the vicinity: many of the finest Egyptian sarcophagi come from the burials of the highest officials along the causeway between the Sphinx and the pyramid of Khafra.

## Interpreting the architecture

From his life of work on the giant pyramid sites, Rainer Stadelmann has observed a precise and revealing correlation between the complexity of the pyramid and that of the complex in which it stands as centrepoint. Where the inner chambers form an intricate, even labyrinthine plan, the outer complex of temples and causeway appears relatively plain. In the Giza group, the pyramids of Khufu and Menkaura have elaborate internal corridors and rooms in contrast to the uncomplicated layout of the temple at the foot of the pyramid. Chronologically the two complexes stand separated by the complex of Khafra, where the inner chambers of the pyramid are extremely plain in layout, but the pyramid temple becomes a web of offering rooms, corridors and pillared halls. The essential plan appears standardized after one last innovatory break during the 4th Dynasty, the cult complex for Shepseskaf at Saqqara. This returned to the form of a cuboid, like the lowest tier of the Step Pyramid, at the centre of an enclosure from which a causeway leads down towards the valley on the eastern side. However, the radical difference in form may derive from prosaic circumstances. The reign of Shepseskaf has left few surviving traces, and the king may have reigned fewer than six years, according to the doubtful historical evidence of the later kinglists. We can only speculate, but it is possible that the king died when only the first stage of pyramid-building had reached completion. In that case, the unusual cuboid may simply represent the swiftest solution to preparing the cult place for the king's burial. The next king would already have been preparing his own cult complex.

## Sun temples and ruler cult

In the later kinglists, there is a break of dynasty at about this point, marking the start of the 5th Dynasty. The temptation to seek kinship and political explanations should be resisted, where not warranted by the evidence. We have virtually no sources for the single events or the family ties, in short for the biographies of Egyptian kings before the Ptolemies. Rather we can follow the self-expression of the civilization on broader lines, in the monumental architecture and above all in the development of the king's cult. Here we do indeed find a distinct group of kings, corresponding to the early and middle reigns of the '5th Dynasty' in later tradition. These kings, from Userkaf to Menkauhor, had cult centres with a double focus. On the one side there remained the now standardized pyramid complex, where the body of the king was laid to rest after his death. On the other, there appeared an entirely new phenomenon, which has been misinterpreted as marking these kings as more sun-fixated than the 4th Dynasty: the sun temple (*ill. 62*). There is no group of kings more solar than the 4th Dynasty, as we have seen in the introduction of the cartouche to enclose the king's name, in the boats of Khufu, the Sphinx of Khafra, and in the very form of the giant pyramids of Sneferu, Khufu and Khafra. The same theme appears also in the title 'son of Ra' first attested under Djedefra. Yet the 5th Dynasty king Userkaf brought in a radical addition to his cult architecture, almost a second pyramid complex, but with a massive stone mound shaped like a squat obelisk, at the back of an open court. The best-preserved example is that of Nyuserra at Abu Ghurab, and here the layout follows closely the model of the pyramid complex. There is a causeway leading up from the riverside temple to the place of the king's cult, where the open altar and squat obelisk form the focus. The shattered relief fragments include some of the finest art to survive from ancient Egypt, notably the depiction of the three seasons of the year, and other images of the fertile life in the Nile Valley. These anticipate by more than a thousand years the lyrical idyll of art under Akhenaten.

*62 Reconstruction of a sun temple of the 5th Dynasty at Abu Ghurab.*

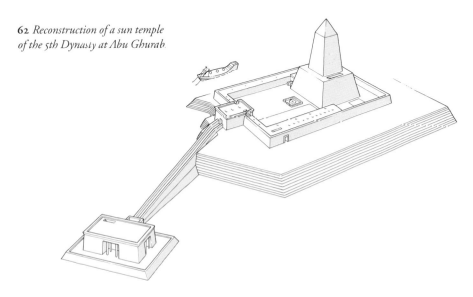

Most of the other kingly sun temples survive only in inscriptions and manuscript references, recording their names and personnel. These indicate the solar flavour of the cult, yet the buildings are less 'sun temples' than temples for the cult of the king.

The motive behind this extraordinary extension of the architecture of king worship becomes clear when we look at the map of sight-lines from Iunu itself, from the temple of Ra (see Chapter Three, *ill. 38*). The 4th Dynasty kings placed their pyramids at Giza within view of Iunu, across the river. By moving back to the plateau at Saqqara, the kings of the 5th Dynasty lost their sight-line to the centre of the solar cult. There was no alternative to leaving Giza, where the restricted desert plateau was entirely covered by the monuments of Khufu, Khafra and Menkaura. The sun temples of the 5th Dynasty seem to provide a solution, a means of retaining the direct link between the cult and burial place of the king and the home of the sun god on earth. As with the pyramid complexes, the names of these establishments provide the clearest statements by the Egyptians on their meaning. As the list shows, the kingly sun temples are tied each to an individual king, and all include a direct reference to the sun god.

| KING | NAME OF KING'S SUN TEMPLE |
|------|---------------------------|
| Userkaf | Nekhenra (birthplace[?] of Ra) |
| Sahura | Sekhetra (field of Ra) |
| Neferirkara | Setibra (place of the heart of Ra) |
| Nyuserra | Shesepibra (recipient of the heart of Ra) |
| Menkauhor | Akhetra (horizon of Ra) |

These names and the massive obelisk shapes in the open courts show the solar affiliation more strongly than the link to the cult of the king. Yet the structures appear in succession reign by reign, and the surviving pyramid complex archives of Neferirkara and Neferefra reveal how intricately the two types of monument shared estates and offerings, in the ancient equivalent of bank accounts. The accountancy papyri date largely to the period after the construction of the sun temples, and this demonstrates that the decision not to build any more did not mark an opposition to the cult they represented. Indeed, in the next phase of the history of pyramids, the solar association becomes still stronger.

## Pyramid Texts – the earliest religious literature

After Menkauhor, the reign of Isesi brought many changes, including an end to the inclusion of sun temples in the architecture of the king's cult. Under his successor Unis, the outward form of the pyramid complex at Saqqara changed little, but a revolution took place within the pyramid itself.

For the first time since the Step Pyramid with its sed-festival reliefs of King Netjerkhet, the walls of inner chambers receive inscriptions. However, the new trend uses hieroglyphs not as captions to great illustrations, but dispenses with image altogether in its focus on the word. This is the earliest large written corpus to survive from Egypt, providing us with the first accounts of the relations between deities, amongst the most ancient religious literature in history. Later historical tradition introduces a break in dynasty between Unis and Teti, as first king of the 6th Dynasty. There is no contemporary evidence to support this, still less to substantiate the late tale of the murder of Teti. Indeed, the theme of regicide recalls suspiciously closely the Middle Kingdom literary references to attacks on the life of Amenemhat I, founder of the 12th Dynasty. Perhaps, as often in the history of writing, a good story has become the model for generally applicable morality tales on grand themes such as rule and right, and undergone seamless transfer to historical settings to which it did not originally belong. The obsession with political events only distracts us from the substantial treasury of information to be gained on the broader ground of history. When we examine the contemporary late Old Kingdom sources, there seems to be a continuum from the reign of Unis to the end of the period, when the unity of Egypt crumbled under centrifugal forces. Throughout this phase, the walls of the burial chamber and adjacent rooms bore hieroglyphic inscriptions in profusion, named by Egyptologists 'the Pyramid Texts', after these their earliest locations. The words echo, or even directly convey, the liturgies and offering rituals accompanying the body of the king to his resurrection as a heavenly body. Yet they offer modern scholarship more than the single moments of kingly burial. Thanks to their rich imagery relating to the world of the divine, they have become the earliest and still one of the largest bodies of evidence for all aspects of Egyptian belief.

## A pyramid at Thebes?

The Old Kingdom disintegrated under centrifugal forces that remain difficult to explain in detail, though major factors doubtless include the seepage of literacy through to the provincial elites, and perhaps climate change affecting the centralized control of resources. In the First Intermediate Period, that is, the century of political disunity, it seems probable that the northern kings continued to construct pyramid complexes, but on a smaller scale. Indeed, the monuments of kingship diminished in size to such an extent that they have either vanished without trace, or remain unrecognized within the known pyramid fields or in unexcavated sectors along the desert edge. The kings in the south were originally provincial governors, and, even when they secured regal status, they retained a funerary architecture local to

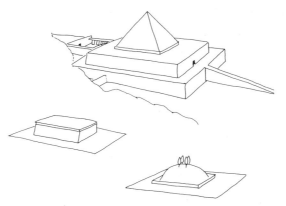

**63** *Three modern reconstructions of the superstructure for the temple of Mentuhotep at Deir el-Bahri, Thebes West. At the top is the interpretation by Edouard Naville, at centre that by Dieter Arnold, and below that proposed by Rainer Stadelmann.*

Thebes. Over the rock-cut tomb a cliff front backed an open courtyard, the Arabic name for which, *saff*, has become the archaeological label for the tomb type. This design lies behind the inspired plan of the terraced temple for the cult of Nebhepetra Mentuhotep, the king who reunited the Two Lands and so founded the Middle Kingdom, the second great period of ancient Egyptian civilization. Edouard Naville excavated his cult complex, at Deir el-Bahri on the West Bank at Thebes, in the early 1900s, and found at the centre of the upper floor of the terraced structure a massive stone feature. Earlier reconstructions interpreted this as the remains of a pyramid, but re-excavation in the 1960s by Dieter Arnold left a challenge to this view. Today scholars attempt to restore a different focus to the structure, viewing it as either a great circular mound like an organic earthen tumulus, or a more geometric, roughly cuboid form with angled sides. The underlying reference to the primeval mound would be the same in all three versions pyramid, mound or cuboid – but a mound or cuboid would echo not the pyramids but such funerary constructions as the tomb of Shepseskaf, discussed above (*ill. 63*). The debate remains open, and it is tempting to revert to the proposal by the first excavators, that the Egyptians cast the primeval mound as a pyramid. Nevertheless, the entire complex displays such ingenuity in its use of the Theban cliff-face that it would be futile to imagine that we have yet recovered its form.

## Ra and Osiris in the pyramids of the Middle Kingdom

The succeeding 12th Dynasty returned both to the pyramid complex and to the area closer to Memphis (*ill. 64*). The first in this group of kings, Amenemhat I, may have embarked on a building programme similar to that of Nebhepetra Mentuhotep. In year 20 of his reign, for unknown reasons, he began instead a new pyramid complex near present-day Lisht, between Memphis and the mouth of the Fayum. He probably founded his residence in the same area, again emulating the Old Kingdom, termed 'Time of the Residence' in Middle Kingdom literature. This has not survived, or been found, but hieroglyphic writings refer to it as a fortified enclosure named Itjtawy, or, in fuller form, Itjtawyamenemhat 'Amenemhat is the one who seizes hold of the Two Lands'. If at first these Middle Kingdom cult complexes recall the 5th to 6th Dynasty model, they add features drawn from other prototypes, and also develop original concepts. The monument at the dawn of the tradition, the Step Pyramid at Saqqara, evidently inspired the design of the enclosure for Senusret I, son of Amenemhat I. A great niched façade runs around the pyramid, though interrupted by vast writings of the name of the king in the Horus frame. In the reign of his grandson Senusret II, new formulations of belief seem to lie behind the original layout of the inner chambers beneath the pyramid. Erik Hornung has compared the plan to that of the Cenotaph of Sety I at Abydos, indicating a common source for both monuments. This can only be the concept of the tomb of Osiris, identified from the 12th Dynasty as the tomb of King Djer in the 1st Dynasty royal necropolis. The central chamber lies surrounded like an island in a lake, with corridors angled around it on each side (*ill. 65*). The motifs of fertility and solar rule, Osiris and Ra, combine in the same alliance of primeval and celestial forces that we have seen in the Underworld Books of the New Kingdom. In the next reign, Senusret III had a more traditional pyramid complex constructed at Dahshur, at the southern end of the Saqqara pyramid fields. Yet he also prepared a cult complex for his eternal worship at the southern end of the Abydos cemeteries (*ill. 66*). Here a vast rock-cut

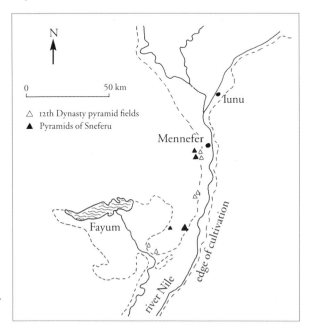

**64** *Distribution of 12th Dynasty pyramid fields in relation to the pyramids of Sneferu.*

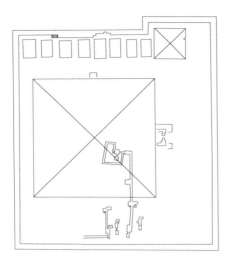

N

0 _____ 50 m

**65** *The pyramid of Senusret II, showing the underground galleries on the same plan later used for the 'Osiris tomb' of Sety I at Abydos. 12th Dynasty. Lahun.*

corridor leads to a burial chamber in the cliff-face. The temple and court in front may have married the classic pyramid complex with the architecture of Nebhepetra Mentuhotep from the similar geographical constraints of the Theban mountain range. The most recent investigators of the two sites, Dieter Arnold and Joe Wegner, have argued that Senusret III was buried not at Dahshur, but at Abydos. The Osirian theme perhaps seemed more apt to the eternal resting place than the machine designed to elevate him to heaven, the pyramid complex. Yet both remained necessary, Dahshur for the solar aspect, Abydos for the chthonic.

In the reign of Senusret's son, Amenemhat III, the cult complex becomes once again centralized. Already at Dahshur the pyramid temple of Senusret III had undergone massive expansion to about double its original intended size. Here thousands of fragments of relief represent perhaps only 5 per cent of the decorated wall surface, but at least indicate the range and quality of the art. Amenemhat III took the same elaboration of the pyramid temple to its extreme, and created a series of pillared halls and chambers, all magnificently carved in relief and equipped with sculpture of king and gods. One and a half thousand years later, this labyrinthine complex astounded the ancient Greek writers, who recorded it as more wonderful than even the Giza pyramids. The name and extent of the structure may be part of the background to the Greek myth of the Labyrinth and its bull-headed man, the Minotaur. Today the pyramid at Hawara resembles a sand dune, the area of the complex a moonscape. The monuments were quarried away, the stone burnt for lime, after the demise of the old religion. However, this fate had not yet befallen the cult of Amenemhat III in the 1st and 2nd centuries AD, when the Egyptian elite in the province chose their burial place in the shadow of his pyramid. In 1888 Flinders Petrie excavated the unpromising

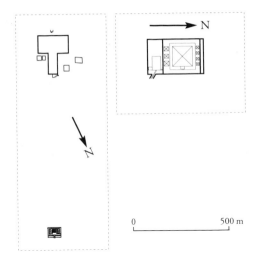

**66** *Scale comparison of the northern and southern cult complex for Senusret III:* right, *his pyramid at Dahshur, compared with,* left, *the cliff-tomb at Abydos. 12th Dynasty.*

terrain, and found, in addition to the fragments of this once awesome labyrinth, a miraculous treasury of Roman art, painted wooden panel portraits set in the mummy wrappings. The efforts of the Middle Kingdom artists had not saved Amenemhat III, but indirectly, through the magnet of the great solar edifice, they helped to preserve on dry ground the largest group of Roman panel portraits to survive from any part of the empire.

## Later, smaller, steeper pyramids

After the 12th Dynasty, the numerous kings of the 13th Dynasty continued to build pyramid complexes, where they reigned for long enough to do so, as shown by the few identified examples, and by basalt or siltstone pyramidia, the capstones for the pyramid. The latest of these names was King Merneferra Iy (reigning in the late 18th century BC), and was found in the Eastern Delta, perhaps removed there like so much other hard stone sculpture from the Middle Kingdom royal cults. Egypt slid into disunity, until the reunification of the country and expulsion of foreign rulers, under Ahmose I, founder of the 18th Dynasty. The New Kingdom kings chose the Theban mountain for their burial place, perhaps partly because the natural profile of the tallest 'horn' of the mountain range vaguely recalls a pyramid. This seems to have left the shape free for non-royal architecture. In some instances, the tomb-chapel was crowned by a pyramid of brick, building perhaps on the tradition of the now lost superstructures of Second Intermediate Period kings at Thebes. Especially after the reign of Akhenaten, the tomb-chapels of officials often include a roof-top pyramidion, or miniature pyramid, as capstone to the brick chapel-pyramid. In the area of Memphis, the angle of the pyramidion follows that of the classic pyramid, whereas at

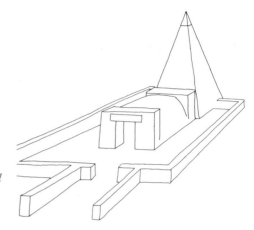

*67 Reconstruction of the pyramid and chapel over the tomb of an 18th Dynasty official at Soleb, in Upper Nubia.*

Thebes and other sites such as Soleb in Nubia the brick pyramid with its limestone tip adopts a steeper angle (*ill. 67*). The sides of the pyramidion might be inscribed, with an image of the tomb-owner on the east side, kneeling and hands raised in adoration of the rising sun. The southern type, and perhaps specifically the New Kingdom cemeteries at Nubian sites such as Soleb, evidently served as model for the last royal pyramids, those of the Napatan and Meroitic kings in present-day Sudan. From the 8th century BC, the kings and queens were buried beneath acute-angled pyramids of stone, with small chapels at the foot, in a small-scale revival of the Old Kingdom tradition. This too is the angle followed by the Roman military officers who must have served in Egypt under Augustus, and returned inspired to build their own monument of eternity. One of these has disappeared from the map of Rome, but another remains remarkably intact. It commemorates Gaius Cestius, and survives incorporated into the later Roman city wall, not far from another solar symbol drawn more physically from Egypt, the Lateran obelisk from Karnak.

PART TWO

OBELISKS

## Early obelisks and kingship at Iunu

The obelisk form extends an idea already implicit in the pyramid, that of gaining maximum height with minimum ground space. Early obelisks in the sun temples of the 5th Dynasty appear squat, with a massive cuboid trunk topped by a pyramid-shaped tip. Later obelisks are monoliths generally of hard stone, as slender as the sculptors of the day could achieve, capped by slender pyramid tips cut within the same tall pillar. The imagery and inscriptions associated with the Egyptian obelisk are predominantly solar, though such a prominent column may well have carried additional phallic symbolism, appropriately enough for the sun as the creator who generated creation. The Egyptian name for the obelisk, *tekhen*, does not seem to refer explicitly either to the sun or to the phallus of the creator, a reminder that the full range of ancient meanings most often eludes us. Like the pyramid, the obelisk has become throughout the world a symbol of Egypt and of the monumental. This diffusion began long before writing reached European shores. In the Middle Bronze Age, at the eastern Mediterranean port of Byblos, the city ruler had small stone obelisks inscribed in Egyptian hieroglyphs and set up at the temple of the city goddess, identified for the Egyptian script as Hathor (*ill. 68*). Thus the fascination and influence began 1,800 years before Augustus moved the first Egyptian obelisk to Rome.

The earliest evidence for obelisks comes, as we have seen, and as is only to be expected, from the city of Ra, in Iunu itself. Whatever structure had required alignment with the cult complex of kings in the 4th Dynasty, it found a slender echo in the monolithic quartzite obelisk of Teti, in the 6th (*ill. 36*). Material and location emphasize the solar significance spelled out in later royal inscriptions of the New Kingdom. The Teti obelisk is the oldest surviving obelisk cut from a single block of stone and inscribed for a king. It may not have been the first in the tradition, but here we are dependent on the shattered archaeological record at the site of the Ra temple complex. On a smaller scale, and perhaps inspired more by the royal monolith than by the original focus of the solar cult, there appear during the late Old Kingdom roughly obelisk-shaped monuments for persons other than the king (*ill. 39*).

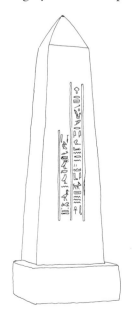

68 *The obelisk inscribed with the name of Ibishemu, ruler of Byblos, from the sanctuary of obelisks at Byblos, Lebanon. About 1800 BC. Beirut Inv 17917.*

69 *Small-scale obelisk of Sheshi, a scribe of work-crews of Iunu, from his tomb at Iunu. Egyptian Museum, Cairo. 6th Dynasty.*

These stood in open courts at the doorways to tomb-chapels. They are attested both at Iunu, as seen in the previous chapter, and in elite cemeteries elsewhere, notably at Memphis where they include monuments for members of the king's family. As we saw in the previous chapter, the Sabni inscription from the last great reign of the Old Kingdom, that of Pepy II, refers to two transport ships for obelisks. This implies that, at least by the end of the period, the monolithic obelisks quarried at Aswan had reached the extreme scale of their later kin. The 6th Dynasty sources also suggest that the obelisks may represent the next stage in the monumental expression of royal solar cult. Where the 4th Dynasty placed its solar focus on the location and form of the royal cult complex, and the 5th Dynasty used the strategy of the kingly sun temple, perhaps the 6th Dynasty developed the giant monolith. These kings no longer either rested for eternity within sight of Iunu (their pyramids all lie too far south in the Saqqara pyramid fields), or had a link to that sight-line through sun shrines at Abusir. Perhaps, then, they simply brought the solar kingship directly into the cult place. The obelisks become part of the device named by the Egyptians 'temple of the *ka*-spirit' (*hut-ka*) of kings. Kingship begins its long history of devolution from the centre to encompass every geographical location in the land. Fittingly this would begin with the centre for the most kingly cult, that of the sun.

None of these Old Kingdom examples quite prepares us for the scale of operation in the Middle Kingdom. The obelisk of Senusret I, now the solitary survivor of the ruin of Iunu, reaches over 20 m (66 ft) in height, still cut as a single block of Aswan red granite (*ill. 70*). It weighs 121 tons, and was only one of a pair. Here we finally find the tangible example of the type of monument implied in Sabni's inscription, a pairing of slender obelisks for the temple of the sun. Although the position in relation to the temple remains disputed, as seen above, the obelisks of Senusret I clearly marked the entrance to the temple. The inscription on the one still standing records the titulary of the king, designated 'beloved of the Powers of Iunu'. It further specifies that the monuments rose at the first occasion of the *sed* or kingship festival, generally ascribed to the 30th year of reign. Kingship and solar cult fuse here to form a single generator and defender of creation. Other obelisks followed in the New Kingdom, both at Iunu and at Thebes in its new guise as the 'Iunu of Upper Egypt' (see also Chapter Two). Between the two periods, the only evidence for the type seems to be the rather smaller pairs placed in front of at least some royal tombs, in the Egyptian kingdom reduced to the region of Thebes. At the same time, the royal monopoly on

70 *The publication of the obelisk of Senusret I at Iunu, produced by the members of the French Expedition to Egypt in 1798-1801.*

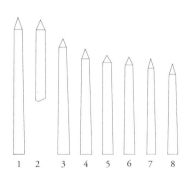 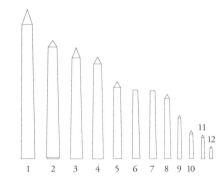

**71** (Left) *Skyscrapers - eight of the tallest obelisks still standing, excluding those in Rome:* from left to right, *with heights in brackets,*
**1** *Hatshepsut at Karnak (29.56 m, 97 ft),* **2** *Thutmose III now in Istanbul (original height perhaps 28.95 m, 95 ft),* **3** *Ramesses II at Luxor, (25 m, 82 ft),* **4** *Ramesses II now in Paris (22.55 m, 74 ft),* **5** *Thutmose III now in New York (21.21 m, 69.6 ft),* **6** *Thutmose III now in London (20.88 m, 68.5 ft),* **7** *Senusret I at Iunu (20.41, ht 67 ft),* **8** *Thutmose I at Karnak (19.5 m, 64 ft).*

**72** (Right) *Twelve obelisks great and small, now in Rome:* from left to right, *with heights in brackets,*
**1** *Thutmose III and IV from Karnak, now Lateran (32.18 m, 105 ft),* **2** *uninscribed, under Augustus at Alexandria, now Vatican (25.37 m, 83.25 ft),* **3** *Sety I from Iunu, now Piazza del Popolo (23.2 m, 76.1 ft),* **4** *Psamtek II from Iunu, then the Augustus sun-dial gnomon, now on Monte Citorio (21.79 m, 71.5 ft),* **5** *commissioned by Domitian for the temple of Isis at Rome, Piazza Navona (16.54 m, 54.25 ft),* **6** *uninscribed, found at Augustus Mausoleum, now Esquiline (14.75 m, 48.4 ft),* **7** *uninscribed, found at Augustus Mausoleum, Quirinal (14.64 m, 48 ft),* **8** *inscribed in Imperial Rome with copy of the Piazza del Popolo obelisk, Trinita dei Monti (13.91 m, 45.65 ft),* **9** *inscribed under Hadrian for temple of Antinous at Rome, now Monte Pincio (9.25 m, 30.35 ft),* **10** *Ramesses II from Iunu, now Piazza della Rotunda (6.34 m, 20.8 ft),* **11** *Apries from Sais, now Piazza della Minerva (5.47 m, 17.95 ft),* **12** *Ramesses II from Iunu, now Villa Celimontana (upper part only, 2.68 m, 8.8 ft).*

the pyramidal form seems to relax. A stela dating to the late Middle Kingdom or early Second Intermediate Period presents the form of a rough rectangular pillar with a tip triangle on two sides, and square on the other, as if hesitating to adopt the precise obelisk form.

## The New Kingdom obelisks at Thebes

The first in the new Theban series seems to be that of Thutmose I. His director of works Ineni left a description in his tomb-chapel, recording the labour expended both on the quarrying and on the transport, a second engineering feat, for two obelisks. The pair rose between what became the 3rd and 4th Pylons at Karnak: one still stands, to a height of just under 20 m (66 ft). The inscription on the face of the monument claims that its tip was of metal, verifying the statements by Arab historians in the 12th and 13th centuries that the peak of the Iunu pair was of beaten metal. This precious

73 *Fragment from the upper part of a granodiorite obelisk of modest scale, inscribed on both sides with a scene of King Ramesses II worshipping the sun god. UC 16319.*

alloy of gold and silver effectively activated the tip as the *benben* symbol, when the first ray of the sun before dawn would catch the polished surface, lighting it almost electrically. The daughter of Thutmose I, Hatshepsut, had two pairs of obelisks raised at Karnak. Only one of these stands, and this exceeds its predecessors, and every one of its surviving successors, reaching a height of almost 30 m (98 ft), with an estimated weight of 323 tons. According to the uniquely programmatic inscriptions for these supreme monuments, the entire surface received a mantle of gold-silver alloy. This seems possible, for small illustrations flank the central hieroglyphic inscription on the faces of the obelisk, and would have provided a suitable background for a metallic covering. Thanks to explicit records on the rocks at the granite quarries near Aswan, we know that Senmut, principal official at the court of Hatshepsut, organized the cutting and, again the key engineering feat, the transport of two of these 'great obelisks of raising Khepri' along the river downstream to Thebes. The raising of the obelisks formed one of the central motifs in the reign of Hatshepsut, a gift to Amun-Ra depicted on one of the blocks from her red quartzite chapel, for the boat of the god. The hieroglyphic inscription reads:

> The king himself, raising the two great obelisks for her father Amun-Ra
> in front of the sacred columned hall;
> worked in electrum very greatly, they rise to the knife-edge of the sky,
> illumination of the two lands like the sun disk.
> Never has the like been done since the beginnings of time.

This phrasing could be said to give the earliest use of the term skyscraper, and Labib Habachi used it as the label for all these extraordinary 'super-obelisks'. As with the pyramids, there are clearly two groups of monument, a division according to which the far greater scale corresponds to, perhaps even generates, the finest quality. There are innumerable obelisks from Egypt, from the smaller Old Kingdom funerary examples to the countless miniature amulets produced for burial in the Late Period. Yet there are now only 16 'super-obelisks', those exceeding 10 m (33 ft) in height (*ills 71–72*). There may never have been very many more. For these, skyscraper seems indeed an apt name.

## Ramesside obelisks, greater and lesser

After Thutmose III, two great builder kings of the 19th Dynasty, Sety I and Ramesses II, aimed to match the achievements of their predecessors. Significantly, though, they did not set up any new massive obelisk at Karnak, concentrating their efforts instead on the temple of Amun at Luxor in southern Thebes, and above all on the precinct of Ra at Iunu. At this time, resources were pooled at the northeastern corner of Egypt, for the creation of a new residence city in the Eastern Delta, Piramesse, 'House of Ramesses'. Iunu lay between this regal city and the ancient administrative fulcrum of Egypt at Mennefer (Memphis), and perhaps benefited from its position at centre stage on the Ramesside world map. Two centuries later, at the end of the 20th Dynasty, Piramesse yielded to a more northerly site, Tanis, perhaps as the result of a change in the course or navigability of the eastern Nile Delta river branch. The kings of the 21st Dynasty at Tanis emptied Piramesse of its monuments in order to adorn their new city. These included monolithic granite obelisks on the superhuman scale attested at Iunu and Thebes. On the western side of the great Amun temple of Tanis, the 21st Dynasty kings set up no fewer than four pairs of obelisks inscribed originally for Ramesses II. These appear to have stood in front of three great gateways along the east–west axis of the temple: one pair in front of the first and the second gateways, and two pairs in front of the third, where there were also four colossal statues of Ramesses II (*ill. 74*). The front pair measured 12.9 and 12.6 m (42 ft 4 in and 41 ft 4 in) in height, while the second reached over 16 m (52 ft). The third and fourth pairs were grouped as an inner pair about 15.2 m (49 ft 9 in) tall, and an outer about 14 m (46 ft) tall. As at Thebes and Iunu, there was also a gateway at the eastern, sunrise end behind the temple sanctuary, and this was marked by a fifth pair of obelisks, each 12.5 m (41 ft) in height (*ill. 75*). There was however no gateway through the enclosure wall on this eastern side. Since Roman times, all the limestone of the Tanis

**74** *Sketch-plan by Pierre Montet of the Amun temple at Tanis, showing the five pairs of obelisks as fallen, with their bases and the fragments of other obelisks.*

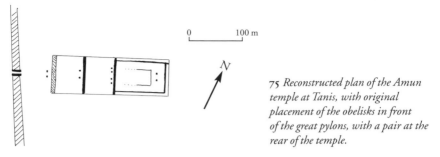

75 *Reconstructed plan of the Amun temple at Tanis, with original placement of the obelisks in front of the great pylons, with a pair at the rear of the temple.*

temples has been quarried away, leaving a jumble of granite and other hard stone blocks. It is not easy today to imagine the magnificence of the temple throughout the 1st millennium BC, when it rivalled Karnak and even the city of the sun at Iunu. It is still harder to reconstruct the original appearance of the temples at Piramesse that provided the stone for the builders of Tanis. It is not certain how the obelisks there would have been grouped, or even whether they adorned one or more than one sanctuary. The main temple at Piramesse was dedicated to Seth, but there was also a cult of 'Ra of Piramesse', and this would have been a more appropriate place for the solar symbols, if they were not set up at the temple to the king's own cult in his city. Another possibility is that one or more pairs came from Iunu, and that the builders of Tanis brought obelisks from both Iunu and Piramesse. However, there is no evidence that monuments were moved from Iunu before the Ptolemaic Period. It seems more likely that Ramesses II commissioned such a great number of these outsize monoliths in order to raise his new city to the level of Iunu and Thebes.

## Smaller royal obelisks and later imperial settings

Alongside the greatest obelisks, the kings of the 19th Dynasty, including Ramesses II, erected smaller-scale versions, up to 7 m (23 ft) in height, principally at sun shrines such as that in front of the great temple at Abu Simbel, and, probably, at the temples to their own regal cult, in Iunu (see Chapter Three). The original architectural settings of royal obelisks, combined with the contents of hieroglyphic inscriptions on many, great and small, may be taken to show specific and intimate links between the obelisk form and the greatest kingship festival, the sed. For both Thutmose III and Ramesses II, inscriptions record the commissioning of the tallest of these solar monuments in connection with the sed festivals of these kings, sometimes specifically at Iunu. The rites of the sed were intended to regenerate the king, leaving him one step closer to his father the sun god. The obelisk effectively expresses this reunion at the most important shrines for the process, those of the king and of the sun (*ill. 73*). A modern feminist reading would draw attention too to the phallocratic message of the granite pinnacles, uniting father and son. It is all the more striking that the most impressive to survive at Thebes, in their form and in their inscriptions, were set up for the woman who would be king, Hatshepsut in the 15th century BC. After the New Kingdom, the northern rulers in the Third Intermediate Period concentrated on the formidable task of moving obelisks from Piramesse to Tanis, rather than quarry new ones. During the Late Period 'renaissance', at least one new obelisk was set up at Iunu under Psamtek II (595–589 BC). Thereafter, it seems that no new giant obelisk was cut until the solar form attracted emperors such as Augustus, after the Roman conquest of Egypt in 30 BC. Kings of the 26th and 30th Dynasties set up the more modest monoliths at sites such as the western Delta city of Thoth, and these, like the great pillars of Iunu and Thebes, were later reused in the adornment of Alexandria and Rome. The Roman emperors were not content to move old monuments. They placed them in new settings of astonishing originality, most notably the gnomon at the eye of the giant sundial in Rome, laid out under Augustus (*ill. 76*). This was the latest known obelisk at Iunu, from the reign of Psamtek II, and became one of the first to leave Egypt, in around 10 BC. The emperor had a pair of smaller obelisks set up at his Mausoleum, while the great monolith from the city of the sun stood a little to the south, in a grid of astronomical lines. Just to the east stood the Ara Pacis principal monument to the peace achieved by the victory over Mark Antony and Cleopatra. On the birthday of the emperor, the shadow from the obelisk fell at the door of the Ara Pacis. In its alignment the ensemble seems to transform Augustus into a new version of the Egyptian sun king (*ill. 77*). The Roman emperors also commissioned great new granite obelisks, such as the uninscribed example intended for the Circus Vaticanus, and now the centre of Saint Peter's Square. The 'last obelisk' in this ancient tradition of solar

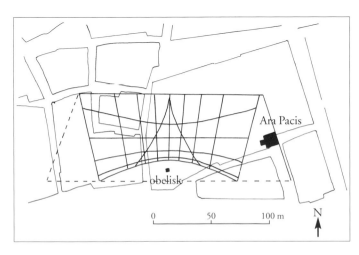

*76 Obelisk as gnomon: the grid of the giant sundial of Augustus beneath the street-map of modern Rome. The Ara Pacis lies on the eastern outermost line of the grid.*

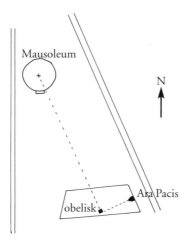

77 *The alignment of the Iunu obelisk as resited in Rome, to the east with the Ara Pacis, celebrating the new Empire, and to the north with the Mausoleum of Augustus.*

sovereignty may be that inscribed with a learned hieroglyphic inscription, one of the latest compositions in that script, set up in Rome for the emperor Hadrian. When the empire adopted Christianity, the obelisks eventually fell, within Egypt and abroad. Several were raised again at Rome, in the wake of the Renaissance, and became symbols of a new faith, surmounted by the Cross and marked with new Latin inscriptions for the papacy. In this new world, the obelisk became reflexively a sign of itself, a symbol of the monumental, and this new meaning has given it a new currency both as landmark of modern cities, from New York to Cairo, and as grave marker, seeking permanence in the face of death. Perhaps this latter form, familiar from cemeteries throughout the Western world, is not so far removed from the original purpose of the obelisk, to capture the spark of life at first dawn, for the eternal regeneration of the king and creation.

# Chapter Five
# The Exclusive Son – Akhenaten

## Logical extremes

The reign of Akhenaten in the 14th century BC represents an extremity of sun worship in Egyptian history, a turning point hailed by some as the birth of monotheism, belief in one god. In certain features, ancient Egyptian civilization displays a very human tendency – to pursue a line of development to a logical extreme. Sometimes the results may strike an outsider as absurd, but some inner impulse powers the creative hand and eye along to its end. When considering the Akhenaten episode, it may be helpful to remember other striking examples where one idea or even a pattern of building led, as if inevitably, to the development of 'new gods'. For example, thanks largely to an overriding desire for symmetry, the architectural spaces for cult fostered a prominent feature of later Egyptian religion, the groups of three gods. The principal image along the central axis required a secondary companion on both sides, to fill the rear wall of the temple. These triads sometimes needed to be conjured out of epithets or images from outside the local cult. In the New Kingdom the god of knowledge Thoth acquired at his cult centre, the city of Khemenu, a consort who had not existed previously. Her name, Nehmetaway 'Rescuer of the Downtrodden', derives directly

78 *Sketch in black, part incised, showing the head of a sovereign with cobra at the brow. From the sheer diagonal stroke to the edge, this is generally identified as Nefertiti wearing the tall crown unique to depictions of her. Excavated by Petrie at Amarna. UC 11.*

from ethical precepts in didactic literature. One and a half thousand years later, at the small temple known by the present-day Arabic place name al-Qala, the supplementary goddesses derived their names from epithets of principal goddesses such as Isis at the local provincial temples in Qus and Qift (Coptos). These deities existed for festival processions, when the architectural space and the performance of cult created a space that had to be filled by a deity. The new name sought to cover a part of divine creation as glimpsed in that place and time. It was not, as we might see it from the outside, an empty artifice, but rather the response to the needs of festival and cult, of religious practice. The all-encompassing pattern of belief embraced these extremities, and nurtured them alongside one another.

Only once, before the arrival of Christianity and Islam, did a line of development lead to a demand that the king avoid all other views, all other beliefs, and, in the case of some cults, even persecute them. This occurred during the 14th century BC, at the height of Egyptian wealth, in the reign of Amenhotep IV, famous under his revised name as Akhenaten. No other reign has provoked as much controversy. Any account of the extraordinary episode must, by the nature of the sources, be read as a speculative reconstruction, this chapter as much as any other study. Yet in this chapter the preceding account should help to highlight both the kingly cult of Ra and the correspondingly mythic expression of Egyptian kingship, in particular as regards the role of women as the goddesses around the solar king.

## Writing a narrative on Akhenaten

In one practical sense, there is a simple reason for the haze of questions surrounding Akhenaten, and that is the mismatch between the sources for his reign and the way we write history. Our histories are journalistic narratives, not tables of data presented as evidence. For the events in this reign only two ancient narratives survive, one near the beginning and the other after its end, and these frame the story with all the art of a great dramatist. The beginning is provided by one of the most remarkable texts from antiquity, an explicit record of the foundation of a new city, set in the mouth of the king, in his fifth year of rule. It is inscribed in hieroglyphs as monumental boundary stelae around the territory of the city, itself established by the terms of these inscriptions as a monument to the sun disk, in Egyptian Aten, and named Akhetaten 'Horizon of the Sun Disk'. Today the city and this unique period often take the name Amarna, from the desert tribe settled in the area in recent centuries. The end of this venture appears in a second composition inscribed in hieroglyphs, on the Restoration Stela set up in the name of the boy-king Tutankhamun (probably Akhenaten's son), by the fourth year of his reign. It describes the preceding decades as a time of heresy, when the temples were abandoned and the gods deserted Egypt, and relates how the young king has rescued the land from disaster by the restoration of their cults. Between and around these two compositions we have a shattered textual record, on one side the accidental survivals of fragmentary hieroglyphic monuments, and on the other the cursive inscriptions on storage and transport jars. In order to complicate the comparison with life before and after Akhenaten, our scriptwriter has thrown in a unique survival at Akhetaten, nothing less than the international correspondence of the king of Egypt with major and minor rulers of the Near East. The letters are in, not Egyptian, but Akkadian, the lingua franca of Western Asia at this time. The script is therefore the cuneiform script of that region, devised around 3300 BC for the Sumerian language, and written with a wedge (Latin *cuneus*) on rectangular tablets of clay. Archaeology adds to this uniquely different set of sources, with the sum of the record from Akhetaten, the only residence city yet excavated on Egyptian soil. Although the residence city of Ramesses II is now being excavated in the eastern Delta, unequal preservation in the damp soil there does not provide a complete picture of the city to the extent allowed by the dry ground along the eastern half of Akhetaten. At Akhetaten, unlike Piramesse, archaeologists have been able to record the full ancient appearance of great palaces and villas, equipped with wall- and floor-paintings, and chapels to the king. These combine to produce exactly the effect one might imagine Akhenaten intended, of utter difference from all that had preceded it.

## Controversial issues

The fragmentary record of these two decades in the 14th century BC has given rise to a series of questions still bitterly contested in Egyptology. Before presenting an account of the reign, it is only fair to note the principal debates.

*Did Akhenaten reign alongside his father, and, if so, for how long?*

The reign of Akhenaten lasted into a 17th year, according to the sequence of wine jar inscriptions from his city. However, some scholars believe he shared the throne for some years with his father, Amenhotep III. Of these, depending largely on how one interprets the date and contents of one of the cuneiform tablets, some favour a co-regency of two years, while others argue for a co-regency lasting a full 12 years.

*What part did Nefertiti play in the reign, and did she rule as king?*

Akhenaten's wife, the famous Queen Nefertiti, holds exceptional status, taking early in the reign the second name Neferneferuaten. She is last seen in depictions of a great festival including the presentation of produce from abroad, in year 12. At some point after this, a second ruler appears alongside

**79** *Fragment of relief depicting Nefertiti in the extreme style typical of the first half of the reign of Akhenaten. Excavated by Petrie at Amarna. UC 38.*

Akhenaten, with the names Ankhkheperura Neferneferuaten, and then there are a couple of sources recording a King Ankhkheperura Smenkhkara. John Harris has interpreted this series of names as evidence for the rise of Nefertiti first to exceptional queenly status, as Neferneferuaten, then, after year 12, to kingly status as Ankhkheperura, and finally, after some other key event, to the briefly attested Smenkhkara. Others have seen Smenkhkara as an ephemeral male heir, succeeded within months by the boy Tutankhaten (renamed Tutankhamun after the restoration of the old cults).

In 1905 Theodore Davies uncovered the body of a young royal male in the Valley of the Kings at Thebes, buried with funeral equipment of Akhenaten and his mother, Queen Tiy. Without forensic examination, it remains uncertain whether the body is that of a man around 20 years of age (a male Smenkhkara) or 30 to 35 (perhaps Akhenaten himself). If the body is that of Akhenaten, it removes the evidence for a male Smenkhkara, and makes it more likely that the name denotes Nefertiti as king.

*Who is the despairing Egyptian queen in the Hittite royal annals?*

German excavators at the capital of the Hittite empire in the mountains of present-day Turkey uncovered a vast archive of royal texts from the century following Akhenaten. One referred back to an episode in which an Egyptian royal woman wrote to the Hittite ruler after the death of her husband, asking for a prince to marry. The Hittite text calls her Dahamunzu, generally interpreted as a rendering of Egyptian *ta-hemet-nesut* (the final t being dropped in New Kingdom and later Egyptian) 'the king's wife'. Which king and which wife? Some see her as Nefertiti, others as Ankhesenamun, the widow of Tutankhamun, who would then be appealing for help after her husband's death at the age of 16 or 17 years.

What is a historian to present to readers from the tattered data and furious scholarly disputes? Whichever version is chosen, both writer and reader must remember that this can only be a tentative reconstruction, as the narrative that seems to her or him most persuasive. What else is any history? For this culmination of the story of the sun in ancient Egypt, I follow here what may often seem extreme interpretations within each of the debates. I do this because at this moment these seem to me the most plausible. Any or every point might be overturned by a single find in the next season of excavation at Akhetaten, at Thebes, or at Memphis and its cemeteries over Saqqara. The reader must read what follows as not so much a history as a story of Akhenaten.

## Amenhotep III – the climax of divine kingship

During the early 14th century BC the Egyptian royal court enjoyed its most brilliant years of luxury, a peace coinciding with control of Nubian gold mines to the south, and of some of the key Levantine trading centres to the northeast. The king Amenhotep III embarked on a spectacular programme of temple-building for his own cult and that of the gods the length of the

80 *Thebes under Amenhotep III.*

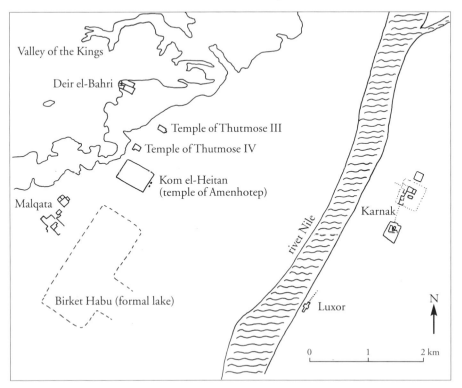

Egyptian-controlled Nile Valley. Near the Third Cataract, deep into occupied Nubia, his engineers and architects established a pair of temples, one to the cult of the king, at Soleb, the other to that of his principal wife Tiy, at nearby Sedeinga. Here the king became the moon, echoing the far vaster enterprise of his temple, palace and ritual lake on the West Bank at Thebes, where he was to occupy the very place of the sun. Other temples have entirely disappeared, but we know of their scope and perfection. At Mennefer (Memphis), the work of David Jeffreys has shown how the course of the Nile shifted fairly swiftly to the east at about this time, leaving behind a new tract of untouched land fresh for building. From this site survives the wrecked but once magnificent quartzite statue of the king's administrator at Mennefer, named Amenhotep like his sovereign, and here depicted as seated on the ground, privileged position of king's secretary. Both the material and the posture indicate exceptional favour from the sun king to his trusty official, and the autobiography inscribed in hieroglyphs on the statue explains why. This estate manager oversaw the revenues for a great new temple to his king in the domain of Ptah, earth-creator of Mennefer. The splendour of the foundation described matches that for the temple of the king at Thebes. Today even the site is uncertain, though Robert Morkot has indicated that its most likely location was the area transformed a century later into a temple to Ramesses II. On the tourist map this appears as the temple of Ptah, but Jaromir Malek has shown that the original temple to Ptah is more likely to lie beneath the mound on which the present village of Mit Rahina stands. The vast precinct to its east would then be not a temple of Ptah, but the temple of the king 'in the domain of Ptah', as the ancient Egyptians phrased it. Another temple may perhaps have risen at Iunu, and yet another at the key central Delta city Hutherib (rendered in Greek as Athribis). Of the latter little survives today, though the mound of ruins remained visible until the 19th century. However, the texts from other places imply that Hutherib contained a substantial population, with national significance. Its most famous son was another Amenhotep, son of a man called Hapu.

Amenhotep son of Hapu held the title 'overseer of recruits', in other words the organizer of manpower resources. Although it seems curious at first, on reflection it is not so surprising that the man with this position received credit for the most spectacular engineering achievement of the reign. Hieroglyphic inscriptions record his role in the quarrying, transport and final positioning of two colossal statues in front of the king's first temple, on the West Bank at Thebes (*ill. 81*). Each measures over 21 m (69 ft) in height and is cut from a single block of shining quartzite from the mountain behind Iunu, city of the sun. In the Hellenistic and Roman Periods these statues became famous as the Colossi of Memnon, in Greek myth the doomed son of the Dawn. A crack in one caused the statue to emit an eerie

**81** *Colossi of Memnon, the monolithic quartzite statues of Amenhotep III at the front of the site of his temple, Thebes West.*

lament every day at that time, until the Roman emperor Septimius Severus piously ordered repairs for the statue, inadvertently blocking the fissure and ending the miracle. Visitors to the site today can see the cloak of Greek and some Latin graffiti left by awe-struck visitors preceding them by 2,000 years. In Greek texts the statues gave their name to the entire district on the West Bank at Thebes, as the Memnoneia. Behind them the great temple fell into oblivion only a short time after the death of its maker, and presents today a desolate and largely unexcavated terrain. Yet its area alone, and the description of it on a stela standing at the rear, indicate how Egypt here reached the peak of her magnificence.

The little-known rules of ancient Egyptian kingship laid down that the king prepare for the *sed*, the mysterious festival marking the end of an old cycle of rule, and the king's regeneration in preparation for a new cycle. Greek texts translate *sed* as 'festival of 30 years', and indeed Amenhotep III enacted the rites from his year 30. This was the first celebration of the *sed* since Thutmose III, a century earlier, and, as Betsy Bryan has shown, it became no mere repetition. Riding on its tidal wave of gold, the Egyptian court prepared to express itself with a power and expense never experienced before or since. The transformation and the difference from all other festivals in history may be appreciated most sharply in the images sculpted from the hardest stones of the Egyptian desert. For Amenhotep III the incantations to appease the Furious Goddess, Sekhmet, at the end of the year became the mightiest litany ever sung, a chorus of perhaps 730 images of the goddess. These depict her as a lion-headed woman holding the sceptre of flourishing and the sign of life, in half of them seated, in the other half standing. In place of rituals marking the journey of the king with the sun through the sky, Amenhotep III met the constellations themselves, in the form of statues. Where other kings had confronted small images of gods and goddesses reunited from all over Egypt, the royal artists created out of quartzite, alabaster and granodiorite each deity for, we must imagine, unprecedented pageants of statuary in which the king truly walked in the company of the gods (*ill. 82*). After the festivals, many of these images made the journey to the cult centres in the provinces, such as the exquisite alabaster dyad of Amenhotep III receiving life from the crocodile-headed Sobek, found at the latter's local temple in ancient Sumenu, south of Thebes. At the culmination of the festival the power of the king reached through the night of renewal, an undisclosed mystery, to the point of melt-down where he revitalized not only himself but all creation.

The potency of the rites, and of the art serving them, may be gauged from the findspot of two of the outstanding masterpieces of Egyptian art, the pair of sphinxes of Amenhotep III, now on the banks of the Neva in St Petersburg. They were retrieved from the point where they had been buried, metres down in the ground on the site of the king's great Theban temple. The false beard of each sphinx has been smashed from its chin, but each still bears the Double Crown over the royal headcloth, and their almond eyes are the unmistakable eyes of the redeified Amenhotep III. Restored to the surface, they still leave the impression that they are too powerful for this world. From the mystery of regeneration, the king emerged as the sun at dawn. Earlier kings depicted themselves sailing beside the sun god in the sky, but Amenhotep III went further. He himself 'took the position of the one who is in the sun disk'. There was a great artificial lake cut beside his *sed* palace on the West Bank at Thebes, and here he could literally sail in the morning boat of the sun god, now his boat. Other kings had merged with the sun disk after death. While still alive, this king had now already become more manifestly the sun god on earth, his status changed from solar king to sun. The most stunning discovery in the cache of statues a decade ago at the temple of Luxor is the colossal image of Amenhotep III, called the Shining Sun Disk of All Lands. It is a depiction not directly of the king, but of a statue of him drawn on a sled. This is an object of cult. All kings of Egypt share in the divinity of the sun god, but, by passing his *sed*, this king of the wealthiest period attained more identity than a share. From now on

82 *Scarab of Amenhotep III beside the Sacred Lake at Karnak. The front of the plinth depicts Amenhotep III offering to Atum of Iunu. The hieroglyphic inscription includes the words of the sun god as Khepri: 'you are the lord of what the Disk (Aten) illuminates'. The winged disk above also reads 'Ra' in the throne-name of Amenhotep III, Nebmaatra, to stress the identification of the king with the sun.*

Amenhotep III becomes a new creature: he appears youthful, there are rings of gold on his arms, he wears the Double Crown over the short braided wig, all to mark a tangible and visible difference in his being.

## The transfer of power to Akhenaten

There is no explicit mechanism for succession to the throne in ancient Egypt: each king 'rises' like the sun, revealing himself as what he has always been, the son of the sun since he was in the womb, or, as the Egyptians phrased it, 'king in the egg'. As suggested in the Introduction, this lack of clear procedures may help to account for a sporadic practice of securing the succession by installing the preferred successor on the throne as co-regent. In this arrangement, the senior king may have been less active, withdrawing into the palace like a god in his temple, while the junior co-regent played the more active role, visible on occasions such as military exploits. When King Amenhotep III became the Shining Sun Disk of All Lands, would he too retire into the sed palace at Malqata? Who then would take the active role in the outside world? It is generally thought that, six centuries earlier,

**83** *The sarcophagus of Tamiy, pet cat of the high priest Thutmose, son of Amenhotep III. From Memphis, Egyptian Museum, Cairo, CG 5003.*

Amenemhat I shared his throne with his son from his 20th year of reign, and indeed I see no other explanation for the dated building work on the pyramid complexes of those two kings. These indicate that the elder king decided in year 20 to return to the Old Kingdom pyramid form for the royal tomb, and that the junior king began work on his own pyramid complex in his year 10. Year 20 of the reign of Amenemhat I is therefore the most likely moment at which the co-regency was established, while the new royal residence, named Itjtawy, was constructed near the tombs of the two kings. So co-regency can open the way to new centres of power, the founding of new royal bases. Would this happen under Amenhotep III?

Hieroglyphic inscriptions record that the king had a son, Thutmose, who held the office of high priest of Ptah. Some have seen this as an elder son and heir apparent, and have asked why he did not ascend to the throne as co-regent. However, there is no instance where a king's son was appointed high priest and then succeeded to the throne. The lack of parallels may imply quite the opposite – that, if Thutmose was appointed high priest of Ptah, he was already excluded from the succession. The reigning king is a manifestation of the sun, and the next manifestation is not made apparent during his life-time except in the most unusual circumstances (as asserted by Hatshepsut in support of her claim to be king). This leaves the biological sons (and brothers) of kings invisible in the sacred textual record, the hieroglyphic inscriptions. We can only ever compile incomplete family trees for the kings of ancient Egypt. Therefore it is hopeless to speculate over the number of princes at the court of Amenhotep III, even worse to imagine that Thutmose was sidestepped or removed to make way for another claimant. We do not know how or when he died: the prince remains as elusive as the pet cat for whose sarcophagus he is most well known in Egyptology today (*ill. 83*). All we know is the existence of another, possibly elder, possibly younger, son of Amenhotep III, also bearing from birth the name Amenhotep. This is the prince who became Amenhotep IV, and then changed history with the adoption of new beliefs expressed in the new name, Akhenaten.

## Patterns in the sed festivals of Amenhotep III and Akhenaten

Ray Johnson has argued strongly that Prince Amenhotep already became king as junior co-regent to his father when the latter began to prepare for his sed, when he would become the Shining Sun Disk of All Lands. The co-regency could have lasted a full 12 years, divided into phases by the *sed* and its three-yearly repetitions. The years of reign do indeed provide remarkable equations, as can be seen in the following tabulation:

| AMENHOTEP III YEAR | AMENHOTEP IV/ AKHENATEN YEAR |
|---|---|
| 26 | 1 |
| 27 | 2 |
| 28 | 3 |
| 29 | 4 |
| 30 First *sed* festival | 5 Founding of Akhetaten, change in name |
| 31 | 6 Renewal of Boundary Vows |
| 32 | 7 |
| 33 | 8 Renewal of Boundary Vows |
| 34 Second *sed* festival | 9 Great festival at Amarna |
| 35 | 10 |
| 36 | 11 |
| 37 Third *sed* festival | 12 Great festival with foreign envoys |
| 38 Dies during this year | 13 |
| | 14 |
| | 15 |
| | 16 |
| | 17 Dies during this year |

Years 1-5 (= 26-30) would mark the Theban programme of Amenhotep IV, followed by the change in his name to Akhenaten at the first *sed* of his father. Years 5-12 would occur at the time that Amenhotep III celebrated his three *sed* festivals, while the renamed Akhenaten established his city. The final phase, years 13-17, would be the most violent, seeing after the death of Amenhotep III a nationwide programme to erase from all hieroglyphic inscriptions the references to Amun, Mut and 'the gods'.

This reconstruction is highly attractive as a cogent and explanatory account of the period. Perhaps the single greatest obstacle remains a cuneiform tablet that mentions the previous Egyptian king as fairly recently deceased. Along one edge the tablet bears remnants of a date in Egyptian cursive script, long read as 'Year 12 (?)', but now conclusively shown by a recently published photograph to be 'Year 2' (*ill. 84*). It seems then either that Akhenaten ruled alongside his father for no more than two years, or that there was no co-regency at all. This is the most probable interpretation of the data currently available, but it is difficult to rule out the theory of

84 *The date 'year 2, month 1 of spring, day 2',
in cursive Egyptian script, on the edge of a
cuneiform letter to a new king. Amarna
Letter EA 27.*

co-regency altogether, because even the Year 2 cuneiform tablet seems
somehow indirect evidence. Perhaps a case can still be made for a long co-
regency, and therefore, though I do not support the theory, I have attempted
to give it space in the following pages as one more possibility in the Amarna
sea of uncertainties. On the whole, it may be said that Year 2 of Akhenaten
probably fell later than Year 38 of Amenhotep III. In this case the recurrence
of great festivals at intervals reveals not co-regency, but a phenomenon no
less interesting – that Akhenaten continued the triennial *sed* festival
sequence of Amenhotep III. At death Egyptian kings 'flew to heaven and
merged with the sun disk', according to the formula. Akhenaten seems to
have insisted on the survival of his father's presence as the sun disk, following on logically from the Luxor Cache statue inscribed as 'Amenhotep III
Shining Sun Disk of All Lands'. Accordingly the new king focused all cult
on his father the sun disk, a practice reinforced perhaps by the assonance of
the Egyptian words *it* 'father' and *itn* 'sun disk' (in Akkadian versions, the 'n'
of Aten is not given, suggesting that the final consonant was only weakly
pronounced). The record is too broken to be sure, but perhaps the young
king planned to renew his paternal partner's powers every three years
throughout his reign. These might be the reasons behind the great festivals
documented in years 9 and 12, and perhaps the consolidation of the city of
Akhetaten in year 6. The *sed* festivals continued to be celebrated for the
Aten, as if the elder king were still alive on earth. The joint rule of Ra and
king would have become a new more closely bound co-regency in denial of
death, between Amenhotep III and IV beyond the former's mortal lifespan.

## The first five years: focus Thebes

Under Amenhotep III, Thebes was transformed on both sides of the river
into one great construction site (*ill. 80*). The West Bank became the soil for
the regeneration of the king. A palace was set up at the desert edge, a great
lake cut, and the vast temple for the eternal cult of the king at Kom el-
Heitan pushed towards completion. On the East Bank, Karnak and Luxor
temples expanded beyond recognition, linked not only by the Ipet festival,
but physically by avenues of ram-headed sphinxes. During the first years of

his son's rule, as Amenhotep IV, the planners opened up a vast tract of land for new temples to the sun god. Thutmose III had recast Thebes as the 'Iunu of Upper Egypt', but now the temple of Amun-Ra would find itself joined by vast new sacred precincts dedicated to the sun alone. At first the presentation of the king and the sun god at Thebes remained within the bounds of traditional principles of depiction. A few surviving relief blocks depict the junior king Amenhotep IV making offerings to a sun god, who is shown as usual with a falcon head and human body so that he can hold his sceptres of power and harmonize with the human form of the king. However, the intentions of the king were already radical, as revealed by one hieroglyphic inscription at the sandstone quarries of Silsila, between Thebes and Aswan. This records the contents of a royal decree despatching an expedition to identify a special vein of stone. The material had to be suitable for quarrying a *benben* as the focus of sun worship at Karnak. Taking up the challenge of the monolithic single obelisk of Thutmose III on the east face of the Amun temple, the new structure must have transformed the balance of worship and festival on the East Bank at Thebes. Soon this radical change brought equally startling innovations in sculpture and relief, a new form of expression which would have stunned the ancients with the same force that strikes any witness today. At a stroke, a new art was born. It is important to remember that these changes did not occur first at Akhenaten's city of the sun at Amarna, at this stage not yet founded: they appear at Thebes, between the second and fifth years of the young king's reign. The fragments of temple reliefs and sculpture began to reappear in the early 20th century AD, as Egyptologists prised from later structures the inscribed and sculpted blocks reused for building work in later reigns. Art historians are still trying to absorb the impact of these fragments, and above all of the great colossal sculptures unearthed in the 1920s (*ills 85–86*).

The novel temple to the east of the Amun temple at Karnak elevated in effect a purified, rarefied image of the sun, or of the senior co-regent Amenhotep III as sun disk, anticipating his reunion with the sun god's celestial body in the *sed* festivals. If they were the homage of the son Amenhotep IV/Akhenaten to the senior sun king Amenhotep III, it becomes easier to explain the initial reason for excluding all other gods, and for seeking a different style of art. This can only be hypothesis, but the senior partner in the sky may alone have been in full contact with the sphere of the divine, leaving the junior partner on earth as intermediary specifically between earth and its closest sun, the senior king merged with the sun disk. How was the relation of senior to junior sovereign to be expressed? The solution to this problem might be the sun disk in its plain physical form, as viewed not on the divine level but by human beings on earth. In place of the rows of gods that had surrounded Amenhotep III and his predecessors,

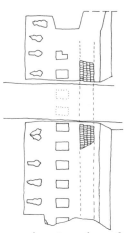

85 *Akhenaten colossus in sandstone, from the Aten temple in Karnak East, Thebes. Cairo 29-5/49-1.*

86 *The sketch plan by Henri Chevrier of his excavation of the Akhenaten colonnade east of the Amun precinct at Karnak East.*

there could only be depictions of the sun over his immediate junior partner. The exclusion of the gods, and exclusive depiction of the sun and royal family, may have rested initially on the interpretation of the reign as a new, divine co-regency. This would account for the creation of the new art alongside the walls of Karnak, which teemed in traditional manner with formal depictions of divinities as human or animal, without any antagonism arising between the two styles at the outset. Instead of the falcon as image of heavenly power, the new sanctuaries around Karnak depicted the disk more prosaically as a deep-cut convex circle with rays ending in hands offering the sign of life to the junior king and, significantly, his wife, Nefertiti. Already Tiy, wife of the elder king, occupied a prominent role, with her own cult centre at Sedeinga complementing and serving her husband's larger temple at Soleb. Nefertiti continues this prominence, acting in part of the new Karnak shrines as sole officiant of the cult of the sun disk (*ill. 87*). She is shown as sole officiant in one part of the new structures, and assumes roles previously reserved for the reigning king alone, such as that of smiting the enemies of Egypt, sometimes in the form of the sphinx to emphasize the sheer physical majesty of the rulers. Most astonishing of all are the colossi depicting a sovereign clasping the crook and flail, insignia of rule. These seem to have stood at the base of vast columns in a temple court, some clothed, others naked. Some have seen these as depictions of Nefertiti, but the naked colossi are entirely sexless: neither male nor female genitalia are marked. They may instead evoke Amenhotep IV as the 'mother and

*87 Reconstruction of the depiction on a column from the Aten complex at Karnak East, showing Nefertiti and her eldest daughter Meretaten in worship of the sun disk.*

father' of humankind, embracing all the impulses of creation. As with almost every detail of the period, they remain open to mutually exclusive interpretations. Yet they serve what may well have been their prime function – to demarcate the new art from all that had gone before, in this eastern focus for the sun at Thebes.

## Years 5 and 6: new name and new city

In the fifth year of his reign Amenhotep IV changed his name to Akhenaten, in English translation a shift from 'Amun is content' to 'light/useful one of the sun disk'. Here *akh* might almost be rendered 'pious', as in the Latin *pius*, with the sense of 'good son'. More importantly the word reunites two strong Egyptian themes – *akh* meaning 'transfigured' (from a series of words connected with the sunlight) and *akh* meaning 'useful'. In co-regency the junior partner would become the active, 'useful' son of the sun, a transfigured status, at the moment that his father withdrew into what we might term retirement. This fifth year brought a new status and name for the young king, and a new centre of royal power and cult dedicated exclusively to the sun disk. Karnak East had been dedicated exclusively to the sun, but alongside the temple of Amun-Ra. The new city at Amarna was explicitly removed from any other god or cult, and lay about midway between Memphis and Thebes. By an extraordinary stroke of fate, we can read the foundation of the city of the sun directly in one of the most evocative inscriptions from antiquity, the royal decree of Akhenaten ordering the creation of Akhetaten 'Horizon of the Sun Disk'. This inscription on the boundary stelae around the city reveals exactly what spatial and conceptual parameters the foundation implied. Three of the surviving stelae bear the original decree issued in year 5; a further 11 are dated to year 6, presumably in the midst of the intense initial phase of construction in the city. The terrain itself is not the most promising soil for a new urban centre, a long strip of desert along the east bank of the Nile. Yet its symbolic importance can be understood both from that position, and from the gap in the eastern Saharan cliffs, which forms with the rising sun every dawn a cosmic writing of the very hieroglyph signifying 'horizon'.

## Akhetaten, city of the sun disk

Since its survey by the French Revolutionary Expedition of 1798–1801, the city of Akhetaten has entered modern histories of Egypt as a model of town planning, where we can see every detail of the ancient city. However, the town is perfectly preserved only over the dry areas along the desert edge. Two crucial elements are lost beneath the fields and, perhaps, the recent course of the Nile: river embankment and royal residence. The director of the current excavations at the site, Barry Kemp, has emphasized the importance of the fragment of a massive walled complex at the north end of the great road running parallel to the Nile from the city's tip to its centre. This can be identified as the place where the king would have resided during his time in the city, not least because the prevailing north wind carries the odours of urban living towards the south, leaving the northern end as the more desirable residential area. The royal residence is unknown, perhaps destroyed beneath the surface and so unknowable, though it would have contained and expressed arguably the greatest concentration of power. The loss may be partly compensated by the survival of the *sed* festival city of Amenhotep III at Thebes, where we can examine the relations between different elements of the court around the kingly halls for eating and sleeping. There are, too, the palaces for the king in the city centre, spaces for the royal family when they visited the central temples, and, probably, where the king and queen received foreign envoys. There is no such compensating parallel for the second major hole in our knowledge of the city, the exact location of the ancient river bank, which has been subject to changes in the course of the river over the centuries. Transport and communication depended almost entirely on the Nile, and the river bank attracted workshops, as would any commercial quayside. The Egyptian language uses the same word for docks and craftshop: the economic and industrial heart of any community would have been here, where the boats docked. It is reasonable to suppose that this area would have formed a densely packed slice of the urban landscape, and this may account for the absence of the humblest level of dwelling on the archaeological map of Akhetaten. Certainly the estimates of the city's population should take into account this invisible space beneath the modern fields and river.

Without its absolute ruler and its humblest populace, Akhetaten seems in archaeology all the more the ideal city, where we can study the town planning skills of the ancients. Despite the disappearance of riverside and northern tip, the city plan does represent an extraordinary survival, the Pompeii of ancient Egypt, much the clearer for its short term of life. The boundary stelae mark out a city in the ancient and medieval sense, an urban centre complete with the surrounding farmland needed to support the inhabitants (*ill. 88*). The largely desert arc runs about 9 km (5.6 miles) from south to north on the eastern bank of the Nile, not far from the area where the West Bank zone contained Khemenu, city of the god Thoth. The core of the city, as it survives, covers a strip about 1 km (0.6 miles) in width and

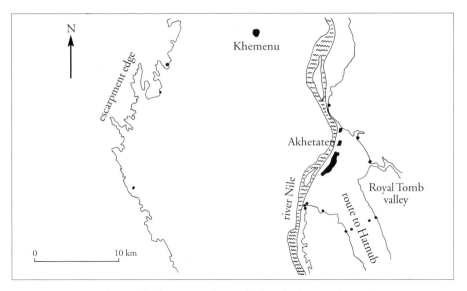

**88** *The city of Akhenaten in the area laid out by the Boundary Stelae (indicated here by black circles).*

about 3.5 km (2.2 miles) in length. At the meeting of north–south and east–west axes, the Great Temple of the Sun Disk provides the orientation from the Nile to the eastern desert valley containing the intended tomb of Akhenaten. This may have served the royal cult, and perhaps, inasmuch as Akhenaten planned anything for the future, would have perpetuated his cult after his death. The smaller Temple of the Sun Disk to the south may have been the principal place of worship for the king and royal family. It adjoins the central palace, across the road that leads from the lost northern residence. Both temples present a stark contrast to most other surviving Egyptian temples to the gods, above all in the vast open courts filled with platforms for offerings to be made directly to the sun in the open sky above. The model for this would doubtless be found at Iunu, had that city of the sun survived. The precise manner in which the sun was worshipped remains uncertain, as the rites of daily cult and festival have not survived. Certainly the royal court spent vast resources on offerings to the sun god, and these did not differ in content from the piles of food and drink presented by the king to the gods in temple reliefs from the Old Kingdom to the Roman Period. Yet we do not know whether the butchers and bakers and gardeners were accompanied by trained specialists reciting correct formulae; in other words we do not know what priests of the sun disk did. The words for the cult did include hymns, as previously, and it is possible that the cult had been pared down to the singing of a now famous text, ascribed formally to the king himself, the Great Hymn to the Sun Disk.

## The Great Hymn

There are two principal compositions from Akhetaten, known today in Egyptology simply as the shorter and the great Hymn to the Sun-disk. These stand out among a range of sun hymns known to us from hieroglyphic inscriptions in the tombs of royal courtiers. In most instances the words are pronounced by Akhenaten himself. Only exceptionally, as in the tombs of the high priest of the sun-god Meryra, and the enigmatic elder courtier Ay, does the tomb-owner pronounce the text of the hymn for himself. Perhaps then these words belong to the climax of the offering rituals, when only the king or, in his absence, the high priest would perform the gesture of offering and recite the necessary words. They describe a belief in one creator, providing for all life on earth, in lyrical phrases anticipating the Psalms of the Old Testament. If we knew nothing else about the sun cult through history, these lines would suffice as evidence for its power. An ancient Egyptian reader or listener would have felt the impact still more keenly, for Akhenaten chose to sing to his god not in the venerable phrasing of the classical Egyptian language, Middle Egyptian, but in the spoken language of his own day, Late Egyptian. This revolution in court life had already occurred with the promulgation of the Boundary Stelae, despite their being formal royal decrees, in Late Egyptian. In the most sacred hymn of kingly ritual, the choice of spoken over classical language must have overturned tradition with the same force as the deliberate proportions chosen for the body in the art of Akhenaten. Translations using an artificially old-fashioned English entirely miss the effect intended by the composer: street slang would probably be inappropriate, but it might capture the shock felt when the Great Hymn was first sung at the court of Pharaoh. The central passage of the Great Hymn reveals a wonder at the diversity of creation, and casts this as the core deed of the creator:

*89 The Aten Temple, with the king offering upon a raised platform, as depicted in the tomb of Panehesy, at Amarna.*

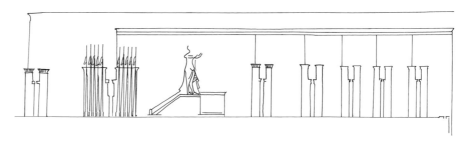

Your works are so numerous, though hidden from sight,
Unique god – there is none besides him.
You mould the earth to your wish, you and you alone –
All people, herds and flocks,
All on earth that walk on legs,
All on high that fly with their wings.

And the foreign lands of Khar and Kush-
You place every man in his place,
You make what they need,
So every one has his food,
His lifespan counted.
Tongues are separated in speech, and forms too –
Their skins are made different,
For you make foreign lands different.

## A new festival and a new name for the sun disk

In year 8 of Akhenaten new inscriptions at several of the boundary stelae of
his city record a renewal of the oaths he made in dedicating the 'monument'
to his father the sun disk. The following year a great festival took place at
Akhetaten, documented in part by the concentration of jar inscriptions for
meat and wine, the food and drink of celebration. It seems likely that the
king and court resided in the new city by this time, allowing a two-to-three-
year period of construction for the principal features. The style of art for the
sun disk becomes softer around year 9 of Akhenaten. In order to understand
what may have happened, we might turn to the early Middle Kingdom
again for a parallel. When the royal court moved to Itjtawy, a fertile union of
Theban and Memphite artistic traditions resulted in the exquisite relief and
sculpture of Senusret I. This draws attention to the effect of a physical fixed
location for the royal court. With each move, the configuration of resources
and talents would have had to change, bringing together artists in word and
image under new combinations and influences. In the context of a long co-
regency, the softer, 'late Amarna' style would have been the product of such
a move. At the same time that the art became less mannered, and its proportions in rendering the human body less extreme, the hieroglyphic inscriptions
suddenly became more insistent on the purity and uniqueness of the sun god.

Dated inscriptions show that by year 9 of Akhenaten the sun disk
received a change in its formulaic name. This change removed any reference
to the traditional expression of gods. The early formula for naming the sun
disk may be translated as 'Ra-Horakhty who rejoices in the horizon, in his
name of Shu/light who/which is in the sun disk' (*ill. 90*). This gives way to
the more neutral later formulation 'the living the sun, ruler of the horizon,

90 *A detailed rendering of the earlier form of the name for the Aten in which the falcon remains prominent – the living Ra-Horakhty. Excavated by Petrie at Amarna. UC 69.*

in his name as Sun-Father (?) coming as the sun disk'. The new name teems with as many problems of syntax and interpretation as the earlier one it replaces, in particular the semicircle loaf sign, for the sound t, but here written after the circle denoting 'sun'. In other contexts the loaf alone can denote the Egyptian word *it* 'father' and this speculative solution would seem to tie the sun disk once again to Amenhotep III, Shining Sun Disk of All Lands. In the celebrations of year 9, the paternal sun disk in the heavens would find his name inscribed over his temple as 'the sun disk, the living, the great, lord of the *sed*'.

If a long co-regency is to be believed, and the celebrations are in fact the second *sed* of the living Amenhotep III, serious problems arise. What, for example, of the officials at Thebes, whose tomb-chapels continue to include depictions of the other gods, in traditional style? How could Amenhotep III take the form of traditional king in one place, and the abstract sun disk in another? The outline of history by proponents of a long co-regency brings these problems to the fore, and helps to remind us how much we assume. The evidence is problematic, and it does not always warrant the confidence in our assumptions. Later Egyptian history includes a phase where the same ruler can appear in one image as a traditional king according to the proportions and aspects of ancient Egyptian art, and in another as a Hellenistic monarch, according to the conventions of classical Greek art. The two world views are incompatible, but suit different contexts and were indeed used at the same time. There is no attempt to resolve the two views, until both are dissolved in the transition to late Roman or Byzantine expressions in art. Such contradictions should help us to keep our minds open regarding the evidence for Akhenaten. Whatever the truth about the co-regency, in some manner a change in the name of the god accompanies the celebrations of year 9. An interval of three years then follows before the next great celebration – echoing the interval of three years between the *sed* festivals of kings such as Amenhotep III and Ramesses II.

## The year 12 festival at Akhetaten

Depictions in the tomb-chapels of high officials at Amarna include depictions of a great festival dated to year 12 of Akhenaten. This involved the delivery of foreign products by envoys, but the motive is not stated. In the tomb of Meryra (the second of that name in Egyptological reference) the inscriptions identify these scenes as a festival of Akhenaten, while those in the tomb of Huya label them a festival of the sun disk. The tomb of Huya includes the latest depiction of the king with his wife and daughters gathered around him, in the grouping so characteristic of his city. One of the most famous wall-paintings from the central palace at Akhetaten provides the names in the king's family at the latest moment, before the name of Nefertiti disappears. Her three elder daughters were Meretaten, Meketaten and the future wife of Tutankhamun, Ankhesenpaaten. Three younger members of the family each had extremely curious names on the pattern of regal accession names or epithets. These were Neferneferuaten-tasherit (or 'Neferneferuaten the younger'), Neferneferura (a variant of Nefertiti's regal name Neferneferuaten), and Setepenra (meaning simply 'chosen by Ra', an epithet often applied to the king in the 18th Dynasty). The two youngest women at the feet of the king were the 'king's daughters' Meretaten-tasherit ('Meretaten the younger') and Ankhesenpaaten-tasherit ('Ankhesenpaaten the younger'). These have been seen as the fruit of father–daughter unions between Akhenaten and, respectively, the elder Meretaten and Ankhesenpaaten. In fact, their parentage is not recorded. The Egyptian language has no special word for granddaughter; the title 'king's daughter' could equally apply to granddaughters of the king. The new princesses could also just have been two more daughters of Nefertiti: the added element 'the younger' simply indicates that there were two persons of the same name in the family; it reveals nothing of their parents.

## Five final violent years under Akhenaten

Year 12 is the latest dated evidence for the family of Akhenaten, Nefertiti and their daughters. Something happened after this year to change the way in which kingship worked in this court. If there was indeed a prolonged co-regency, that event was the death of Amenhotep III in the 38th year of his dazzling reign. This would be the moment of truth for the junior co-regent, the court, the expression of belief in word and art, all that was associated

*91 Ring-bezel of faience, bearing in hieroglyphs the name Ankhetkheperura-beloved-of-Waenra (i.e. beloved of Akhenaten). The feminine ending –t after both the element Ankh- and the word 'beloved' indicates that Ankhkheperura was a new name for a royal woman, perhaps Nefertiti. Excavated by Flinders Petrie at Amarna.*

with him. When Amenhotep III died, his wife Tiy would change in status, no longer in ritual 'king's wife' and 'king's mother', but now only 'king's mother'. In traditional terms her role as Hathor and Isis would give way to her role as Nut, the sky. It would leave to Nefertiti the principal role of female complement to the now solitary sun king. However, if there was no such long co-regency, there is another explanation for the changes in status and attitude at court: the birth of a son to one of Akhenaten's wives. The child prince Tutankhaten came to the throne in the year after Akhenaten's year 17 and death, and the boy then ruled for a decade before dying at about 16 years of age. The arithmetic seems to suit the interpretation that the future king was born around year 12 of Akhenaten.

Either change at court might explain the apparent disappearance of the king's wife Nefertiti after year 12. She already had a status far above the usual level of king's wife, with her name not only in the oval name-ring or cartouche, to denote solar sovereignty, but from the early years of the reign accompanied by the regal second name Neferneferuaten 'perfect is the perfection of the sun disk'. The structure of this additional name, always written first in the cartouche for the queen, mirrors the throne name of the king himself, Neferkheperura 'perfect are the forms of the sun'. In the final years of Akhenaten, even allowing for a 12-year co-regency, his father Amenhotep III was dead. There now appears in the absence of Neferneferuaten Nefertiti an enigmatic co-regent for Akhenaten with two names, each in its own cartouche as was usual for a king: the dual king Ankhkheperura, son of Ra Neferneferuaten (*ill. 91*). John Harris proposes to see in this new name pairing a new status for Nefertiti herself. After year 12, then, the king's wife appears elevated to the perfect, divine feminine complement to the sole sun king. This changes not only the relation between the kingly husband and wife, but also the relation between them and the world. Tiy might continue as king's mother, but the solar pair now have the status of twinned sovereigns, a new and very different style of co-regency.

The known precedent for this – though not quite a precedent – is the joint rule of the king's wife Hatshepsut as king alongside the young ruler Thutmose III, a century before Akhenaten. Hatshepsut and Thutmose III provide a model of the co-regency of a man and woman, but their relation is not that of husband and wife, but of nephew and aunt. It would not have been an endorsement of any future co-regency of man and woman, for the name and image of Hatshepsut was edited out of the sacred hieroglyphic record after her death. Yet their case demonstrates the range of possibilities at the Egyptian royal court. With Nefertiti elevated to the position of co-regent, a gap opened for the ritual position of king's wife at court. Just as Amenhotep III had taken his daughter Satamun to perform the role of king's wife after the elevation of Tiy to higher status, so too Akhenaten took his eldest daughter Meretaten to fill this gap. We have no means of knowing whether the union included sexual relations between father and daughter: the sun king operated on such a different level from humankind that it is possible, but simply unknown. The two new king's wives appear to produce like-named king's daughters at the royal court, in the hieroglyphic images and inscriptions at Akhetaten. At face value, these must be daughters of Akhenaten by his own daughters. However, there is no space in this ritual-ized court for the son-in-law, and we have seen that the Egyptian word daughter is also used for granddaughter. If the two young ritual 'king's wives' had born children by other men, those men would be invisible in the record, and their children would still correctly in Egyptian terms carry the title 'king's daughter' in hieroglyphic inscriptions. The evidence of the hieroglyphs is direct data not for a family tree, but for a series of ritual relationships emulating cosmic circuits. This can be seen on the plan of Akhetaten, as the following paragraph shows.

## The royal women at Akhetaten

At the new city of the sun, the women closest to the king figured promi-nently in special cult enclosures set around the city at the desert edge (*ill. 92*). These ritual spaces included formal rectangular pools, and corridors and chambers painted with the now famous scenes of animals and birds in the marshes. The location of the enclosures reflects the natural environment of the Nile Valley. When the river flooded after midsummer, the waters lin-gered longest in low-lying marshy reaches between the main strip of fields and the desert edge. The 'backwaters', as the Egyptians named them, teemed with wildlife, and provided a dramatic contrast to both the orderly irrigated fields on one side and the arid Saharan desert on the other. They must have struck the Egyptians as echoes of the prototypical primeval marsh out of which creation emerged at the beginning of time. In myth the god-desses beside the creator embodied the principle of primeval fertility, and at the court the royal women provided the same feminine complement of fer-tility for the solar king. The lake and garden shrines around the city gave a highly formalized expression to this principle of fertility. At the southern and northern tips of the city lay the most substantial of these desert-edge sanctuaries, named 'sun-shades of Ra', or at the southern end *maru*, a word of uncertain meaning but perhaps signifying a 'viewing platform'. For a time

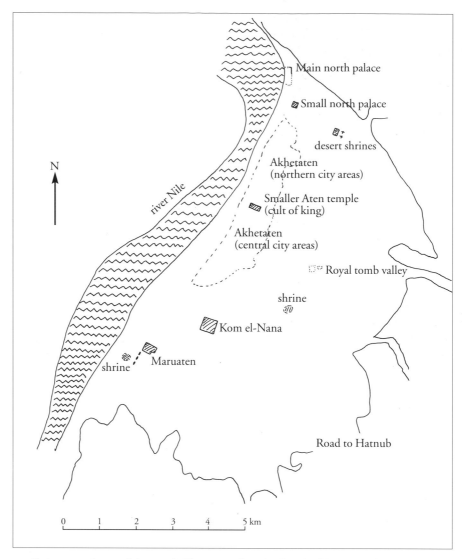

**92** *Shrines in and around the city of Akhetaten, perhaps for the cult of the king and the royal women. Kom el-Nana, recently uncovered, may have been for the cult of Nefertiti.*

these supplementary shrines around the city gave prominent place to a lesser king's wife named Kiya. At a point late in the reign, her name was removed and replaced by that of the king's daughter Meretaten. Earlier Egyptologists interpreted the erased name as Nefertiti, and suggested that the latter had fallen from grace. In 1959 Kiya's name was recognized on a vase now in the Metropolitan Museum of Art, New York, and since that time it has been read throughout the city in the erasures formerly attributed to a fall of Nefertiti. It is not known what role Kiya played, though some have seen her

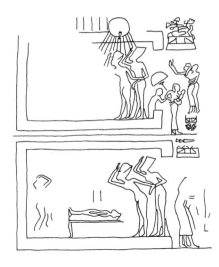

*93 Akhenaten, Nefertiti and the court in mourning at the death of a royal woman. The presence of a nurse with baby to the right suggests to some that this indicates the death of Kiya at the birth of a son, the future Tutankhamun. Wall F of Room Alpha, in the Royal Tomb at Amarna.*

as the mother of the future king Tutankhamun. Whatever her duties in ritual, Kiya disappears from the hieroglyphic inscriptions, without any recorded reason being given, whether political or natural. She left little mark on the outward appearance of the court, and it is difficult to know whether Egyptologists have exaggerated her significance. Yet at one point she was the prominent name in the ritual defence system of the king's city against the forces of the desert, in the lake shrines around Akhetaten. Death struck the family of Akhenaten at some point in the middle to later years of his reign, but how is uncertain. The king's tomb includes several wall reliefs depicting him with his wife at a funeral, once that of their second daughter Meketaten, and the nurturing of a child: this could be interpreted as death in childbirth, a recurrent nightmare in Egypt throughout antiquity. The inscriptions, though, do not provide dates or details for each of the dramatic scenes, without parallel in all the kingly monuments of ancient Egypt (*ill. 93*).

## The ritual destruction of Amun

The constellation of cosmic forces at the end of the reign appears to have been the following. King Neferkheperura Akhenaten sole one of Ra reigned with a co-regent who appears to have been none other than his powerful wife, Ankhkheperura Neferneferuaten, the former Nefertiti. It is not known in which year the king's mother Tiy died, but her death would have provided a logical point for the most violent eruption in the reign, the programme to destroy the names of the god Amun and his consort the goddess Mut. Once both father and mother had departed this earth, the faith in the sun disk confronted a new reality, the earthly absence of the Shining Sun Disk of All Lands, and of the mother of his son King Akhenaten. This painful absence

94 *Cursive inscription on a jar from Amarna, recording the contents as 'Year 17, sweet wine of the estate of Sehetep-Aten'. This is one of a handful of wine-jars bearing the highest year-date recorded for Akhenaten. UC 32931.*

contrasted with the claim in the very names Amun 'Hidden' and Mut 'Mother'. Those traditional expressions for divinity effectively refuted the claim of the distant sun disk to divinity. Either the king could return to the traditional pattern, following his father in the company and cult of all deities, and abandoning his exclusive focus on the sun disk his father. Or else he could pursue that exclusivity to a new and dramatic climax, the rejection of the ancient formulae Amun, Mut, and even the phrase 'the gods'. It was the latter course that Akhenaten chose.

There may have been powerful economic incentives driving in the same direction. The vast new temples of the sun disk required supporting estates, and the kings of Egypt traditionally balanced their books by a technique labelled *wedjeb-khet* 'reversion of offerings'. This allowed offerings to pass from one cult to another, satisfying the religious requirement but directing the actual food and drink and cloth to a single destination. The Abusir Papyri of the late Old Kingdom demonstrate the system very neatly, with new kingly foundations draining the resources of older cult centres lower on the list of priorities. Every so often the reversions of offerings needed a complete overhaul, and a Great Revision would take place. This must have been one of the most feared decisions from any ruler, the assessment of current needs, where black and white replaced the grey compromise of the reversions of offerings. At Great Revisions cults would lose their estates, temples would close, and title-holders lose their shares in revenue. The religious iconoclasm launched against Amun and Mut may well have been secondary to the Egyptians, when compared with the economic impact of a full revision of royal (and this included temple) estates. This may have been the point at which Akhenaten broke most forcefully with the past. What was most significant in this respect was not his idiosyncratic art, not his focus on one father, the sun disk, but the exclusion of all other approaches. We cannot know whether violence against the gods included attacks on men and women. Inevitably our own recent history of dictatorships worldwide must leave us with a chill of suspicion. It is difficult in modern times not to see every religion and ideology, from agnostic consumerism to the fanatic sect, as a crime of hate against creation and humanity. Inevitably, then, we may suspect Akhenaten and his agents of the same crimes. There is, though, no evidence, either way.

The programme to eradicate the name of Amun from the sacred hiero-glyphic record, from the monuments establishing eternity, reached every height, every corner and every scale (*ills 5, 26*). If the enemy word lay within a name, it was hacked out there too: every visible instance of the name of the father, Amenhotep III, lost its first element to the iconoclasts. At the tips of obelisks, on the humblest stelae, the hated word fell to the chisel. At Iunu itself, these physical editors of the sacred record did not spare even a faience chalice bearing a scene of the old king offering Maat to the sun god: the throne name Nebmaatra survived, but the element 'Amun' was erased from the king's birth name Amenhotep (fragment Turin Inv. Suppl. 3591). However long it took, the task of eradication was comprehensive, if not complete, by the time that Akhenaten died, at some point in his 17th year of reign (*ill. 94*). At this point a new kingly figure appeared, in place of Ankhkhepe-rura Neferneferuaten an equally enigmatic Smenkhkara. Following John Harris in his theses, this may have corresponded with the final rise to power of the former Nefertiti, perhaps as her husband died. An inscription at Thebes records a third year of this sovereign, already served by a temple in the territory of Amun. Within days of Akhenaten's death, it seems, the cause of his Aten cult had been lost. Smenkhkara disappears soon after, perhaps in that same third year, leaving a boy from the old royal family to ascend the throne as King Tutankhaten.

## The restoration – Tutankhaten to Tutankhamun

On the stela of a middle-ranking subject, the new king Tutankhaten is depicted offering to Amun, and by year 3 or 4 the court issued in his revised name Tutankhamun a decree authorizing the return to the inclusive worship of all gods. Two versions of this decree survive as hieroglyphic inscriptions on stelae, found at Karnak. Their message is echoed in the great number of colossal images of the gods Amun and Mut bearing the features of the young king. Presumably the new statues filled the place of images destroyed under Akhenaten. In year 8 a decree in the name of Tutankhamun proclaimed a Great Revision, under the direction of the Treasurer, Maya. This may have been the point at which the temples to the sun disk forfeited their estates, and when Akhetaten lost its economic base, but there had already been a move fatal to the flourishing of the city. The highest officials of Tutankhamun, notably Maya and the general Horemheb, had tomb-chapels prepared at Memphis. It seems that the court returned to that area to rule. It remains difficult to assess how long a substantial population remained at Akhetaten. The city may have lived as long under Tutankhamun as under Akhenaten, and this makes it very difficult, across 3,300 years, to date specific finds to before or after the 'heretic' king's death. Many small images of gods and goddesses have been excavated across the city, and the South Tombs even contained wooden figures of the ibis and the crocodile, emblematic of the gods Thoth and Sobek. These may all, though, postdate the death of Akhenaten and the phase of exclusive sun worship. One late find from the city is a crude inscription of Horemheb, after his accession to the throne. Its mediocre quality already indicates the absence of a royal court and royal craftsmen, though it shows that there were still craftsmen creating work at Akhetaten in the name of the reigning king. Fifty years later, under Ramesses II, the city became a quarry, its statues hacked apart, and its stone blocks removed wholesale to Khemenu for vast new temple-building projects for the god Thoth. The same had happened at Thebes, where Horemheb began to dismantle the Akhenaten temple blocks and sculpture, and have them safely packed into his great gateways, for Egyptologists to rediscover in the 1920s. Until the reign of Sety I, it seems that the heretic king was not demonized, curiously perhaps, given the attack on Amun. Only under the Ramessides did the horror at the episode take hold. Akhenaten and his court were removed from the record of eternity, and his name, and that of his wife and successors, was eradicated as viciously as his agents had eradicated the name of Amun. Yet the worship of the sun continued. The formula Amun-Ra remained vibrant and effective for the Egyptians for another 1,500 years, until Greek, Roman and finally Christian forms of expression came to replace this acknowledgment of the visibility and invisibility of the creator in our lives.

# Epilogue

## After Akhenaten

When kingship reverted under Tutankhamun to the worship of many gods, the Egyptians removed first the city, and then the very memory, name and image of Akhenaten. Yet they never attacked the object of his cult, the sun, and the sun god Ra remained at the centre of ancient Egyptian religion until the end of its long history. In the two centuries after the death of Akhenaten, many of the craftsmen working on royal tombs set up small stelae in which they appeared with the hieroglyphic inscription 'excellent spirit of Ra'. The same men were employed in covering the tombs of their kings with the scenes of the solar journey through the night. We have seen how Ramesses II established no fewer than five pairs of colossal monolithic obelisks at his new residence, Piramesse, calling it 'the sustaining spirit (ka) of Ra'. At the beginning of the 1st millennium BC, these ten obelisks must have been the most difficult monuments to move to the new residence of the 21st Dynasty at Tanis, where their fragments still lie. The old formula Amun-Ra continued to express most cogently for the Egyptians the universal rule of the creator, and the sun god remained central to this experience of supreme divine power, both as Atum and as Ra-Horakhty. During the mid-1st millennium BC, many funerary stelae depicted in place of Osiris a triple vision of the sun god as three forms upon the solar boat: the form with scarab for head, Khepri, the falcon-headed Ra, and the human form of Atum wearing the Double Crown (*ill. 95*). The three could, as in New Kingdom hymns, express dawn, midday and dusk in the solar cycle. As the divine powers presented on funerary stelae, they reveal how strongly the Egyptians relied, with their kings, on the daily rebirth of the sun as guarantee for their own resurrection.

Ancient Egypt did not vanish overnight. Essentially its fusion of kingship, religion, art and script was a product of the era we name the Bronze Age. All four were expressions of a society in which the ruler and his rule seemed as superhuman, as divine as the force behind creation. The use of bronze in the 3rd and 2nd millennia BC denotes more than a stage in the narrower history of technology. It corresponds to a particular scale of com-

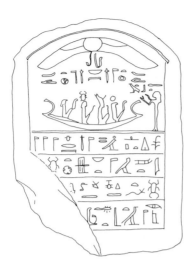

95 *Ra after Akhenaten: the stela of Tabekhet, showing her worshipping the three forms of the sun god in the solar barque: falcon-headed Ra, human-headed Atum, and the scarab-bearing Khepri. 26th Dynasty. Dublin NMI L917.*

munications between peoples, and to the social strata in settled life within each area. The Bronze Age world involved separate territories each populated on a large scale, more in sporadic than in continuous contact. Over the course of the 2nd millennium BC in the Near East, the distinct areas developed more frequent contact, which culminated in wars between 'superpowers' such as Egypt and the Hittite empire. By 1200 BC, growth in scale and density of population accompanied a new technology, for which we brand the following era the Iron Age. In this new and different world, Egypt no longer stood isolated among separated kingdoms. Instead it lay precariously on the margin of a new series of far vaster empires, first the Assyrian, then the Persian empire, absorbed by Alexander the Great of Macedon, and finally the Roman empire. Until the very end of the 1st millennium BC, ancient Egyptian kingship and its religion and art continued to function, and in many of its centuries they flourished. Denigrated as a 'Late Period', the last ten centuries of ancient Egyptian history in fact provide a large proportion of the masterpieces in art and architecture that attract a modern audience to the civilization. From magnificent bronze votive figures to the mighty sandstone temples of southern Upper Egypt, the output belies the gloomy judgment passed by hindsight on a thousand-year 'twilight'. The age of Ra was not yet over.

How then did it meet its end? After the arrival of Alexander the Great in 332 BC, for almost a thousand years the rulers of Egypt spoke not Egyptian, but Greek. In 305 BC General Ptolemy declared himself king, and until Cleopatra VII the Ptolemaic dynasty governed Egypt, respecting and promoting her ancient cults, alongside new Hellenistic initiatives such as the Great Library and Museum (centre of learning) at the new residence Alexandria. The Ptolemies were still, in hieroglyphic inscriptions, 'Horus' and 'son of Ra', but there is little evidence that they ever learned an Egyptian script. Probably too they never commissioned any new temple building at Iunu, the heart of the solar cult: as mentioned in Chapter Three, two statues of Ptolemy II and Arsinoe refer to Atum and Ra, but there was a temple of Atum at Sais, in the western Delta, and the statues are not known to have stood at Iunu. The sun was still creator in the Egyptian belief system, but the Ptolemaic lacuna at Iunu echoes a fundamental separation of kingship from hieroglyphic script and formal Egyptian art. Where the Ptolemies cast themselves as celestial gods, their model was Zeus, the Greek sky god, as much as Helios, the sun. In 30 BC the dynasty met its end, when Cleopatra VII committed suicide, after the defeat of her ally and lover Mark Antony at the hands of his rival Roman general Octavian. In 27 BC the young victor declared himself princeps, 'emperor', and received the name Augustus. He set about transforming Rome, and the solar monuments of Iunu and Thebes became central pieces in his strategy incorporating East and West. On the Field of Mars in the heart of his new Rome, a vast sundial arose, with an obelisk as its midpoint or gnomon. Here the ancient monoliths remained focal symbols in the claim of imperial rulers to celestial divinity. Perhaps these emperors saw themselves more as sun kings than had the Ptolemies, though the strongest influences here seem to have been Syrian. The imperial cult culminated in the reign of Diocletian, who crushed rebellion in Egypt, and transformed the entire temple of Luxor (and perhaps that at Kheraha, south of Cairo) into a legionary fortress centred on the worship of the divine emperor. His persecution of Christians was so fierce that his reign still inaugurates the Christian era as the Era of Martyrs in the calendar of the Coptic Church (the Christian Church in Egypt). From this point, late classical Roman art obliterates any earlier form of expression: at Luxor we see this quite literally, as the Roman paintings overlaid the Egyptian reliefs of Amenhotep III. In the 4th century, the tables turned, Constantine embraced Christianity as he became emperor, and sealed the conversion of his territories. A new god ruled Egypt.

The 3rd and 4th centuries AD witnessed the last temple-building, formal art production and hieroglyphic inscriptions under official commission. These years extinguished pharaonic civilization, which was already weakened by foreign rule. In the final flowering of funerary literature, the last Documents for Breathing from the 2nd century AD, we find the sun at the heart of the belief in creation and rebirth, as firmly as in the first inscriptions of the same tradition, in the pyramid of Unas 2,500 years earlier: 'I am Ra in his rising, Atum in his setting.'

# Bibliography

### Preface and Introduction

For the Egyptian language, a clear recent introduction is provided by Mark Collier and Bill Manley, *How to Read Egyptian Hieroglyphs*, London 1998.

On chronology see now Ian Shaw (ed.), *Oxford History of Ancient Egypt*, Oxford 2000.

On the contact between northern Europe and Egypt, see Patrick Connor (ed.), *The Inspiration of Egypt*, Brighton 1983.

On the concept of kingship in ancient Egypt, see Oleg Berlev, 'The Eleventh Dynasty and the Egyptian concept of kingship', in Dwight Young (ed.), *Studies presented to Hans Polotsky*, East Gloucester Massachusetts 1981, 361–377.

On the women near the king, see Lana Troy, *Patterns of Queenship in Ancient Egyptian Myth and History*, Acta Universitatis Upsaliensis – Boreas 14, Uppsala 1986.

On the composition 'the King as Priest of the Sun', see Jan Assmann, *Der König als Sonnenpriester*, Glückstadt 1970.

### Chapter One

James P. Allen, *Genesis in Egypt*, Yale Egyptological Studies 2, New Haven 1988.

Werner Forman and Stephen Quirke, *Hieroglyphs and the Afterlife*, London 1996.

On early stamp-seals and scarab development, see Andre Wieser, *Die Anfänge der ägyptischen Stempelsiegel-Amulette*, Freiburg Schweiz and Göttingen 1996; on early scarabs in Egypt and the Aegean, see Lesley Fitton and Stephen Quirke, 'An Aegean origin for Egyptian spirals?', in Jacke Phillips (ed.), *Studies in Honour of Martha Rhoads Bell*, San Antonio 1997, 421–444.

On the benu bird, see Laszlo Kakosy, 'Phönix', in Wolfgang Helck and Eberhard Otto (eds), *Lexikon der Ägyptologie IV*, cols 1030–1039.

For the Litany of Ra, see the original edition of the principal hieroglyphic sources, Erik Hornung, *Das Buch der Anbetung des Re im Westen*, Geneva 1975–1976, and by the same author the general account of New Kingdom royal funerary compositions, *The Valley of the Kings: Horizon of Eternity*, translated by David Warburton, New York 1990.

For the 'Destruction of Mankind', see the edition by Erik Hornung, *Der ägyptische Mythos von der Himmelskuh. Eine Ätiologie des Unvollkommenen*, Freiburg/Schweiz and Göttingen 1982.

On the goddesses of Iunu, see J. Vandier, 'Iousâas et (Hathor)-Nébet-Hétépet', in *Revue d'Egyptologie* 16, 1964, 55–146; 17, 1965, 89–176; 18, 1966, 67–142.

On Middle Kingdom rituals in the Coffin Texts, see Harco Willems, *Chests of Life*, Leiden 1988, 141–159.

For the Late Period account of conflicts under Shu and Geb, see Jean-Claude Goyon, 'Les travaux de Chou et les tribulations de Geb', in *Kêmi* 6, 1936, 1–42.

For the god Seth, see H te Velde, *Seth, God of Confusion*, Leiden 1967.

Edition of the Deir el-Medina tale of Horus and Seth: Alan H. Gardiner, *Papyrus Chester Beatty I*, London 1935.

The Roman Period account of the episodes

involving the family of Osiris is Plutarch, *De Iside et Osiride*, translation and commentary by J. Gwyn Griffiths, University of Wales 1970.

**Chapter Two**

On Egyptian time-keeping, see Jurgen von Beckerath, 'Kalender', in Wolfgang Helck and Eberhard Otto (eds), *Lexikon der Ägyptologie III*, cols 297–299.

For the Amduat, see the original edition of the principal hieroglyphic sources, Erik Hornung, *Das Amduat. Die Schrift des Verborgenen Raumes*, 3 volumes, Wiesbaden 1963–1967, and by the same author the general account of New Kingdom royal funerary compositions, *The Valley of the Kings: Horizon of Eternity*, translated by David Warburton, New York 1990.

On the morning and evening accompaniments, and the hourly sun hymns, see Jan Assmann, *Egyptian Solar Religion in the New Kingdom*, London and New York 1995.

On solar features at Thebes, note the detailed description of the principal Amun temple by Paul Barguet, *Le Temple d'Amon-Re a Karnak*, Cairo 1962.

Richard Parker and Jean-Claude Goyon, *The Edifice of Taharqa*, London 1979.

For the sun hymns, see Jan Assmann, *Sonnenhymnen in Thebanischen Gräbern* (Theben I), Mainz-am-Rhein 1983.

**Chapter Three**

On Iunu see now the extensive monograph by Dietrich Raue, *Heliopolis und das Haus des Re. Eine Prosopographie und ein Toponym im Neuen Reich* (Abhandlungen des Deutschen Archäologischen Instituts Kairo, Ägyptologische Reihe, Band 16), Berlin 1999.

An account of recent excavations and finds in the area is given by M. Abd el-Gelil, M. Shaker and D. Raue, 'Recent excavations at Heliopolis', in *Orientalia* 65, 1996, 136–146.

For the excavations by Hekekyan, see David Jeffreys, 'Joseph Hekekyan at Heliopolis',

in Anthony Leahy and John Tait (eds), *Studies on Ancient Egypt in Honour of H.S. Smith*', London 1999, 157–168.

The Petrie excavations were published by W. M. F. Petrie and E. McKay, *Heliopolis, Kafr Ammar and Shurafa* (British School of Archaeology in Egypt 24), London 1915.

The excavations in the northern enclosure and western gateway areas are published by A. Saleh, *Excavations at Heliopolis* volume I, Cairo 1981; volume II, Cairo 1983.

On the stela of Ramesses II from the quarries at Gebel Ahmar, see A. Hamada, 'A stela from Manshiyet es-Sadr', in *Annales du Service des Antiquités d'Egypte* 38, 1938, 217–230.

On the fossil of Tjanefer, see S. Curto, in Anna-Maria Donadoni-Roveri, *Le credenze religiose*, Milan 1988, 50 fig. 51.

On the two quartzite lintels of Senusret III, see Stephen Quirke, *British Museum Magazine*, summer 1995.

For the predynastic remains, see F. Debono and B. Mortensen, *The Predynastic Cemetery at Heliopolis*, Mainz-am-Rhein 1988.

For the relief fragments of Netjerkhet discovered by Schiaparelli, see Raymond Weill, 'Monuments nouveaux des premieres dynasties', in *Sphinx* 15, 1911, 1–35.

On the great platform, see Herbert Ricke, 'Der "Hohe Sand" in Heliopolis', in *Zeitschrift für Ägyptische Sprache und Altertumskunde* 71, 1935, 107–111.

For the record of an inscription of Senusret I at Iunu, see Hans Goedicke, 'The Berlin Leather Roll (P Berlin 3029)', in *Festschrift zum 150 Jahrigen Bestehen des Berliner Agyptischen Museums*, Berlin 1974, 87–104.

On the sight lines from Iunu to the pyramids, see David Jeffreys, 'The topography of Heliopolis and Memphis: some cognitive aspects', in *Stationen. Beiträge zur Kulturgeschichte Ägyptens, Rainer Stadelmann gewidmet*, Mainz-am-Rhein 1998, 63–71.

For the Piy stela, see N. Grimal, *La stèle triomphale de Pi(ankh)y au Musée du Caire*, Cairo 1981.

On balustrades, see Ian Shaw, 'Balustrades, stairs and altars in the cult of the Aten at el-Amarna', in *Journal of Egyptian Archaeology* 80, 1994, 109–127.

On the model shrine of Sety I, see A. Badawy, 'A monumental gateway for a temple of King Sety I – an ancient model restored', in *Miscellanea Wilbouriana* I, Brooklyn, 1972, 1–20.

On the inventory plaque discovered by Schiaparelli, see Herbert Ricke, 'Eine Inventartafel aus Heliopolis im Turiner Museum', in *Zeitschrift für Ägyptische Sprache und Altertumskunde* 71, 1935, 111–133.

On the Greatest of Seers, see Bettina Schmitz, 'Hoherpriester von Heliopolis', in Wolfgang Helck and Eberhard Otto (eds), *Lexikon der Ägyptologie II*, cols 1249–1254.

On the *ished*-tree, see Laszlo Kakosy, 'Ischedbaum', in Wolfgang Helck and Eberhard Otto (eds), *Lexikon der Ägyptologie III*, cols 182–183.

For the inscription of Ramesses IV at Karnak, relating the miracle of the *ished*-tree at Iunu, see Wolfgang Helck, 'Ramessidische Inschriften aus Karnak', in *Zeitschrift für Ägyptische Sprache und Altertumskunde* 82, 1957, 98–140.

On the Menwer bull, see M. Moursi, 'Corpus der Mnevis-Stelen und Untersuchungen zum Kult der Mnevis-Stiere in Heliopolis I', in *Studien zur Altägyptischen Kultur* 10, 1983, 247–267, and 'Corpus der Mnevis-Stelen und Untersuchungen zum Kult der Mnevis-Stiere in Heliopolis II', in *Studien zur Altägyptischen Kultur* 14, 1987, 225–237.

On the tomb of a late Middle Kingdom healer at Iunu, see Janine Bourriau, *Pharaohs and Mortals. Egyptian Art in the Middle Kingdom*, Cambridge 1988, 120–121, cat. no. 112.

The block from the house of Yery at Piramses is cited by Raue, *op. cit.*, 450.

For the Late Period cemeteries, see S. Bickel and P. Tallet, 'La nécropole saïte d'Héliopolis', in *Bulletin de l'Institut Français d'Archéologie Orientale au Caire* 97, 1997, 67–90.

On the eclipse of Iunu by Kheraha from the 30th Dynasty, see J. Yoyotte 'Prêtres et sanctuaires du nome héliopolite à la Basse Epoque', in *Bulletin de l'Institut Français d'Archéologie Orientale au Caire* 54, 1954, 83–115

**Chapter Four**

On orientation and the stellar aspects of Old Kingdom pyramids, see especially Kate Spence, 'Ancient Egyptian chronology and the astronomical orientation of pyramids', in *Nature* 408, 320–324.

On pyramid names, see Wolfgang Helck, 'Pyramidennamen', in Wolfgang Helck and Eberhard Otto (eds), *Lexikon der Ägyptologie V*, cols 4–9.

Mark Lehner, *The Complete Pyramids*, London and New York 1997.

Rainer Stadelmann, *Die ägyptischen Pyramiden. Vom Ziegelbau zum Weltwunder*, Mainz am Rhein 1991.

For the Khufu boat, see Nancy Jenkins, *The Boat Beneath the Pyramid*, London 1980.

On Giza after the Old Kingdom, see C. Zivie-Coche, *Giza au deuxième millénaire* (Bibliothèque d'Etude 70), Cairo 1976.

Pyramid Texts: for English translations for the whole corpus so far published, see Raymond Faulkner, *The Ancient Egyptian Pyramid Texts*, Oxford 1969.

On the form of the Middle Kingdom monument at Deir el-Bahri, see Barry Kemp, *Ancient Egypt. Anatomy of a Civilization*, London and New York 1989.

On the monuments of Senusret III, see the contributions by Dieter Arnold and Joe Wegner to the magazine *KMT* 6, 1995.

On obelisks, see Labib Habachi, *The Obelisks of Egypt. Skyscrapers of the Past*, London 1978.

For the Middle Bronze Age obelisks at Byblos, see *Liban. L'autre rive* (exhibition at the Institut du monde arabe, Paris, 1998–1999), 1998, 66–70.

On Piramesse see Eric Uphill, *The Temples*

of *Per Ramesses*, Warminster 1984.

For obelisks at Rome, see Erik Iversen, *Obelisks in Exile I. The Obelisks of Rome*, Copenhagen 1968.

On the sundial of Augustus at Rome, see Edmund Buchner, *Die Sonnenuhr des Augustus*, Mainz am Rhein 1982.

**Chapter Five**

For Akhenaten and his reign, see now Nicholas Reeves, *Akhenaten, Egypt's False Prophet*, London and New York 2001.

Note also the works by Cyril Aldred: *Akhenaten, King of Egypt*, London and New York 1988.

*Akhenaten and Nefertiti*, Brooklyn 1973.

The cuneiform tablets with correspondence between the rulers of the Near East in the Amarna Period are translated with commentary by W. Moran, *The Amarna Letters*, Baltimore and London 1992.

For the reign of Amenhotep III, see Arielle Kozloff, Betsy Bryan and Larry Berman, *Egypt's Dazzling Sun. Amenhotep III and his World*, Cleveland 1992.

On the cult temple of Amenhotep III at Memphis, see Robert Morkot, 'Nebmaatra-united-with-Ptah', in *Journal of Near Eastern Studies* 49, 1990, 323–337.

For the interpretation of Amenhotep III temple sculpture as a ritual star-map, see Betsy Bryan, 'the statue program for the mortuary temple of Amenhotep III', in Stephen Quirke (ed.), *The Temple in Ancient Egypt: New Discoveries and Recent Research*, London 1997, 57–81.

On the theory of a long co-regency between Amenhotep III and Akhenaten, see Ray Johnson, 'Amenhotep III and Amarna: some new considerations', in *Journal of Egyptian Archaeology* 82, 1996, 65–82.

The hieratic inscription on cuneiform tablet EA 27 is published by W. Fritz, 'Bemerkungen zum Datierungsvermerk auf der Amarnatafel KN 27', in *Studien zur Altägyptischen Kultur* 18, 1991, 207–214.

On the monuments of Akhenaten at Karnak, see D. Redford, *Akhenaten, the Heretic King*, Princeton 1984.

For the Boundary Stelae, see W. Murnane and C. Van Siclen, *The Boundary Stelae of Akhenaten*, London and New York 1993.

A dynamic structural account of the city of Akhenaten is given in Barry Kemp, *Ancient Egypt: Anatomy of a Civilization*, London and New York 1989.

For the Great Hymn to the Aten, see M. Sandman, *Texts from the time of Akhenaten*, Bibliotheca Aegyptiaca 8, Brussels 1938 (for the hieroglyphic handcopy), and M. Lichtheim, *Ancient Egyptian Literature* Volume II, Berkeley 1976, 96–100 (an accessible translation with introduction).

Royal Tomb: Geoffrey Martin, *The Royal Tomb at El-Amarna*, 2 volumes, London 1974 and 1989.

The original article on the identity of Nefertiti and Smenkhkara: John Harris, 'Neferneferuaten' in *Göttinger Miszellen* 4, 1973, 15–17.

On the principal wife of Akhenaten, see the measured account by Joyce Tyldesley, *Nefertiti, Egypt's Sun Queen*, London 1998.

For the shrines of the royal women at Amarna, see Barry Kemp, in *Amarna Reports* VI, EES London 1995, chapter 15 'Outlying temples at Amarna', 411–462.

On great revisions, see A. Spalinger, 'Some revisions of temple endowments in the New Kingdom', in *Journal of the American Research Center in Egypt* 28, 1991, 21–39.

On the reign and burial of Tutankhamen, see Nicholas Reeves, *The Complete Tutankhamun. The King, the Tomb, the Royal Treasure*, London and New York 1990.

# SOURCES OF ILLUSTRATIONS

All pictures were supplied by the author unless otherwise indicated.

# INDEX